"[AN] ARTICULATE AND ENGAGING HISTORIAN."
—USA Today

"Clarke describes the Pearl Harbor attack in vivid detail, and dissects the myths and symbols that grew around it. He skillfully recreates the Hawaii of 1941, and the events of Dec. 5–7, based on contemporary records and accounts, on several of the better histories and on his own interviews with survivors of that unforgettable Sunday morning."
> —New York Newsday

"Fascinating . . . The racist attitudes toward the Japanese that Clarke has collected tell a story that goes far beyond the confines of the Hawaiian archipelago."
> —Entertainment Weekly

"Thurston Clarke's *Pearl Harbor Ghosts* stands apart from other examinations of that tragic day."
> —Chicago Tribune

"Evocative . . . [Clarke's] book resonates."
> —San Diego Union

"No other event in this century has riveted America's attention as did the Japanese attack on Pearl Harbor in 1941. . . . Clarke says the Pearl Harbor attack was not merely a clear-cut, singular military event. Rather, he persuasively argues that the aerial assault opened a Pandora's box of questions that were not then addressed, have never been successfully dealt with, and the 'ghosts' of these issues still remain with us, even after a half century."
> —Dallas Times Herald

Please turn the page for more reviews. . . .

PEARL HARBOR GHOSTS

PEARL HARBOR GHOSTS

DECEMBER 7, 1941—
THE DAY THAT
STILL HAUNTS THE
NATION

THURSTON CLARKE

BALLANTINE BOOKS   NEW YORK

A Ballantine Book
Published by The Ballantine Publishing Group

Copyright © 1991, 2001 by Thurston Clarke

All rights reserved under International
and Pan-American Copyright Conventions. Published
in the United States by The Ballantine Publishing Group, a division
of Random House, Inc., New York, and simultaneously in
Canada by Random House of Canada Limited, Toronto. Originally published
in different form by William Morrow and Company, Inc., in 1991.

Ballantine is a registered trademark and the
Ballantine colophon is a trademark of Random House, Inc.

www.randomhouse.com/BB/

Maps by Mapping Specialists, Ltd.

The Cataloging-in-Publication Data for this title is available
from the Library of Congress.

ISBN 0-345-44607-0

Manufactured in the United States of America

Text design by Holly Johnson

First Ballantine Books Edition: May 2001

10 9 8 7 6 5 4 3 2 1

FOR SOPHIE

CONTENTS

PART THREE: DECEMBER 7, 1941

PART FOUR: AFTER THE ATTACK

POSTSCRIPT: DECEMBER 5–7, 2000

APRIL 1990–OCTOBER 2000

B y World War II standards, Pearl Harbor was neither a very bloody nor complicated battle, and it can easily be summarized. In the early hours of December 7, 1941, a Japanese task force containing six aircraft carriers sailed to a point 230 miles north of the Hawaiian island of Oahu and launched 354 warplanes in two waves. These flew undetected to Oahu, surprising the American military. During a raid lasting about an hour and forty minutes, Japanese pilots attacked every important air and naval installation on the island, destroying 188 Army and Navy aircraft, most of them on the ground, and sinking or damaging four auxiliary ships, three cruisers, three destroyers, and eight battleships. Japan lost twenty-nine planes and five midget submarines. Its fleet withdrew without having been sighted, having won one of the century's more one-sided victories.

This raid has since become one of the most obsessively examined engagements in military history, described and analyzed in thousands of articles and monographs, in over a hundred books listed under "Pearl Harbor" in the Library of Congress, and in the reports of nine military and congressional investigations. We know, in many instances, which pilots sank which ships, and sometimes which gunners downed which planes. We know what happened to every Pearl Harbor vessel—that the light cruiser *Phoenix* was sold to Argentina, where it was renamed the *Admiral Belgrano* and torpedoed by a British submarine during the Falklands war, that the Coast Guard cutter *Taney* was the only Pearl Harbor ship to serve in Vietnam, and that Navy Tug 146 became a fireboat in San Francisco Bay.

Any piece of an aircraft present on Oahu at the time of the attack has become a valuable relic. A wing section from an American P-40 fighter (or "pursuit plane," as fighters were then called) shot down on December 7 sold for several thousand dollars fifty years later. World War II archaeologists have continued searching for the crews of six American planes that disappeared on December 7. A Honolulu resident has collected the names and curricula vitae of the Japanese pilots and can account for all but six of the downed Japanese aircraft. He is looking for the rest, hoping to find one that might become the centerpiece of a projected museum. Texan David Aiken has spent thirty-two years compiling a roster of every airman who was airborne on December 7 and locating witnesses to every aerial battle. He plans using this information to create a roster of the Japanese and American airmen he hopes will become the foundation for an organization of these men and their descendants, something like the Daughters of the American Revolution.

I think we remain fascinated by Pearl Harbor because it was the first attack on American soil by a foreign power since the War of 1812, the worst naval catastrophe in United States history, and a landmark battle, like Yorktown or Gettysburg, that changed the course of history, in this instance by forcing the United States to play an active role in world affairs. There is also the romance that surrounds spectacular military defeats such as the Little Bighorn and the Charge of the Light Brigade, and the belief that, in the words of Admiral Thomas Fargo, who spoke at Pearl Harbor on December 7, 1999, "No single event is more central to our concept of national tragedy and national conviction than the events of December 7." There is also the suspicion that, like the assassination of

President Kennedy, Pearl Harbor is a watershed separating an innocent past from a corrupt future.

My own fascination with Pearl Harbor began in grade school during the 1950s, when no December 7 could pass without a bulletin board filled with old clippings or a visit from a veteran. I learned that the Japanese had been treacherous for mounting a sneak attack, then an indisputable evil rather than the approved "preemptive strike" of today, and remembered Pearl Harbor during our duck-and-cover air-raid drills, and worried that if those poky Japanese propeller planes could appear without warning over Hawaii, then why not Russian jets over Connecticut?

I considered Pearl Harbor a purely military engagement, and pictured warships spewing fire, planes exploding on the ground, gunners surrounded by rings of flame, and naval bands completing "The Star-Spangled Banner" before breaking for cover. I saw Marine officers emptying their revolvers at Zeros as tears ran down their cheeks, and admirals wearing pajamas standing in their gardens, staring in disbelief. But what I ignored, or never knew, was that this had happened on the edge of an American city where 40 percent of the 1941 population was the same race as the pilots of those dragonfly planes.

When I first arrived in Honolulu more than ten years ago I found it hard to believe that a modern city of 900,000 could have time for the relics of a 1941 city less than a third its size. But I was soon finding them everywhere. Bullet holes still scarred buildings at Hickam and Wheeler Fields, and although the teahouse patronized by a spy from the Japanese consulate had changed its name, it still catered to homesick Japanese.

The more time I spent in Honolulu, interviewing Pearl Harbor witnesses, and reading the 1941 newspapers and diaries, the more I suspected that the bitterness, failed reconciliations, and touchiness of survivors were products of both 1941 and the present—of the unique nature of Pearl Harbor, and of its ghosts. I was soon seeing Honolulu with a double vision, juxtaposing the 1941 city and the current one, and finding myself unable to visit a neighborhood without comparing it to its past, or to listen to witnesses without connecting their memories to their current lives. This is why I decided to recount the attack while also placing 1941 and the present alongside, hoping this might help to explain why, when far bloodier battles have been forgotten, Pearl Harbor remains so controversial and capable of stirring up such painful memories.

Pearl Harbor Ghosts was originally published in 1991, for the fiftieth anniversary of the attack. Like most survivors attending the December 7 ceremonies in Hawaii that year, I had assumed I was witnessing a last hurrah, the last great Pearl Harbor landmark anniversary before death decimated the World War II generation and interest in this pivotal day waned. As it turned out, I could not have been more wrong.

Pearl Harbor continues to haunt its survivors, as well as their descendants. Poignant requests for information about dead fathers, and from survivors attempting to locate old comrades, fill several Internet sites. One survivor laments that it has taken him almost sixty years to realize that his Pearl Harbor friendships were more precious than any others. A man asks for help in finding a sailor stationed on a battleship during the attack who was "the best boyhood friend I *ever* had." A Pearl Harbor son wants a 1941 crew list from the U.S.S. *Pennsylvania*, so he can determine where his father was standing on December 7, and exactly what he had seen and heard.

Throughout the 1990s, survivors, their children, and a large cadre of amateur and professional Pearl Harbor historians have continued documenting the most arcane aspects of the attack, and attempting to solve every mystery and preserve every relic.

Nanette Purnell of Kailua, Oahu, has gathered so much information about the professions and family backgrounds of the forty-eight civilians killed on December 7 from interviews, obituaries, archives, police reports, and hospital records she can pinpoint the exact spot where her "forgotten victims" were killed or mortally wounded. In 1997, an article by John De Virgilio in *Proceedings*, the magazine of the U.S. Naval Institute, traced for the first time the precise path of the Japanese bomb that destroyed the U.S.S. *Arizona*. In July 2000, underwater archaeology students from the University of Hawaii located the remains of a Catalina flying boat the Japanese had sunk at its moorings in Kaneohe Bay. Two months later, the Pisces deep-diving submarines of the University of Hawaii's Underseas Research Laboratory spent weeks crisscrossing the mouth of the channel leading to Pearl Harbor, searching for a Japanese midget submarine sunk by an American destroyer before the aerial attack. And also in 2000, it was revealed that an urn containing the ashes of Nancy Wagner, the baby daughter of Albert Wagner, who had been chief yeoman on the U.S.S. *Utah*, still remained on board the sunken ship, and that Wagner's twin sister had been coming to Hawaii every Thanksgiving since 1990 to cast a lei onto the water.

The 1990s also saw more memorials to Pearl Harbor. The U.S.S. *Hoga*, the tugboat that dragged the damaged battleship *Nevada* to shallow water during the attack, was listed on the National Register of Historic Places; Colorado's Interstate 70 was christened the Pearl Harbor Memorial Highway; and a Pennsylvania Turnpike extension was renamed the Pearl Harbor Memorial Highway Extension. During the decade, survivors of the U.S.S. *Arizona* held their first memorial service at the *Arizona* Memorial, California observed its first Pearl Harbor Remembrance Day, the Department of the Navy finally dropped its long-standing objections to naming a ship after the attack and commissioned the U.S.S. *Pearl Harbor*, and President Clinton proclaimed December 7, 1996, the fifty-fifth anniversary of the attack, to be National Pearl Harbor Remembrance Day.

To mark the sixtieth anniversary I have revised and updated this book. The story of the attack and its immediate aftermath of course remains the same, but the ways in which Pearl Harbor continues to haunt the nation, and those who survived it, is a continuing and changing one. The attorney representing Admiral Husband Kimmel, who commanded the U.S. Pacific Fleet at the time of the attack, had it right when he wrote, "Pearl Harbor never dies, and no living person has seen the end of it."

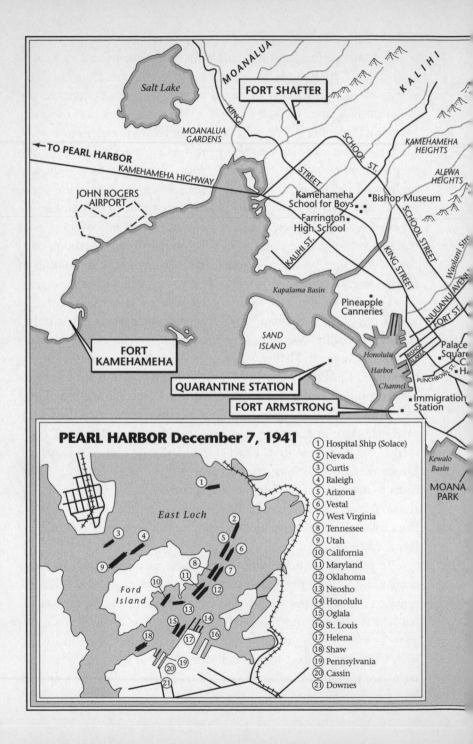

Salt Lake

MOANALUA

KALIHI

FORT SHAFTER

KING ST.

MOANALUA
GARDENS

SCHOOL ST.

KAMEHAMEHA
HEIGHTS

← TO PEARL HARBOR

ALEWA
HEIGHTS

KAMEHAMEHA HIGHWAY

STREET

SCHOOL STREET

JOHN ROGERS
AIRPORT

Kamehameha
School for Boys

Bishop Museum

KING STREET

Waokani Stre

Farrington
High School

KALIHI ST.

Kapalama Basin

Pineapple
Canneries

NUUANU AVENU

FORT ST.

SAND
ISLAND

BISHOP
ALAKEA

Palace
Square

**FORT
KAMEHAMEHA**

Honolulu

C.
H.

QUARANTINE STATION

Harbor

PUNCHBOWL ST.

Channel

FORT ARMSTRONG

Immigration
Station

PEARL HARBOR December 7, 1941

Kewalo
Basin

MOANA
PARK

East Loch

① Hospital Ship (Solace)
② Nevada
③ Curtis
④ Raleigh
⑤ Arizona
⑥ Vestal
⑦ West Virginia
⑧ Tennessee
⑨ Utah
⑩ California
⑪ Maryland
⑫ Oklahoma
⑬ Neosho
⑭ Honolulu
⑮ Oglala
⑯ St. Louis
⑰ Helena
⑱ Shaw
⑲ Pennsylvania
⑳ Cassin
㉑ Downes

Ford
Island

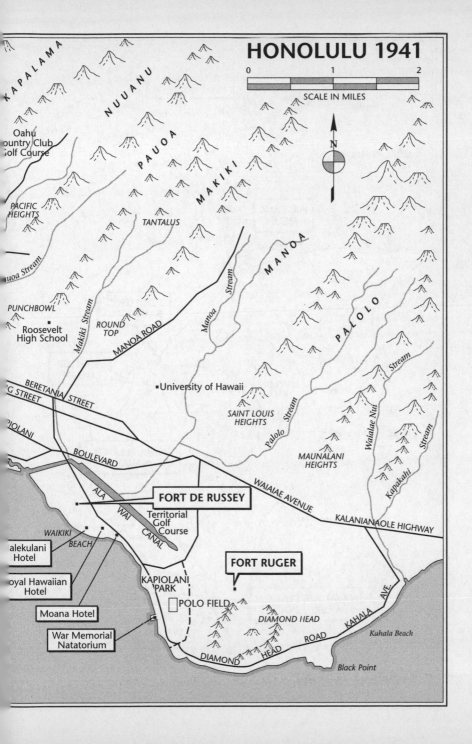

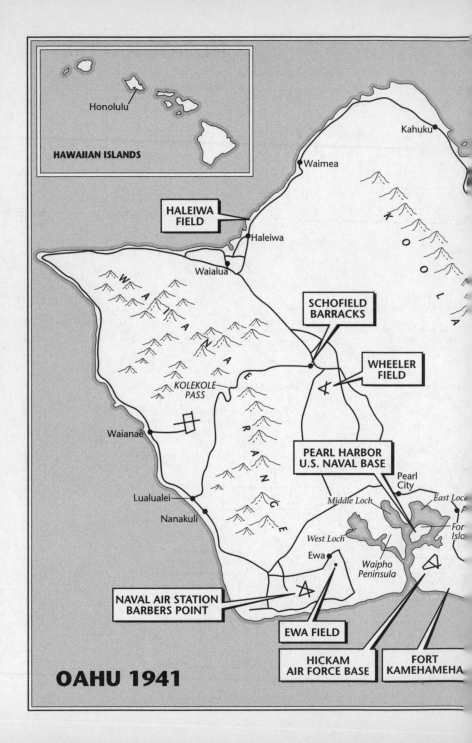

HAWAIIAN ISLANDS

Honolulu

HALEIWA
FIELD

Haleiwa

Waialua

Waimea

Kahuku

K
O
O
L
A

SCHOFIELD
BARRACKS

WHEELER
FIELD

W
A
I
A
N
A
E

KOLEKOLE
PASS

R
A
N
G
E

Waianae

Lualualei

Nanakuli

PEARL HARBOR
U.S. NAVAL BASE

Pearl
City

Middle Loch

East Loch

For
Isla

West Loch

Ewa

Waipho
Peninsula

NAVAL AIR STATION
BARBERS POINT

EWA FIELD

HICKAM
AIR FORCE BASE

FORT
KAMEHAMEHA

OAHU 1941

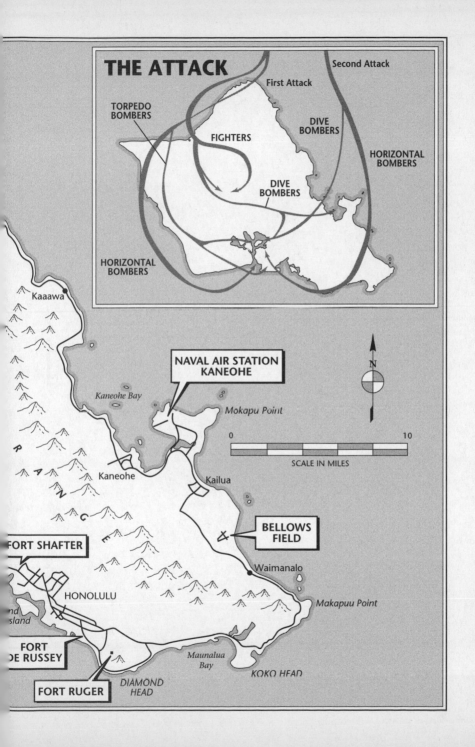

THE ATTACK

Second Attack

First Attack

TORPEDO
BOMBERS

FIGHTERS

DIVE
BOMBERS

HORIZONTAL
BOMBERS

DIVE
BOMBERS

HORIZONTAL
BOMBERS

Kaaawa

R A N C E

Kaneohe Bay

**NAVAL AIR STATION
KANEOHE**

Mokapu Point

N

0   10

SCALE IN MILES

Kaneohe

Kailua

**BELLOWS
FIELD**

FORT SHAFTER

Waimanalo

HONOLULU

Makapuu Point

and
Island

**FORT
DE RUSSEY**

FORT RUGER

DIAMOND
HEAD

Maunalua
Bay

KOKO HEAD

PART ONE

DECEMBER 5, 1941

CHAPTER 1

THE GREAT WHITE SHIP
LEAVES HONOLULU

Ever since I read about the last peacetime sailing of the S.S. *Lurline* from Honolulu on December 5, 1941, the words "Pearl Harbor" can set her sailing in my mind.

I like the contrast: the Great White Liner of the Pacific leaving peacetime Honolulu and docking five days later, in wartime San Francisco, its passengers having traveled from peace to war. The abrupt change traumatized them. They learned about the attack when a porter brought their morning coffee in a tin pot, because the expensive silverware was already in storage, or when a crewman sloshed blackout paint across their portholes, with each stroke darkening their staterooms. They lived in that eerie twilight for two days, fully clothed and wearing life preservers, knowing there were casualties in Hawaii, but not knowing which of their loved ones were already corpses.

The *Lurline*'s passengers may not have been escaping an enemy occupation or certain death, but had they stayed behind they might have been among the twenty-five hundred servicemen and civilians killed on December 7. The *Lurline*'s last peacetime sailing is compelling because it separated people into two groups: those who would be strafed by Japanese planes, live under martial law, and see dead American soldiers and sailors; and those aboard the *Lurline* who, like mainland Americans, would always remember December 7 in terms of where they were and what they were doing, much as my generation recalls the Kennedy assassination.

So imagine the S.S. *Lurline*, the Great White Ship of the Matson Lines, as she loaded passengers in Honolulu on December 5, 1941. First, picture her from a distance, perhaps from the observation deck of the eight-story-high Aloha Tower—The Gateway to the Pacific—that winked colored signals and was the tallest building for thousands of miles. From here, several hundred feet above the docks, there appeared to be little to distinguish this Boat Day from others marking a liner's arrival or departure from the most isolated archipelago in the world. There were spiderwebs of streamers, blizzards of confetti, and celebrities posing for photographers. The Royal Hawaiian Band played its tearjerking melodies and hula girls danced. Local boys dived for coins thrown from the top deck, and there were flower leis everywhere.

Earlier that day, Japanese women had gathered blossoms from slopes of the saw-toothed mountains overshadowing Honolulu. Elderly Hawaiian women had sat along the sidewalks leading to the docks all morning, plucking wild ginger and plumeria from old cereal boxes and releasing clouds of perfume, as they strung the fifteen hundred leis necessary for the average Boat Day. The leis were long and full, fragrant necklaces of yellow ilima and sweet mountain maile hanging to passengers' knees.

Seen from the Aloha Tower, the Boat Day crowds of December 5 resembled earlier ones. So many people were dressed in white the scene appeared as if in an overexposed photograph. Women wore white-cotton dresses and carried white parasols. Naval officers were in dress whites and civilians were in linen suits. Nursemaids in white uniforms minded the scrubbed children of the kamaaina (native born) aristocracy, an elite of about one hundred Caucasian families descended from nineteenth-century New England missionaries who, as the expression goes, "Came to do good and did well." During the last half century, these families had overthrown the Hawaiian monarchy, supported the immigration of Chinese, Japanese, and Filipino laborers, and through intermarriage and interlocking directorates seized control of the land, commerce, and political life of these islands as completely as the oligarchy of any banana republic. Yet, within three days of the *Lurline*'s sailing, this elite would see logs rolled across its polo fields, its private schools and country clubs turned into barracks, and its political power swept away forever.

As on every Boat Day, the crowds beneath the Aloha Tower numbered in the thousands, many more than might be warranted by the departure of eight hundred passengers. But on a remote island the arrival or departure of a boat for the mainland was always an event. Large Alexander and Baldwin calendars advertising the Matson Lines schedule hung in most Honolulu kitchens and so on Boat Day office workers left their desks to see who was arriving or leaving, and young men met every liner, hoping to discover a pretty girl. Beachboys from Waikiki came to play ukulele serenades to women they had romanced. Businessmen and politicians gathered in huddles, closing deals and exchanging gossip. The leis, hula dancers, and Royal Hawaiian Band reminded everyone that they lived on an island with an exotic history and culture that had, so far, escaped the horrors of the century.

But descend from the Aloha Tower, mingle in the crowd, and you might notice that this Boat Day was unlike any other. Her passengers might not imagine that the *Lurline* would be dodging Japanese submarines, and officers embracing their departing wives might not imagine that in two weeks some would be carried aboard this same ship on stretchers, but there were clues.

Because of a sudden increase in boisterous young defense workers and servicemen, there were more police on the pier and more cars clogging Fort and Bishop Streets, even though traffic lights had recently replaced the Hawaiian policemen who directed traffic from beneath umbrellas. Because so many passengers were defense workers, the Matson Line had engaged two Los Angeles policemen to make the round-trip voyage on their vacation time, giving them free accommodation in exchange for keeping order on board. Because war with Japan was feared—although few believed it would start in Hawaii—and 40 percent of Hawaii's population was Japanese, the authorities feared sabotage, and so the piers were guarded by soldiers of the Hawaii Territorial Guard, who were Japanese.

The *Lurline*'s sister ship, the *Matsonia*, was already being turned into a troopship, meaning there had been no transportation to California for the previous two weeks except a few seats on the Pan Am Clippers. Thus there was a record number of passengers on this voyage, so many that seventy were assigned cots in a main lounge once described as "the last word in maritime trimmings . . . until someone puts a keel under the Louvre and floats it." There was also a record number of letter pouches and parcels, more American diplomats and Pan-American Airways employees than usual (evacuated from the Orient because of the danger of war), more stowaways, more people without leis, since they had not been in Hawaii long enough for anyone to make an event of their departure, more women than men, and a sizable contingent of military wives, some of whom would discover, when the *Lurline* docked in San Francisco, that they had become widows.

There were Japanese-Americans on the passenger list, too, including an Army officer who would soon suffer some embarrassing moments, and Japanese families sailing from a place where their incarceration in a detention camp would be unlikely to a place where it was almost certain.

The *Lurline* usually filled several staterooms with starlets and socialites, but that day there was only Miss Marjorie Petty, the model for her father's drawings of the scantily clothed "Petty Girl" in *Esquire*. Many passengers were defense workers who had been turning Hawaii into America's "Fist in the Pacific" and were returning home after shocking Honolulu by being the first haoles (Caucasians) seen to engage in heavy physical labor. Because these workers did not consider Hawaii home, and were glad to be leaving, you could see at that Boat Day something unthinkable even the year before, people leaving Honolulu with dry eyes.

The last prewar sailing of the *Lurline* seemed to indicate that everyone *knew* war was coming. Why else the crowding? The stowaways? The Army wives? The contingent of panicky prostitutes who were more sensitive than anyone to the military mind?

There were passengers like Mrs. P. R. Sellers, who still remembers how servicemen had been telling their wives for months that they were concerned about a war with Japan, and that her husband, then at sea on the carrier *Enterprise*, wanted her out of Hawaii. But she was in the minority. Most military wives were leaving because their husbands worried that a war in Asia would restrict travel to the mainland. Most local residents were going on vacation and business trips, confident they would be able to return to the islands whenever they wished. Bob Stroh's father, who was a salesman for Primo beer, was taking his family along on a West Coast business trip, never imagining they would all be stuck in California for three years. Stroh recalls the sailing as a glorious occasion, with the *Lurline* steaming away through a cloud of confetti and streamers.

More than anything, the December 5 Boat Day reflected how confused Honoluluans were during their last week of peace. Assembled on the pier were people fleeing because they feared war, and staying for the same reason; those leaving because they believed war was remote, and remaining for the same reason.

Honolulu's newspapers reflected this uncertainty. If you wanted to prove that everyone must have known war was imminent, you could pick out headlines like, "Kurusu Bluntly Warned Nation Ready for Battle," "Pacific Zero Hour Near," "U.S. Army Alerted in Manila—Singapore Mobilizing as War Tension Grows," and "U.S. Demands Explanations of Japan; Moves Americans Prepare for Any Emergency; Navy Declared Ready." If you wanted to prove peace was equally likely, there was, "Japan Called Still Hopeful of Making Peace with U.S.," "Hirohito Holds Power to Stop Japanese Army," "Further Peace Efforts Urged," and, on December 6, "New Peace Effort Urged in Tokyo—Joint Commission to Iron Out Deadlock with U.S. Proposal."

The *Lurline* passenger who best reflected the nervousness and overconfidence characteristic of December 5 was a Colonel Tetley of the Army Signal Corps, who commanded the Army's radar system in Hawaii. Radar was only installed in mid-November, and was largely ignored or treated with contempt by military and civilian authorities on Oahu despite its importance in winning the Battle of Britain. Governor Poindexter and the National Park Service had forbidden Tetley to install his radar on mountain peaks, where it would be most effective, because they feared radar installations would ruin scenic vistas and defile mountains sacred to the Hawaiian people. The commander of the Army's Hawaiian Department, General Walter Short, believed Tetley's five mobile radar stations were good training tools, but not important enough to operate twenty-four hours a day. But there was great enthusiasm for radar in the lower ranks and, as Tetley told me, his radar operators were "exceptional people, the brightest young men from Signal Corps."

Whenever Tetley's whiz kids plotted a Japanese attack in their training exercises it was carrier-based, and hitting the island at dawn. They expected an attack at Thanksgiving. When it never materialized Tetley thought Oahu was safe until Christmas. Still, he was dumbfounded when the Army ordered both him and his antiaircraft liaison officer to San Francisco to observe how its radar stations handled a simulated attack by carrier-based planes against its Navy Yard. He was so convinced an attack on Hawaii was imminent he had prepared his household goods for shipping and had decided to evacuate his wife and infant son to the mainland, even though the only accommodations available were expensive ones in first class. As his family waited for the *Lurline* to sail, his wife met Pan Am and State Department employees being evacuated from Wake and Midway Islands. She asked Tetley, "Why are they pulling people back from Asia and the islands?" He replied, "For the same reason you're on this boat."

But most civilians and servicemen in Hawaii discounted the chance of a Japanese raid. Certainly none of the passengers arriving on the *Lurline* two days before believed they were sailing into a war zone. After all, if war was expected, would two football teams have arrived from the mainland? The Willamette team would play the University of Hawaii on December 6, while San Jose College was scheduled for the following week. Would Hollywood cameramen have come to film background scenery for *To the Shores of Tripoli*, a historical drama about the first Marine Corps victory? Would noted European war correspondent Joseph C. Harsch have planned to catch the westbound Pan-American Clipper on December 7 so he could spend the winter reporting from Japan? Or would Earl Thacker, a respected local executive, have told reporters meeting the ship on December 3 that the opinion in Washington was that there would be no war with Japan and that the present attitude was bluff although, he added, "if the Japanese military want a fight, the United States is fully prepared for them."

Walter Dillingham, a member of a wealthy and influential Honolulu family, remembers the *Lurline*'s last peacetime crossing to Honolulu as "a normal *Lurline* voyage, except there were no pretty girls." He told me, "Most of the passengers were defense workers who came to the main dining room—which was a very posh place— with rubber bands around their sleeves and wearing sweat-stained hats." He was so confident Hawaii was safe he had proposed via radiophone to his girlfriend, who was temporarily in San Francisco. "You're going to have a problem getting back to the Islands," he told her. "The military are not letting people on the boats now unless they're bona fide citizens of Hawaii. Perhaps you should tell them you're about to be one because you're going to marry me."

The most complacent of the arriving *Lurline* passengers was Brigadier General Howard C. Davidson, commander of Wheeler Field's Fourteenth Pursuit Wing, the planes assigned to intercept an airborne attack on Oahu. A formation of these planes buzzed the *Lurline* in his honor, and upon arriving he announced that during a tour of mainland airfields he had been particularly impressed by a civil-defense exercise in Seattle. Eight thousand volunteer civilian spotters there had quickly reported a flight of attacking airplanes, and reports piled in to defense headquarters in time for interceptor squadrons to rise and meet them. He promised to duplicate this scheme in Hawaii and recruit civilian spotters who would keep their eyes peeled for the approach of enemy aircraft, even though it is difficult to imagine a plan more unsuited to Hawaii's geography or more useless to its defense. Wheeler Field was nine miles from the north shore, and twelve from the south, so civilian spotters standing at the water's edge could provide less than five minutes' warning. Furthermore, after Davidson's fighters had completed their aerial tricks over the *Lurline* on December 3, he ordered them disarmed and parked in a tight antisabotage formation on Wheeler's tarmac, which would make it impossible to launch them all in under four hours.

Late on the afternoon of December 5, after a five-hour delay caused by the last-minute arrival of military families, loudspeakers in the *Lurline*'s corridors finally sounded "All ashore going ashore." Like every departure from Hawaii, this one unfolded in an atmosphere of hysteria, melancholy, and recklessness. Strangers embraced, laughter became hoarse, corridors filled with cigarette smoke, and the thick perfume of flower leis choked staterooms. The delayed departure made the parties more boozy and emotional than usual, and tears appeared even in the eyes of those hardened Boat Day veterans, the Royal Hawaiian Band.

Finally the *Lurline* blasted her whistle, the band played a last "Aloha Oe," people shouted "Good-bye . . . see you in a month, six months, a year," and men, even men in uniform, wept.

As she pulled away her passengers threw streamers at friends on the pier, creating a colored spiderweb that straightened, tightened, and, just before breaking, appeared to be binding her to that dock, and to that peaceful day, forever. Outrigger canoes followed her to the mouth of the harbor and bombers from Hickam Field circled overhead, their bellies just feet above the water. Fighters swooped across her decks, their pilots waggling their wings in farewell to their wives.

Some husbands raced to Diamond Head Lighthouse to wave a

final good-bye, or hired speedboats to escort the *Lurline* from the harbor, cutting recklessly across her bow. Some passengers tossed their leis overboard, the legend being that if they washed ashore, their owners would return to Hawaii.

The people seeing them off walked or drove back through a low-rise little colonial city of palm trees, pink stucco, and red-tiled roofs, past the granite trading house of the haole (Caucasian) elite, the rococo palace of the deposed Hawaiian monarchy, and the handsome schools that children, even wealthy children, attended barefoot. They returned to homes whose sliding doors, louvered windows, and flimsy wooden walls made them vulnerable to air raids, all in all, an architecture spectacularly unsuited to war.

CHAPTER 2

VICE-CONSUL MORIMURA
SEES THE SIGHTS

On the same day, and perhaps at the same time that pursuit pilots flew over the *Lurline* to salute their departing wives, Vice-Consul Tadashi Morimura of the Japanese consulate in Honolulu was observing Wheeler Field and Pearl Harbor from the passenger seat of a Piper Cub, counting planes and warships, and searching for the barrage balloons rumored to have arrived from the mainland. Morimura was in fact Ensign Takeo Yoshikawa of the Imperial Japanese Navy, a wispy, boyish-looking man who, since arriving in Honolulu under diplomatic cover nine months earlier, had become the most effective and important spy in a world with many contenders for that title.

Spying on Pearl Harbor from a commercial sightseeing plane while dressed in linen trousers and an aloha shirt was very much in character for Yoshikawa. He checked out the depth of Kaneohe Bay by taking a glass-bottomed excursion boat, accompanied by several young women from the consulate. He disguised himself as a Filipino laborer and washed dishes in the Pearl Harbor officers' club so he could eavesdrop on conversations. He went swimming at the mouth of Pearl Harbor to look for submarine nets, avoiding detection by scattering moss on the water and breathing through a reed. He purchased rounds of drinks in sailors' bars, and traveled as a tourist to Maui to inspect the anchorage at Lahaina, staying at a hotel owned by a Japanese alien with a glass eye. He hiked through the forested hills and cane fields of Aiea Heights that enjoyed unobstructed views of Pearl Harbor, memorizing the movements of the warships below. He joined a Japanese fencing club popular with American servicemen, becoming known there, according to a later intelligence report, as "an attentive listener." He spent evenings carousing with the consulate staff at the Shuncho-Ro teahouse on Alewa Heights, romancing geishas and observing Pearl Harbor through a high-powered telescope its owners had thoughtfully installed on a second-floor balcony. He could not drive, so he was chauffeured in a Packard limousine by John Mikami, a Japanese-American taxi driver, and accompanied by Richard Kotoshirodo, a clerk at the Japanese consulate who held dual American and Japanese citizenship.

Yoshikawa commanded two agents of dubious value: a lazy German playboy named Otto Kuehn, who was related by marriage to Heinrich Himmler and was already under FBI surveillance, and the chief chemist of the Honolulu sake brewery, who often drank too much of his own product and boasted that his father-in-law was a Japanese admiral. He resisted recruiting agents from Honolulu's Japanese residents because he thought them "just trash" and "insufficiently educated" (an attitude still expressed, although more subtly, by some present-day visitors from Japan). Add up the teahouse, telescope, drunken sake chemist, German playboy, glass-eyed hotel owner, and Yoshikawa's missing finger (a device used by Alfred Hitchcock in *The 39 Steps* to identify a German spy), and he becomes a spy out of a radio serial or Hollywood B film, a caricature of a Japanese spy, the most obvious Japanese spy in the world.

He was an unlikely combination of dedication and recklessness, not unlike the archetypal Japanese businessman of today who puts in a serious, productive day, then heads off to a karaoke bar for an infantile binge. He was frequently drunk, often entertained girls in his quarters, and wrote sugary love poems to the Shuncho-Ro geishas, boasting the first joint of his left index finger was missing "on account of love." Yet he gathered intelligence carefully and methodically, varying his clothing so he would not be remembered, never carrying binoculars or a notebook, never taking photographs, and relying only on maps printed by the Hawaii Visitors Bureau. He told one consulate employee that the first rule of information collecting was "no get caught."

He used diplomatic cables to file his reports on the number of ships in Pearl Harbor and the reconnaissance activities of American aircraft. A September 24, 1941, cable from Tokyo ordered him to place an imaginary grid over Pearl Harbor, dividing it into five areas and reporting regularly which warships were anchored where. After the attack, this cable became known as the "bomb plot" message because of its obvious value for planning an air raid on Pearl Harbor. The American military had broken the Japanese diplomatic codes, and Yoshikawa's previous messages had been deciphered by top-secret Navy and Army units in Washington, Manila, and on the West Coast that were collectively known as "Magic" because their cryptanalysts were "magicians" at breaking codes. But this September 24 message, after being processed in Washington, was filed and forgotten like much of the intelligence transmitted by Yoshikawa, not considered important enough to be communicated to military commands in Hawaii. That happened because of bureaucratic rivalries and the military's obsession with secrecy, and because it was believed unlikely that any information of a tactical or operational military value could be found in the routine communications of minor Japanese diplomats.

Yoshikawa transmitted some of his most valuable espionage to Lieutenant Commander Suguru Suzuki, who arrived aboard the *Taiyo Maru* on November 1, 1941, disguised as a ship's steward. The *Taiyo Maru*, the last Japanese liner to call at an American port, had been sent via a northerly route, to chart the course that Admiral Yamamoto's strike force would use a month later. Its other mission was to collect intelligence material that Yoshikawa could not easily cable to Tokyo. Because Suzuki feared arrest by American counterintelligence agents, he met aboard ship with the Japanese consul, Nagao Kita, slipping him a ball of crumpled rice paper bearing ninety-seven questions such as "Are there antisubmarine nets at the entrance of Pearl Harbor?" "Each week, the fleet goes to sea. Where do they go; what do they do, particularly aircraft carriers?" "This is the most important question: On what day of the week would the most ships be in Pearl Harbor on normal occasions?"

Back at the consulate, Yoshikawa provided detailed answers to Suzuki's questions. Many of these answers were essential to the last-minute planning and timing of the attack. He reported that aerial reconnaissance to the north was "poorly organized" and "downright bad," and identified Sunday as the day most ships were in harbor and their crews most relaxed.

American counterintelligence agents believed the greatest threat to Hawaii's security came from its Japanese residents and so, despite all the FBI, customs, and intelligence agents watching the *Taiyo Maru's* gangplank, and despite searches of departing passengers that delayed its sailing several days, consulate staffers were given only cursory inspections and managed to smuggle aboard Yoshikawa's answers and the Souvenir of Honolulu photographs on which he had divided Pearl Harbor into numbered squares. Copies of those photographs would later be found in the cockpits of Japanese planes shot down on December 7.

Tokyo increased its demands on Yoshikawa during the ten days preceding the attack. On November 28, his superiors ordered him to "report upon the entrance or departure of capital ships (battleships, cruisers, and carriers) and the length of time they remain at anchor." They told him the next day, "We have been receiving reports from you on ship movements, but in future you will also report even when there are no movements." (A clue Japan was interested as much in ships remaining in harbor as in their sorties.) On December 2, his Tokyo control inquired about observation balloons and antitorpedo nets, adding, "In view of the present situation, the presence in port of the battleships, aircraft carriers, and cruisers is of the greatest importance. Hereafter report to me daily to the utmost of your ability." On December 4, Yoshikawa was ordered to "wire immediately the movements of the Pacific Fleet subsequent to [December] 4." The following day he made his penultimate information-collecting expedition.

After Yoshikawa's sight-seeing flight of December 5, he drove to the Pearl City peninsula and bought a soda pop from a stand opposite the Pearl Harbor gate. He returned to the Japanese consulate and drafted a cable to Tokyo reporting, "(1) During Friday morning . . . the three battleships mentioned in my message #239 arrived here. (2) The *Lexington* and five heavy cruisers left port on the same day. (3) The following ships were in port on the afternoon of [December] 5: eight battleships, three light cruisers, sixteen destroyers . . ."

As with every coded message sent by the Japanese consulate since December 1, the manager of the RCA office in Honolulu gave a copy to Captain Irving Mayfield, the chief intelligence officer for the Fourteenth Naval District. These Japanese diplomatic cables, containing obvious clues to the attack, were ungarbled originals, delivered on the day of their filing. Neither Mayfield nor Admiral Husband Kimmel, Commander in Chief Pacific Fleet, nor any Navy or Army officer on Oahu knew of the existence of the Magic codebreakers in Washington, who could have deciphered these messages. Instead, on December 5, Mayfield took this and other Japanese consulate messages of the last several days to Commander Joseph Rochefort, who headed the naval communications intelligence unit on Oahu responsible for intercepting and deciphering Japanese naval codes. Because Rochefort's unit was busy attempting to discover the location of the Japanese carrier groups, Yoshikawa's cables were given a low priority and assigned to Farnsley Woodward, a young warrant officer. Because the Navy was not supposed to tackle any intercepted Japanese diplomatic messages, Woodward did not have the key to the Japanese code, and so on December 5 he began the laborious task of breaking the diplomatic code from scratch, a task he made even more difficult by erroneously lining up the text of the messages backwards, a mistake he only discovered on December 9.

Since Pearl Harbor, the importance of the cable traffic between Tokyo and the Japanese consulate in Honolulu has been widely recognized. These messages not only gave the Japanese task force crucial information about Oahu's defenses and the ships in harbor, but also provided some of the last and best clues that Japan was preparing a surprise attack. Former fleet intelligence officer Edwin T. Layton concludes in his book, *And I Was There*, that any of Yoshikawa's cables "would, at the very least, have brought an increase in the level of alert on Oahu. Air patrols would have been stepped up, and Kimmel might well have reversed his decision not to send the battle fleet to sea."

These incriminating cables were also sent to Washington for deciphering by the top-secret Magic program. Yet by the morning of December 7, only one had been decoded and translated, while the rest sat in low-priority in-boxes. And it appears this single translated cable, the revealing December 3 "lights" cable, was discounted because it had been translated by a woman.

The Japanese consulate had transmitted the "lights" cable to Tokyo on December 3. It described an elaborate system devised by Yoshikawa's bumbling German agent, Otto Kuehn, to signal intelligence to offshore Japanese submarines using lights placed in the dormer windows of Kuehn's beach house (although he had at that point rented it to two Army couples), stars and numbers displayed on the sail of his boat (although he did not own one), bonfires lit on high points in Maui, and radio want ads such as "Beauty Parlor Operator Wanted," and "Chicken Farm for Sale."

Kuehn did not know an attack was imminent, but the intelligence officer in Tokyo who requested that he devise this code did know. Had Oahu's defenders seen that cable, it would have rung alarm bells because it indicated a strong interest in the Pacific Fleet anchorage, and described a visual system assuming the presence of Japanese vessels in Hawaiian waters.

On December 6, this "lights" message was deciphered in Washington and awaited only translation into English, a process that could be delayed several weeks for low-priority documents. Instead, Dorothy Edgers, the only woman among the Navy Department's cryptographic section's six Japanese-English translators, happened to choose it from a half dozen similar intercepts. Three years later, she told a court of inquiry, "At first glance, this seemed more interesting than some of the other messages I had in my basket. I selected it and asked one of the other men who was also a translator working on other messages whether or not it shouldn't be done immediately." Although Edgers had been employed in the section only three weeks, she had lived in Japan for thirty of her thirty-eight years, and held a diploma authorizing her to teach Japanese to Japanese pupils at the high-school level. Yet, as a novice in the cryptographic section, she was not trusted to translate top-priority work, such as cables transmitted in the code used by the Japanese embassy in Washington.

Although Edgers was supposed to quit at noon on Saturday, and although one of her superiors said the "lights" message did not warrant any special attention and would keep until Monday, she continued working on her translation. She showed a rough version to Commander Alwin Kramer, the chief of the section, who criticized her for staying late to work on a "deferred" intercept, saying he did not think the message was of "sufficient importance." He made some trivial changes in her translation—to make it more "professional," he would later testify—and said, "This needs a lot of work, Mrs. Edgers. Why don't you run along now? We'll finish the editing sometime next week."

She protested, saying the intercept should be disseminated immediately.

"You just go home, Mrs. Edgers," he replied. "We'll get back to this piece on Monday."

She stayed nonetheless, finishing the translation and giving it to the chief clerk. On December 8, it sat on Commander Kramer's desk, waiting for him to make it more "professional."

When you examine the "lights" message story, and the justifications Commander Kramer manufactured later to excuse himself, it becomes obvious that the principal reason Edgers's suspicions were dismissed and her translation ignored was that she was a woman.

The story of how radio intelligence data from the Japanese consulate in Honolulu, such as the "lights" message, was misused in the months and days preceding Pearl Harbor is maddening and complicated. Had the diplomatic cables been decoded in a timely manner, and their contents been communicated to the Army and Navy commanders in Hawaii, the catastrophe of December 7 might have been averted. Historians and former military officers have chronicled this saga of bad luck, and of rivalries between the Army and Navy, and between staff officers in Washington and those in Honolulu. At fault was an obsession with secrecy that kept the Hawaii commanders from knowing of the existence of Magic, much less receiving crucial information from it. There was too much faith placed in technology—on the technical side of intercepting and deciphering—and too little analysis and interpretation, and too much confidence that the ability to read Japanese diplomatic correspondence would protect the United States from any surprise military action.

Less attention has been paid to the larger flaws behind these shortcomings—appeasement and racism. Although the government had closed all German and Italian consulates in the United States by the fall of 1941, Japanese ones were permitted to remain open because it was feared closing them might upset Japanese-American negotiations, and because of the perception, shared by counterintelligence agents in Honolulu and cryptographic officers in Washington, that the staff of the Japanese consulates such as the one in Honolulu were bumbling amateurs, unable to produce valuable intelligence. German spies were seen as efficient and dangerous, but Japanese spies had the image of being small and bespectacled, easily identified, and slightly ridiculous.

Yoshikawa was never named by intelligence officials testifying at the nine Pearl Harbor investigations. Yet forty years later, J. Harold Hughes, an FBI agent at the time of the attack, would claim, "We all knew he was a spy." Hughes said he had broken silence because "I'm just so tired of reading this kind of story about 'Master Spy' Yoshikawa. It just isn't so, by dang." He also claimed that the FBI had spotted Lieutenant Commander Suzuki when he arrived on the *Taiyo Maru*, that none of Yoshikawa's information had had any bearing on the attack, and that there had been no great change in Yoshikawa's routine in the last week indicating the attack was coming, statements all contradicted by every known fact.

Another former naval intelligence officer, Don Woodrum, told me Yoshikawa had been identified as a possible agent, but added that his spying had not mattered much because he had collected mostly negative information, such as that there were no sub nets, or any long-range reconnaissance on weekends. "People were suspicious of him, but suppose he had been followed, what would you really have seen?" Woodrum asked.

The significance of Yoshikawa's activities might have become more obvious had counterintelligence agents employed Japanese-Americans as informers. Many local Japanese worked as cooks, secretaries, and drivers in the consulate, where Yoshikawa's erratic habits, lack of official duties, and interest in intelligence gathering were widely known. In hearings convened a month after the attack, Navy Intelligence chief Mayfield said, "It has been my experience, [with] which I believe the other two investigative agencies [the FBI and Army] agree, that to investigate a Japanese is exceedingly difficult and can really only be done by another Japanese." Yet, when asked, "Aren't there amongst those American-Japanese some persons whom you could trust as American agents?" he replied, "I have not found one."

The FBI had only one Japanese-American staff member, and he was a translator. The FBI agent in charge of the Honolulu office, Robert Shivers, admitted being unable to gather information about Japanese activities from Caucasian sources. He had made a tour of the islands himself, all the while asking Caucasian businessmen and plantation managers about the Japanese. "I got just about as many different answers as the number of people I talked to," he reported. "So far as I could learn, the haole populace in Hawaii was not in a position to give any accurate information about the Japanese populace [because] there had been very little intercourse between the two."

Yoshikawa's task was also made easier by the military's obsession with the loyalty of the local Japanese. A month after the attack, Admiral Reeves, a member of the Roberts Commission, asked a young naval intelligence officer named George Kimball, "Is it possible, then, that both the Navy and the FBI may [have] concentrate[d] on subversive activities among the Japanese populace and have overlooked the espionage activity?"

"I think there has been that tendency," Kimball admitted, adding that, "Of course, a good Japanese agent is not going to be actively pro-Japanese and offensively so. So, I think perhaps they may have overlooked some of the most important [agents]."

Captain Mayfield himself finally conceded in 1943 that, "The type of investigation indulged in was well suited for the purposes of internal security, that is, determining whether certain persons in wartime would likely be loyal to or sympathize with the cause of, or give to, nations at war with the United States. It was not suitable for counterespionage purposes."

In the last days before the attack, instead of searching for Japanese spies by staking out such obvious Pearl Harbor observation points as Pearl City and Aiea Heights, counterintelligence agents became obsessed with deciding which of Hawaii's 160,000 residents of Japanese ancestry should be detained in the event of a war. FBI agents drew elaborate organization charts showing connections between Japanese religious, social, business, and educational groups and the Japanese consulate. They compiled meticulous lists of Japanese corporations and trade organizations, Japanese consular agents, language-school principals, Shinto priests, and consulate staff members, but omitted Vice-Consul Tadashi Morimura (aka Yoshikawa).

In late November, Army Intelligence officers and FBI agents

compiled rosters of potential detainees, including all the German and Italian aliens on the Islands and residents of the Territory of Japanese descent who would be considered security risks. An Army Intelligence report boasted that, "Representatives of this office and the FBI carefully scrutinized the list of Japanese residents," concluding that fifteen hundred posed a potential threat. These were divided into an "A" group of five hundred believed dangerous to the internal security of the United States, and a "B" list of "doubtful" loyalty, who would be kept under tight surveillance.

Lieutenant Colonel George Bicknell of Army Intelligence reported that during November, "individual investigations of persons suspected to be dangerous to security were intensified with all available trained personnel being assigned to this highly important requirement." In the weeks preceding December 7, counterintelligence agents worked twelve and fourteen hours a day, seven days a week, checking the addresses of targeted detainees. They made a reconnaissance of detainees' homes, familiarizing themselves with their neighborhoods and, according to an Army report, "Detailed instructions were drawn up for each squad, including the most minute details." The agents prepared maps showing the exact location of potential detainees' rural residences and made plans for cutting telephone service to their homes, so they could not warn friends. They organized riot squads that would man key intersections, on the assumption other Japanese residents might attempt to free the detainees. They revised the lists of detainees for the last time on December 1, then forwarded them to the chiefs of military intelligence and the FBI on December 4, the day before Ensign Yoshikawa, who was on none of their lists, embarked on his last weekend of espionage.

CHAPTER 3

GEORGE AKITA
DELIVERS A SPEECH

In the days before Pearl Harbor, no one in Hawaii was more concerned with what "Americanism" was, and how it could be attained, than young Japanese-Americans, so it is not surprising that a fifteen-year-old Japanese student at Farrington High School named George Akita should win the ten-dollar first prize in the fourth annual speech contest sponsored by the Aloha chapter of the Daughters of the American Revolution (DAR), held in the McKinley High School auditorium on the evening of December 5.

The contest's theme was "Americanism," a word that now sounds dated but was no joke then for Japanese-Americans wishing to prove their loyalty. They knew it was not enough to vote, pay taxes, serve in the Army, and observe patriotic holidays. "Americanism" was also required. Like every "ism," this was an all-encompassing way of living and thinking, reflecting a knowledge of American history and geography and a taste for approved books, movies, and sports. Akita's prize-winning speech, "American Citizenship and National Defense," ended with, "From tropical Hawaii to the rock-bound shores of Maine, from the snow-clad plains of the Dakotas to sunny Texas, let us, Americans all, rally around the Stars and Stripes in the defense of our way of life. With the love of democracy burning in our hearts and minds, we cannot fail—we must not fail."

Did Akita really believe this? Did he really think he was an American like any other? Apparently he did, if his December 7 diary entry is any indication: "Planning to stay at Central [the school where he was assigned as a student civil-defense volunteer] tonight. Mom didn't want me to go. She was afraid. Pop told her that no matter how young I am since I was a citizen of America I have to help America whenever I am able to. Even to die for America. I like his attitude. . . . I guess we Japanese are in for it now. Especially Mom and Pop, they're aliens. But the U.S. Government has promised not to molest the nationals unless they by their actions and deeds make themselves detrimental. I have faith in the U.S. Government."

It is enough to make you cry. Like most Japanese residents of Hawaii, Akita and his parents were not interned, but 110,000 mainland Japanese were, and on December 5, many of them must have also believed in "Americanism" as fervently as he did.

It is possible Akita won the DAR contest fairly (particularly since the year before he had won the *Honolulu Star-Bulletin* oratory contest on the Constitution) and that his speech was better than "What Is Americanism?" by Christine Weatherby, or "Americanism Marches Onward" by Irene Makaiau, or Peggy Engstrom's "I Am an American." But it is also possible he won because in those final months of 1941, the DAR judges were as obsessed as anyone in Hawaii with the loyalty of the Japanese, and believed it was their patriotic duty to encourage it.

The determination of young Japanese-Americans like George Akita to become "100 percent American" becomes all the more extraordinary when you know that at the turn of the century Honolulu's electric trolley cars had caused an epidemic of broken bones among Japanese customers who, after forgetting to press the stop button, departed a trolley with several traditional, deep-bowed alohas, grandly stepping off the moving car backward into space. Such accidents were so commonplace the Rapid Transit Company mounted a public-education program directed at the Japanese. By 1941, however, transit company officials and passengers were complaining about the loud conversation and boisterous manners of the children and grandchildren of those overly courteous trolley departees, and passengers on the city's new electric buses sometimes witnessed the spectacle of Japanese children shushing parents who spoke Japanese, and looking embarrassed if their parents made a deep-bowed aloha or engaged in any display considered too "Japanesy."

By 1941, the distance between the first and second generation of Japanese immigrants had become greater than the usual wide gap America drives between recent immigrants and their offspring. The issei (first-generation immigrants) were Japanese citizens, prevented from becoming American by discriminatory laws, while the nisei (second-generation immigrants) had American citizenship, or were dual citizens, and were almost wholly American in their attitudes. The issei wanted their children to study Japanese, follow traditional codes of etiquette and familial piety, and adopt the Yamato spirit, which taught loyalty to the Emperor and the uniqueness of the Japanese people, values the nisei found inimical to their crash program of "Americanization." The issei spoke English poorly, if at all, while the nisei spoke Japanese poorly, forcing many families to communicate in pidgin. Children slept on beds while their parents used futons, sat in chairs while their parents rested on zabutons, and used American dressers while their parents' kyodis (traditional chests) stood in another corner of a room. Some issei parents encouraged the Americanization of their children, but were often appalled at the results. They heard their sons adopt American slang, and watched their daughters holding hands with boys who called them "sweetheart."

The determination of the nisei to Americanize themselves now seems touching and quaint, but after Pearl Harbor it often meant the difference between freedom and imprisonment. The Loyalty Hearing Boards instituted in 1942 to determine which Japanese internees should be released favored those demonstrating "unbridled Americanism." These boards were unable to define what Americanism was, but they knew what it was not: anything smacking of Japan.

"Are you truly an American citizen, or are you partly loyal to Japan?" one board member asked a detainee. "It seems by reason of the fact you act Japanese, and you have all the habits and customs of the Japanese indicates you are not wholeheartedly American."

Other ethnic groups in Hawaii also judged the Japanese by the extent of their assimilation, and tended to consider the retention of any Japanese customs as prima facie disloyalty. An essay written by an Army wife for the War Records Depository at the University of Hawaii reflects this loathing for anything Japanese: "Even these Polynesians, the most loving of all peoples, have not learned to love their Japanese neighbors. The polite Japanese smiles had long ago been learned to be nothing more than masks of deceit in many cases. They had come to the islands years ago, these people of Nippon, but most of them still slept on their wooden pillows, wore their colorful but awkward kimonos, ate their rice and drank their sake wine, read their Japanese newspapers and sent their children to long hours of language school. . . . Yes, they had remained a thing apart; they did not know the meaning of assimilation."

Imagine the obstacles niseis like George Akita faced in trying to prove their Americanism. They lived in Oahu in great numbers, among servicemen sent to defend the island against an enemy looking exactly like them. No matter how many patriotic speeches they gave, rallies they attended, or hours they spent as civil-defense wardens, they were still suspected of disloyalty.

The Japanese of Hawaii were encouraged to raise hogs, a job other races scorned as demeaning, and to find scraps to feed their animals, they branched into garbage-collecting. But in 1941 they were accused of using this enterprise as a pretext for rummaging through the refuse of military families in search of discarded national secrets. They were criticized for being clannish and shirking the responsibilities of American citizenship, yet if they ran for public office they were denounced for trying to colonize Hawaii for Japan. They were attacked for not becoming more assimilated, yet many plantations, to improve morale and productivity, encouraged the erection of Shinto temples and subsidized the entertainment of visiting Japanese priests, dignitaries, and military officials. The Hawaii Visitors Bureau promoted the preservation of Japanese dress and customs as a quaint "attraction," and the same haole housewives who feared being poisoned by their Japanese servants took lessons in flower arranging, decorated their homes with Japanese prints, and encouraged their maids to wear kimonos.

By 1941, an individual's opinion of the loyalty of Hawaii's Japanese residents depended more on race, money, and politics than objective fact. Supporters of Hawaiian statehood depicted them as red-blooded Americans, while opponents described them as untrustworthy aliens who might take over the state. A haole with pleasant relations with his Japanese servants might argue for their loyalty, while many Koreans and Chinese, whose homelands were occupied by Japan, believed them evil and treacherous. Plantation owners claimed 99 percent of their Japanese laborers were loyal, but military officers from the mainland argued that that still left Hawaii with sixteen hundred potential saboteurs and fifth columnists.

The antipathy toward the Japanese in Hawaii was so pervasive that even those defending their loyalty felt compelled to express their general distaste for them. A retired general who had described them as "law-abiding and quiet, and industrious and provident and thrifty and not quarrelsome" to an Army Board investigating Pearl Harbor felt compelled to add, "They are not very pretty to look at." The author of "Our Hawaii Is Absolutely American," published in the December 1939 issue of *Paradise of the Pacific*, praised the loyalty of Hawaii's Japanese, but then said, "Now I wish to deny emphatically that I am holding a brief for the Japanese. My natural bias is rather against that race."

The Japanese knew that summary conclusions about their loyalty were overstated, and that their supporters or detractors could easily find individuals to prove their prejudices. There were splits in the community invisible to outsiders: antagonism between Okinawan and mainland Japanese, and between recent immigrants who considered themselves more cultured and the pidgin-speaking kamaaina Japanese. Many nisei joined the ROTC at the University of

Hawaii but others returned to Japan for college, where they were drafted into the army. Most niseis were loyal Americans, but some had been embittered by racial discrimination, and while some issei felt some loyalty toward the Emperor, many others felt little attachment to Japan.

Despite these divisions, and despite the confusing signals from Caucasian Hawaiians, the Japanese of George Akita's generation tried to prove their Americanism in fanatical, heartbreaking ways. Young men joined the Army in numbers far exceeding their proportion of the population. The Hawaiian-Japanese Civic Association contributed the most impressive display to the 1941 Armistice Day parade, a float carrying grim-faced AJA (Americans of Japanese Ancestry) soldiers from the Territorial Guard wearing World War I uniforms, and standing against a banner saying, "We Did It in '17, We'll Do It Again." A group of Japanese-American notables formed a Committee for Inter-Racial Unity and sponsored an annual New Americans Conference, which met for six days in July 1941 at the Honolulu YMCA. It passed resolutions calling on AJAs to renounce their dual national status, and issued a report full of slogans such as "Sincere Loyalty Is the Keynote" and "Find a True Man and Know True America."

Throughout 1940 and 1941, individual Japanese proclaimed their loyalty and Americanism in public letters and articles. Miss Anne Kuaoka contributed "No Less American," an essay ending with this pathetic sentence: "It is deplorable to have enemies of these fair islands bear malice against this racial group [the Japanese] which is so sincere in its multitudinous endeavors to live up to the standards of its white brothers."

Lawrence Nakatsuka, a Japanese-American reporter for the *Star-Bulletin*, wrote a twenty-part series examining problems faced by young Japanese in Honolulu and exhorting them to become better Americans. "There are many American-Japanese who are not worthy citizens of this country," he admitted. "They have failed to prove to other Americans by actions and words that they are truly trustworthy countrymen." He urged Japanese to avoid Japanese clubs and associate more freely with other nationalities. He told admiring stories about Japanese-Americans who were "positive and aggressive in their stand as American citizens." He raged against the public use of the Japanese language, saying he had been "embarrassed and infuriated on many occasions when the first-generation Japanese, in public places, have used Japanese indiscriminately," and advised readers to use Japanese only when it was necessary and they were positive other Americans would not be slighted or made suspicious. He cautioned the younger generation against being overly influenced by their parents, saying, too many Hawaiian-born Japanese were dominated by parents who were "dyed in the wool" Japanese nationals.

For niseis such as Nakatsuka and Akita, the months before Pearl Harbor were a precarious time that found them struggling to convince other Hawaiians of their Americanism, while being reproached by their parents for abandoning Japanese culture. December 7, 1941, would catch them at a bad moment: suspended between the Japanese customs they had rejected and an America that still rejected them. Their tricky position on that day helps explain much of what happened afterward, and why, on subsequent Pearl Harbor anniversaries, some still feel compelled to prove their "100 percent Americanism."

CHAPTER 4

THE VIEW FROM WALTER DILLINGHAM'S WINDOW

A newspaperman visiting Honolulu in 1893 reported that more of its citizens wore evening dress than in any other American city. A half century later dressing for dinner remained the custom, so it is not at all surprising that Walter Dillingham was wearing a dinner jacket on the evenings of December 5 and 6. After all, as he told me, his family was so prominent that when President Roosevelt visited Hawaii in 1936, the only man he really cared to meet was his father, and when the Prince of Wales visited Hawaii, he borrowed Dillingham's polo clothes. "My claim to fame," he said, "is that the Prince of Wales wore my polo helmet and breeches."

Dillingham cannot remember why he dressed up on December 5, but he knows that on December 6 he attended a party at the north shore plantation town of Haleiwa. He had been living at the Haleiwa airstrip all week because he was a reserve officer in the Army Air Corps and his pursuit squadron had two weeks of gunnery practice. He brought dinner clothes to those exercises because, "In those days if you were going anywhere, you always wore a tuxedo." Nowadays almost no one in Honolulu, including members of families like the Dillinghams, dresses for dinner, and the city has gone from being one of the most formal, as colonial outposts always were, to one of the most casual places in the nation, where fewer than a half dozen restaurants require a tie, executives and attorneys wear aloha shirts, and even funeral notices specify "aloha wear."

There is no better place for appreciating how Honolulu has changed since 1941 than Dillingham's sixteenth-floor office at 1750 Kalakaua Avenue, a shimmering blue skyscraper across the Ala Wai canal from Waikiki, and one of many such buildings that by deflecting trade winds and heating the atmosphere has made a necessity of central air-conditioning. Inside, Dillingham's office is determinedly old-fashioned, a reproach to everything outside his windows. There is an ancient manual typewriter, a dusty globe, and stacks of old newspapers. Because Dillingham dislikes air-conditioning, the room is boiling hot.

The effect is disorienting. I sit perspiring and surrounded by these dated furnishings and clutter while staring out at modern Waikiki, a neighborhood shaped by Dillingham's ancestors but now largely owned by Japanese interests. Before his family's company, Hawaiian Dredging, reclaimed Waikiki in the 1920s, 85 percent had been a waterland of duck ponds, rice paddies, and taro patches. Now I see hotel skyscrapers and the multilevel Ala Moana, developed by the Dillinghams in 1959 and once the largest shopping center on earth.

Most of what Walter Dillingham sees from his windows has resulted from the labors of other Dillinghams, but it still does not please him. "Too many people, too many buildings, too many cars," he complains. "We need a moratorium on the number of new cars that can be licensed on this island, and I wouldn't want to see any more development either. If we have more places for people to sleep, where are they going to find room to walk on the street? Oh, Jesus, it's terrible. . . . I liked it better in the old days when you got dressed up in a tuxedo to go to the Royal Hawaiian."

From Dillingham's office, Honolulu appears to be an American city like any other, where anything, good or bad, might happen. But as he loses himself in describing the Honolulu of 1941 I realize it must have been difficult, if not impossible, for him—for anyone—to imagine anything bad happening in a place so beautiful, and realize that if there was a fifth column undermining Hawaii's defense, then that fifth column was Hawaii herself.

Because the Islands have changed so much, it has become easier to overlook how their beauty must have unhinged the purpose of their defenders. Headlines might have read, "Japan Prepared to Strike Over Weekend," and cables from the Navy Department might have declared, "This dispatch is to be considered a war warning," but when their recipients looked out windows and up from breakfast tables, they saw paradise.

They rose to soft and flower-scented breezes, ate papaya or mango from backyard trees, and took cool showers, because in a climate that may be the most perfect on earth, many houses lacked water heaters. On weekends, women dressed in loose-fitting muumuus or kimonos, and men wore aloha shirts, a recent invention of a local Japanese tailor, who made them from the colorful silk fabrics used for children's clothing in Japan. On weekdays, people worked in the mornings and relaxed in the afternoons. After the attack, a captain commanding a field artillery battery at Schofield Barracks told the Army board of inquiry, "Because it was in the tropics we did very little work in the afternoon. It was just the opposite of a warlike attitude."

Everyone lived surrounded by flowers. Hedges of hibiscus and morning glory flowered underneath jacaranda and poinciana trees, and lavender blossoms fell from shower trees, carpeting streets and lawns. Orchids bloomed in ramshackle hothouses and in coconut shells hanging from backyard monkey pods, and cut flowers decorated parlors and bedrooms. Crimson and white oleanders were so fragrant they stopped pedestrians in their tracks, and purple and rose-colored bougainvillea climbed over stone walls and blanketed houses, making them appear to be in flames.

Imagine Honolulu without the roar of the Lunalilo Freeway, carpets of roofs covering mountain slopes, or processions of glittering jets crossing the sky. Imagine, instead, a low-rise little city buried under palms, banyans, and flowering shrubs, with little to distract the eye from the lurid green cane fields or volcanic cliffs eroded by rain and wind into fantastic folds, like thick and velvety curtains.

On the mornings of December 5 and 6, as on many mornings, trade winds blew strongly across Oahu, bringing the landscape alive—rippling cane fields, shaking palm fronds, and stirring up surf. The sky was clear, the light sharp, and the air fresh. In the afternoon, clouds piled up across the Koolaus, releasing gentle showers that threw up rainbows and drifted on wind currents down the Nuuanu Valley, falling from a clear sky so predictably that trolley stops were known as "first shower," "second shower," and "third shower" stops.

The Depression scarcely touched Honolulu, and in 1941 a defense boom was making it as rich as it was beautiful. Gardens and foliage planted at the turn of the century had matured and grown so that palm trees towered over telephone and electric poles, creating tunnels of unbroken shade. Regulations prohibiting outdoor billboards and posters were so strict that Libby could not write its name on the outside of its pineapple cannery. The less attractive necessities of urban life, the factories, pumping station, electric plant, and piers, were confined to a circle a mile and a half from City Hall. There were fine Greek Revival office buildings, airy and superbly designed public schools, and sturdy white Congregational churches, set on lawns resembling New England greens. The homes of wealthy haoles were unpretentious, and one traveler described even the poorest neighborhoods as "slums that have wandered off into a garden."

In the Honolulu of 1941, there was not a single practicing psychiatrist, perhaps because the profession was considered unnecessary in paradise. Crimes were infrequent and minor. A front-page newspaper story appearing after Thanksgiving 1941 was headlined, "Crimes Keep Police Busy over Holiday." It described a "crime wave" consisting of a stolen car, a man pummeled by sailors in a street brawl, an attempted suicide with a pocketknife, a missing piggy bank, and the theft of some bananas from Mr. Issya Tanimoto's front-yard tree.

Oahu was still a place of taro patches and stray pigs, sugar camps, and empty beaches where Hawaiians netted fish. Airmen stationed at Wheeler Field saw pineapples and pink mountain ranges. Sailors looking north from battleships moored in Pearl Harbor saw watercress fields, boys with fishing poles, and a rattletrap sugar mill. To the east was the naval base, a reassuring world of manicured lawns and officers wearing white gloves making social rounds and dropping off calling cards.

Even in 1941 people were complaining that Waikiki was "ruined," "overbuilt," and a honky-tonk without charm. A 1940 article in *Fortune* magazine claimed residents "contemptuously stay away from the visitors' compound around Waikiki." But since the Ala Wai drainage canal, responsible for transforming Waikiki from marshland to resort, had only been completed in 1928, it is perhaps more accurate to say that during those last prewar months, Waikiki was at its best, nicely balanced between the smelly backwater it had once been, and the skyscraper resort of hookers, time-share barkers, and bewildered Japanese honeymooners it would become. It was still slightly bohemian, with room for bungalows and fishermen's shacks, picket fences, and vacant lots. There were no traffic lights, and every cottage had a garden or lawn. In the evenings, you heard strolling musicians, surf, and the clang of a trolley, in the mornings, a muffled radio, the clink of milk bottles, and a distant car. Palm trees leaned at crazy angles over flowered lanes, and traffic detoured around banyans growing in the middle of highways. From the air, it was a carpet of trees, occasionally broken by a peaked roof; from the sea, a coconut plantation sprinkled with hotels.

The biggest hotels were the stately Ala Moana and the flashy Royal Hawaiian, soon to become a symbol of "Old Hawaii," even though its art was French, its cherubs Italian, its carpets from Tunisia and Trenton, and its Moorish architecture inspired by Valentino's *The Sheik*. The only cinema in Waikiki had clouds floating across its ceiling, imitation palms planted along walls, and murals depicting scenes from Hawaiian history. The souvenir program from its 1936 opening proclaimed that its "sheer beauty" was "a complement to all Hawaii."

In 1941, Honolulu was a city where people advertised for a "Hawaiian yard boy who can sing, dance, and play the guitar," and taxi drivers used call boxes attached to palm trees, and you requested a favorite driver by name. It was a city where a siren ordered minors off the streets at eight o'clock, beachboys had names like Hankshaw, Steamboat, Panama, and Tough Bill, who played the ukulele and tucked hibiscus blossoms behind their ears, policemen wore leis and sat on high stools under umbrellas, waving at friends as they pulled "Stop" and "Go" levers, and Pete the "Hula Cop" directed traffic with the arm motions of a hula dancer, and was honored by a downtown plaque thanking him for having "smiled his way into the hearts of the people." It was a city where the most serious civic nuisances were an absence of shade trees along Kalakaua Avenue and bad-mannered children on the trolley buses, politicians wore white suits and panama hats, and promised the moon in several languages, and hostesses descended from early missionaries used ti leaves as tablecloths and sang the doxology before dinner.

Despite its huge new military installations and thousands of defense workers and servicemen, Honolulu still deserved its 1941 advertising slogan, "A World of Happiness in an Ocean of Peace." On December 5, posters bearing that slogan hung in the city's hotels, travel agencies, and restaurants. They depicted native Hawaiians dressed in flower capes and leis, and said, "You can pin a definition on the peace of Hawaii. It is tangible, universally desired, even though almost universally discarded elsewhere. It explains in one word the overwhelming trend to Hawaii. Here life is lived as it was meant to be lived, happily, close to flowers and warm surf." And no doubt that poster reassured Hawaiians and the servicemen who saw it that here, on these remote and idyllic islands, they were safe.

Honolulu's small-town customs also made war and destruction seem inconceivable. Doors were so seldom locked that many house keys had been mislaid, a fact reflected in the title of the first Charlie Chan mystery, *The House Without a Key*. At bars and parties, people entertained themselves by singing. The piano was popular, and children gave recitals and servicemen played in hotel parlors. People believed in being "good Americans," and men spoke the language of the country-club locker room. When Walter Dillingham's uncle testified before the Army board investigating Pearl Harbor, he used expressions such as, "I didn't like the cut of his jib," and "I think he is a clean-cut, straightforward, hard-hitting man." Young people were relatively chaste and a descendant of an old missionary family told me, "People then just did not go around jumping in and out of one another's beds. Women were virgins when they were married, and now in rehashing our lives, so many of us seem to comment on how incredibly pure we were."

Honolulu was not a perfect paradise, however, not an unblemished Eden on the eve of destruction. By December of 1941 it was already suspended between its past and its future, and you could see both what it had been and what it would become: see its easygoing past coexisting nervously with the housing shortages, traffic jams, and suburbanization resulting from the defense boom. By December, the boom had increased the population by 10 percent in a single year, and increased construction expenditures tenfold in two years. Sixty new trolley buses were running on seven new lines, and the boys who had once dived for quarters off passenger liners earned twenty dollars a day in Pearl Harbor's workshops. You could see the new wealth and hustle reflected in the crowded sidewalks, the shopping districts spreading into residential suburbs, and the fad for speedy weddings. The liners brought so many fiancées of servicemen and construction workers that a competition arose to see who could marry the fastest on arrival. The record holder had boarded the *Lurline* on the pilot boat and upon landing rushed his fiancée to the license bureau, completing the formalities in half an hour.

The changes in Honolulu were most evident to kamaainas returning after a lengthy absence. Patricia Morgan, a college student coming home in July 1941, noticed that, "The air seemed charged with activity: the slow Hawaiian tempo had speeded up. As we drove through town there were more cars, traffic was thicker . . . many more soldiers and sailors were in the streets than I had ever seen in Honolulu before. There were new grills, new cafes, new dance halls, new stores. . . . The people in the street looked different, the buildings were new, the smoke of industry was heavier in the Hawaiian sky. Still, the old Honolulu was here, and the combination of carefree Hawaii and mainland efficiency was far from uninteresting."

Unlike Morgan, many kamaainas greeted every change, and every new wave of immigrants, with dismay, insisting Hawaii's "best time" had been ten, twenty, or thirty years earlier, like the old-timer in *The House Without a Key* [1925], who complained, "I knew Honolulu in the glamorous days of its isolation, and I've watched it fade into a . . . copy of Babbittville, USA. The waterfront's just a waterfront now—but once, my boy! Once it oozed romance at every pore."

Kamaainas particularly disliked the changes brought by the defense boom. An editorial in the December 1941 *Paradise of the Pacific* groused that, "Old landmarks are disappearing. There is a faster tempo in the business community. . . . The number of traffic mortalities is appalling. The kamaaina sees few of the old faces. . . . It was not like that ten years ago—five years ago." Another article complained of "thousands of men and women, new to Hawaii, new to the life of Hawaii," who had "swarmed" into the city, bringing with them "the Mainland's rush and crush, hurry and bustle."

But even a booming economy could not change Hawaii's reassuring geographical isolation. On September 6, 1941, a *Honolulu Star-Bulletin* reporter wrote that "A Japanese attack in Hawaii is regarded as the most unlikely thing in the world, with one chance in a million of being successful. Besides having more defenses than any other post, it is protected by distance."

Anyone arriving from the West Coast by liner traveled almost five days across an empty ocean, without sighting another island or reef. Anyone coming on the Pan Am Clipper was aloft for fifteen hours over an ocean marked only by cloud shadows. Despite this isolation, Caucasian Hawaiians took a keen interest in the war in Europe, instead of in the much closer one in China, and founded a British War Relief Society to raise funds, roll bandages, and collect Christmas presents for bombed-out British children. The same *Star-Bulletin* front page reporting Navy Secretary Frank Knox's remarks that the Orient was "a vast powder keg potentially ready to explode with a roar that will be heard across the Pacific" also featured a photograph of a local debutante holding chrysanthemums to be used as decorations for the British War Relief Ball. One local matron, a Mrs. Philip Kahala, adopted a European refugee dog, a German shepherd named Kenos von der Misenger who was said to crawl under a bed at the sound of "Hitler" and had been sentenced to death by Nazi authorities in Denmark for eating too much. At a time when Jewish refugees found it difficult to enter the United States, he had been shipped halfway around the world at Mrs. Kahala's expense.

Hawaii was reminded of the European war by newsreels, freighters that arrived from the Middle East marked by shrapnel, and passengers on the Pan Am Clipper. Almost every day one of these planes brought celebrities, diplomats, and generals from the West Coast or the Orient. On November 12, Japan's new special envoy to Washington, Saburu Kurusu (who would be meeting with Secretary of State Cordell Hull as Japanese planes returned to their carriers on December 7), arrived on a Clipper en route to Washington. He became so flustered by the crowd of journalists and dignitaries meeting him that he fled into the ladies' room and gave a news conference there. His comments were bland, but afterward one of his fellow Clipper passengers said, "Kurusu appears to have little hope for an amicable settlement of the issues."

The Soviet Union's new ambassador to Washington, Maxim Litvinov, arrived on the Clipper on December 4 and went into seclusion in his hotel room, refusing to attend a Chamber of Commerce dinner in his honor and saying only, "I am happy to be in your beautiful islands." (Later it would be suggested that Stalin, and perhaps Litvinov, too, knew of Japanese war plans, so perhaps there was more than fatigue behind his seclusion.) One journalist saw the shadow of war in Litvinov's shabby suit and unpolished shoes, but like many of the reminders of war brought to Hawaii by the Clipper, he was gone the following morning.

The wars in Europe and China reinforced Hawaii's complacency by sending it a colorful band of refugees and expatriates. The European playboys who kept pet chimpanzees and banded together into a motorcycle gang, the princess who worked as a taxi dancer, and the dubious counts who worked as chefs and waiters all confirmed the widespread belief that Hawaii was a safe haven.

Hawaii's physical isolation was matched by a cultural one that, for all the territory's flag-waving, made it seem not quite American.

Hawaii had its own singular obsession with flowers. It had originated with native Hawaiians, been adopted by other races, and found its most feverish expression on Lei Day, when leis decorated everything from car radiators to the straw hats of Japanese gardeners. Hawaii had its own peculiar history. A half century earlier, before American sugar planters engineered a coup leading to its annexation as a United States Territory, it had been a Polynesian kingdom, and evidence of the toppled monarchy remained visible. The elderly Hawaiian men sweeping grass in front of the offices of the territorial governor at the Iolani Palace had performed this same service for King Kalakaua and Queen Liliuokalani. A Hawaiian employee of the Sans Souci Hotel removed his hat, snapped to attention, and shouted "Ka moi! Ka moi!"—The king! The king!—whenever he saw Governor Poindexter. Just ten years before, in 1931, the daughter of Hawaii's deposed queen, Princess Kawananakoa, had thrown a luau for the visiting king and queen of Thailand. According to the *Advertiser*, "The pomp and pageantry of a fallen kingdom was displayed in all its panoply . . . Arriving guests found 18 stalwart Hawaiian youths wearing red capes and malos and bearing spears like the young warriors of old, lining the driveway to the house. They stood beside flaming torches which lighted up the grounds. . . . [and] softly muted music filled the beautiful home throughout the evening." (In 1960, the grandson of this Thai king visited Honolulu. None of the descendants of the monarchy was invited to the dinner given in his honor by Hawaii's governor at Washington Place, the former home of Queen Liliuokalani, and the evening's entertainment was furnished by the Dixie Cats Jazz Band.)

In 1941, native Hawaiians had no political or economic power. They lived on the margins and in the shadows of Hawaiian society, comforted by their large families and wrapped in nostalgia for a romanticized past. Haole artists had stolen their music, composing hapa-haole (half-haole) ditties such as "The Cockeyed Mayor of Kauanakakai," and "When Hilo Hattie Does the Hilo Hop." Missionary families had tried to eradicate their national dance, the hula. As late as the 1920s, letters to the editor were denouncing this dance as a "vile obscenity" and the *Advertiser*'s owner was claiming it represented the "licentiousness of old Hawaii" and promising to "wipe the smirch [of the hula] . . . from the fair name of Hawaii."

By 1941 the hula was one of several Hawaiian customs that had been adopted by the Islands' other racial communities. Native Hawaiians may have lived on society's margins, but their customs still exerted influence on Hawaii's atmosphere, and no custom had more influence than the spirit of aloha, the Polynesian tradition of friendliness and generosity. As aloha spread to other ethnic groups, through intermarriage and its promotion by the tourist industry, it also came to connote a certain *mañana* attitude. This bastardized aloha was embraced by newly arrived defense workers and servicemen, encouraging the postponement of unpleasant tasks and decisions, and further convincing them that nothing bad could ever happen on such relaxed and beautiful islands.

PART TWO

DECEMBER 6, 1941

CHAPTER 5

OMENS ARE SEEN

Some remember December 6, 1941, as a late-autumn Saturday like any other, with Honolulu preoccupied with Christmas and football. Because of Hawaii's climate and Asian population, Christmas was less of an event there than on the mainland. Wreaths were fashioned from cellophane and tinsel looped through backyard trees, and many street-corner Santas were Japanese. But in 1941, homesick defense workers and servicemen were insisting on a more traditional and commercial Christmas, and so gaily wrapped presents hung from palms in the Sears Roebuck parking lot, a canopy of colored bulbs illuminated Fort Street, and, on that last Saturday before the Japanese attack, when the *Advertiser* was warning of the possibility of war breaking out in Asia with the headline "JAPANESE MAY STRIKE OVER THE WEEKEND," it was also sponsoring the arrival of Santa Claus. He circled the city in one of the silvery planes of the 86th Observation Squadron and landed in Kapiolani Park to the screams of three thousand spectators, leading the *Advertiser* to conclude that "an all around richer Honolulu . . . [is] ready for the merriest Christmas on record."

On the afternoon of December 6, 10 percent of the city's population of 250,000 had packed Honolulu's stadium to watch the University of Hawaii play the Willamette Bearcats. One Honolulu company had sponsored an essay contest on "How does football promote national unity?" It was won by Corporal Harry F. Dittmer, Jr., whose essay, "How Football and Americanism Define True Democracy," declared, "Football makes one think of America. Democracy makes one think of America. And . . . we find they both define true Americanism."

The halftime show of the Shriner-sponsored Willamette game was lavish and patriotic. Fireworks exploded and a miniature parachute carrying the Hawaiian flag floated to earth. As fourteen marching bands paraded across the field playing the Shriner anthem, "I'm Forever Blowing Bubbles," a Shriner flag fell from a rocket. As they played "The Stars and Stripes," another rocket rose into the sky, although this one, it was reported, seemed to hesitate before unfurling its patriotic symbol, and those later searching for other portents would recall that the Shriners' cardboard tank had broken down in midfield.

December 6 would also be remembered for its exceptional beauty, with clear skies and puffy clouds over the Koolaus. "Calm" and "still" are the words used most often to describe a day that, even sixty years later, reappears in some memories with the clarity of sharp Pacific sunlight, while in others it is a slow-motion day, with time stretched like taffy.

Compare December 6, 1941, with August 31, 1939, the day before the German attack on Poland that precipitated the European war. Even if Poland had learned of this attack the day before, and even had its army not been taken by surprise, the final outcome would have been the same. But in Hawaii, if cables had been deciphered, telephone calls made, and intelligence properly evaluated on December 6, history might have turned out quite differently. Oahu was not the impregnable fortress described by the press, but the U.S. military was also not like the Polish Army, facing German panzers with cavalry. There were enough planes and warships on Oahu to blunt a Japanese attack and inflict serious losses. Had American forces not been humiliated on December 7, more than the first six months of the Pacific war might have been quite different, and if you believe, as I do, that the humiliation of Pearl Harbor contributed to the willingness to drop atomic weapons on Hiroshima and Nagasaki, then December 6 was a last chance to avoid more than a single day of carnage.

Even today, people who were on Oahu continue to reexamine December 6, breaking it down into hours and minutes, slowing time, and discerning omens. Their belief in such omens perhaps arises from the conviction that catastrophes are usually preceded by warnings, and that just as screeching birds and nervous animals precede earthquakes, so, too, did Pearl Harbor have its harbingers.

On November 27, the same day the Japanese task force sailed into the North Pacific, unusual cloud formations were seen over the Big Island. The next day, the *Star-Bulletin* reported that, "What to most Big Islanders today was just a nice bright sunny morning, to old time Hawaiians was ominous of impending woe. Native legend has it that when Zeppelin-shaped clouds hang over Mauna Kea and Mauna Loa some catastrophic event is due." It is also remembered that Hawaiian women sitting on the lawn of the Kawaihao Church on December 6 saw clouds pile up and take the form of a monster, with a long tongue lashing from side to side. One woman reported the miracle to the wife of Honolulu's mayor, and the story circulated all afternoon.

Jokes about Japanese attacking Hawaii were common, but those made on December 6 are remembered as premonitions. This is why we know that as Commander Roscoe F. Good strolled past the naval headquarters building on his way to lunch, he looked at Battleship Row with its line of double-moored warships, and remarked, "What a beautiful target that would make." We know that as the wife of Captain James W. Chapman reached a point in the Kamehameha Highway where all of Pearl Harbor was spread out below, she said, "If the

Japanese are going to attack Hawaii, this would be the ideal time, for there sits the entire Pacific Fleet at anchor"; that Lieutenant Commander Edwin Layton, upon hearing "The Star-Spangled Banner" played in the Royal Hawaiian Hotel ballroom, experienced a sudden urge to shout, "Wake up, America!"; and that while returning home from a charity dinner dance, General Walter Short, upon seeing the lights of the warships and dry docks blazing in Pearl Harbor, remarked to his wife, "What a target that would make!"

If a Japanese resident of Honolulu offered a drink to a serviceman on December 6, it was later considered proof that Hawaii's Japanese had somehow been tipped off. If a Japanese person appeared excessively nervous or calm, sullen or happy, well, that too was suspicious.

Catherine Mellen thought it sinister that her Japanese maid announced she would not be coming back to work on December 7 because, as Mellen wrote in an unpublished autobiography, "Five men from the island of Kauai were arriving to spend the weekend at her home (already filled to overflow with her family). When I asked who they were she said she . . . thought they were friends of her husband. She was greatly agitated so I did not press for further information but that night I wrote in my diary: 'I am sure she is not a traitor but this news does alarm her because her home is near enough the waterfront to be of importance.' "

Mrs. Mellen also found it suspicious that her Japanese yardman should appear on December 6 bearing a large package. She wrote: " 'A Christmas gift,' he said, nervously. Amazed at this early arrival of a Christmas present I opened it to find a full assortment of expensive toilet articles. His previous gifts had never exceeded one dollar."

A month after the attack, Governor Poindexter revealed that on December 8 the city's rice supply was discovered to be "unusually short." He added, "Our investigation showed that these Japanese merchants, or some of them, when customers would come in to buy a sack of rice, would tell them, 'You better buy two sacks.' Now, that may have been due to either one of two reasons: one, of course, that they had advance notice of what was coming . . ."

When the Roberts Commission convened in Honolulu on January 5, 1942, to investigate the attack, its members had already heard rumors that, as one said, "certain Japanese places of refreshment were serving free drinks to white people on the night of December 6."

The commissioners were particularly suspicious of a party thrown by a Japanese-American to celebrate the opening of his Chinatown fish market because of the free alcohol served. The chief of the Honolulu Police Department testified that serving free liquor at this opening was "a custom of the islands here." In 1944, the Army board investigating Pearl Harbor concluded, "The attack was such a surprise to the Japanese residents themselves that they were stunned and incoherent for a few days . . . [and] stories of maids, garbage collectors, small merchants and laborers [knowing beforehand of the attack] can be dismissed as idle talk and the product of fantastic imagination." But despite such forceful denials, and although it defies logic that Japanese Consul General Kita would have had no warning of the attack while a Japanese bartender would, a half century later I was to hear about how local Japanese had thrown wild parties and bought drinks for sailors on December 6.

I heard that the Yokohama Bank in Honolulu had refused to execute transfers during the last week of peace, and that numerous family servants had vanished for good after December 6. One Pearl Harbor survivor insisted that a tavern near Schofield Barracks provided free drinks to anyone in uniform on December 6, and was owned by a commander in the Japanese navy. Another wrote that, "A Lt. Commander, retired from the Japanese Navy . . . invited all the pilots in the American Armed Forces to attend a Hawaiian luau at Wahiawa. Plenty of food, liquor, music, and beautiful girls were provided to entertain our pilots far into the wee hours of the morning. Most of our pilots were still drunk [on December 7], and not capable of flying their planes if they could have gotten them off the ground."

You might imagine that what would be remembered and saved from the Honolulu newspapers published during this weekend would be articles warning of a possible war with Japan, or copies of the *Star-Bulletin* extra of December 7 headlined, "WAR! OAHU BOMBED BY JAPANESE PLANES." Instead, I repeatedly heard about an advertisement placed by the Japanese-owned Hawaii Importing Company that appeared on an inside page of the *Advertiser* on December 5, and two days earlier in the *Star-Bulletin*, and was allegedly conclusive evidence that Hawaii's Japanese residents had been warned of the attack. It announced "Fashions by the Yard— Look! Our Silks on Parade," and gave the price per yard for silks with exotic names like TipHi, Cantona, Jungo, and Yippee.

On December 8, FBI agents searched the home of the manager of Hawaii Importing, and its employees were besieged by Caucasian customers asking for the advertised fabrics by name, then leaving without making a purchase. In 1942, Margaret Yates, wife of a Pearl Harbor naval officer, wrote *Murder by the Yard*, a mystery premised on the silk ad having been a Japanese code. She said in her introduction, "Those of us who had thrown out our papers dashed madly over the landscape snagging whatever discarded copies we could find, not hesitating to rob our neighbors' garbage cans if our own were empty." Two months later, she found the West Coast flooded with copies, and wrote that, "Sleuths, amateur and professional, were burning the midnight oil and coming up with as many answers as there were decoders."

Some of the advertisement's decoders claimed it warned Japanese to stay home on December 7, thus explaining why so many Japanese maids and gardeners had called in sick. Others believed it had enabled Japanese spies to report on which warships were in Pearl Harbor. One man who decoded it for me explained the dot over an i was the symbol of the Rising Sun of Japan and the "yard" in "Fashions by the Yard" represented the U.S. Navy Yard. I was told that letter combinations in the silk names represented battleships, so that "Cantona" was the *California*, "Romaine" was the *Nevada*, and "Matelasse" the *Maryland*, or perhaps the *Tennessee*, or the Mutual Telephone Company of Honolulu, and "Silk Broadcloth" meant "broadcast," the price of "$1.15/yd." was a clue to the date, since its three numbers added up to seven, and a black background represented "black clouds for the bombing" or, according to another version, "clouds at dawn."

I heard about the famous silk ad from a survivor in Honolulu, a Navy veteran in my hometown in upstate New York, and from a mainland teenager who admitted knowing two things about Pearl Harbor: that President Roosevelt knew about the raid in advance, and that a newspaper advertisement had tipped off the Japanese living in Honolulu. I received a copy of it pressed in pages of *I Was at Pearl Harbor*, a self-published book sent to me by its author, John E. Ollila, a Navy veteran of the attack. "Look in the back of this paper against the light and see 'raids,' " Mr. Ollila had written along the bottom of the silk ad. I held it to the light, I turned it upside down, and placed it opposite a mirror. I was supposed to notice that "fashions" had been written in a tricky script that, when reversed, became "raids." But I only saw "fashions" backwards. Ollila devoted a whole chapter to the ad. "No one wanted to admit that the silk sale advertisement existed or that there was any truth to it, just keep it HUSHED UP!!" he wrote. "You will have to see this advertisement decoded, as it was shown to myself and others and then find your own answer to this mystery which has eaten at me."

I received another copy of the silk ad from Richard Van Dyke, a photographic archivist in Honolulu who had an envelope stuffed with them and boasted of owning the original negative. "Turn it backwards, to the light," he urged. "Can you see it? How 'fashions' becomes 'raids' spelled backwards?"

Navy wives like Mrs. Yates, people advocating the internment of Japanese-Americans, and even mainstream magazines like *Collier's* and *Time* all spread the tall tales that supposedly proved Japanese treachery. An article in the January 5, 1942, *Time* declared that, "Last week Honolulu was fluttering with stories of fifth column activity. . . . One story was that a display advertisement in a newspaper, ostensibly pushing bargain sales of silks, was actually coded instructions to spies. . . . There were many others, and the average Honolulu citizen did not know which was true and which false, but he did know one thing; fed on tolerance, watered by complacency, the Jap fifth column had done its job fiendishly well and had not been stamped out."

The silk ad has enjoyed greater longevity than other Pearl Harbor rumors because it comes with a piece of paper you can decode. It makes no difference that this "code" has no logic or pattern, no difference that it is inconceivable the Japanese military would have risked the success of the raid in order to alert Japanese residents of Hawaii, that an identical advertisement appeared a year earlier in the same newspaper, or that within weeks FBI agents had dismissed the silk ad story and did not even bother to interview the advertisement's designer. Instead, some military and civilian survivors persist in believing that this advertisement proves the disloyalty and treachery of Hawaii's Japanese, and that the Japanese victory at Pearl Harbor was not therefore the result of Japanese bravery, skill, and tactics, or of American incompetence and complacency, but of subversion and sabotage.

CHAPTER 6

THE SUBMARINERS' WIVES
THROW A PARTY

For Kathy Cooper, December 6 was a time of feverish anticipation. She and Bud Cooper had been apart almost continuously since being married in August and the next morning his submarine, the *Pollock*, was scheduled to dock at Pearl Harbor after being at sea for two and a half months. Because she was looking forward to their reunion, the evening seemed particularly long, and its details remain engraved on her memory.

At a party for the wives of *Pollock* officers the conversations dwelt on two subjects: the possibility of war with Japan and the possibility of sabotage on the part of Honolulu's Japanese residents. Cooper worried most about war because her father, then in charge of all Navy construction projects in the Pacific, had told her the United States was preparing for it. Like their husbands, Cooper and the other wives assumed any war would start in Southeast Asia, and would quickly be won by the United States. The wife of Bud Cooper's skipper, Mrs. Stanley Moseley, told the other wives attending the party not to worry because, she said, "We can lick the Japanese with our hands tied behind our backs."

None of the wives feared the Japanese might attack Hawaii.

They worried instead about Japanese spies in Honolulu and passed the evening trading stories about the suspicious behavior of their Japanese servants, with some insisting that even a casual question from a Japanese maid about the proposed guest list for a party might be a devious method of discovering which ships were in harbor.

After spending a lifetime in Hawaii, watching it evolve from a segregated colonial society into a multiracial one, and raising eleven children, two of whom married native Hawaiians, Kathy Cooper is amazed by the racial fears of prewar Honolulu. "Two of our grand-sons are part-Hawaiian," she told me, "but I can remember back then school friends telling me they were forbidden to play with someone because she was rumored to have Hawaiian blood."

Hawaii may be the most successful multiracial society on earth. The rate of mixed marriages is the highest of any American state or foreign country, over half the children are of mixed ethnic parentage, and at any public gathering you see the kind of idealized multiracial mixture common to UNICEF posters. Private schools that largely excluded Orientals in 1941 have a student body reflecting the popula-tion. Japanese who were once barred from working for the telephone company or operating streetcars dominate the state's economic and political life. If you compare what passes for racial tension in Hawaii today with the tensions afflicting other multiracial and multinational societies, Hawaii's would scarcely register on the most sensitive in-struments, all of which makes it even harder to imagine the racial fears of 1941, and to forgive the submariners' wives for scrutinizing their maids and gardeners for signs of disloyalty.

At the time of the attack, Cooper had been living in Hawaii for several years and had a relatively mature understanding of its Japa-nese community. But consider Hawaii from the perspective of the other submariners' wives. Their husbands had recently been trans-ferred to the Islands because of a possible war with Japan, yet they found themselves suddenly in a U. S. Territory where 40 percent of the population was Japanese, and in a city that was the most Japa-nese anywhere outside of Japan itself. Moreover, one-quarter of the territory's 160,000 Japanese were first-generation immigrants who continued to hold Japanese citizenship, while two-thirds of the second generation held dual citizenship. Nor did it escape their notice that many Japanese residents supported Japan's war against China by buying Japanese war bonds, sending "comfort bags" of blankets, shoes, and candy to Japanese soldiers, and collecting money for the Japanese Red Cross to buy a hospital ship, which somehow became a bomber named *Hawaii*.

The submariners' wives would have discovered that Japanese owned half of Honolulu's restaurants and food stores, built most of its houses, repaired most of its cars, and worked behind the counters of most of its retail shops. Japanese fishermen with fast boats and powerful shortwave radios caught all the Islands' fish. Japanese cooks owned lunch wagons topped with overhanging Japanese roofs. So numerous were the Japanese customers and enterprises that they could afford to discriminate against other races, and for every classified advertisement seeking "Haole fountain girls for the Waikiki Milk Bar," there were ones saying, "Night Cashier—Japanese," "Automobile Mechanic—Japanese preferred—OK Service Station," and "Barbecue Inn, prefers Oriental."

Honolulu had dozens of Japanese teahouses, two fish-cake factories, two shops selling nothing but kimonos, and the only sake brewery outside Japan. There were movie theaters showing only Japanese movies, two Japanese-language newspapers, a Japanese Chamber of Commerce, Japanese professional and charitable associations, associations for Japanese from the same prefecture, and language schools that 85 percent of all Japanese children attended after school and where they received instruction in Japanese language and culture. On Japanese holidays, skies filled with paper kites and banners, and when a circus paraded through town, the clowns were met with silent stares from Japanese spectators, who considered it rude to laugh in public.

The largest Oriental neighborhood was known as Chinatown, but Japanese and Filipinos far outnumbered its Chinese residents. When the wives went there they saw Japanese women wearing silk kimonos in brilliant pinks and purples, carrying children on their backs. They saw bathhouses, Shinto shrines, Buddhist temples puffing smoke, and alleys so narrow tenement balconies almost met overhead. They saw garish Japanese signs, restaurants displaying photographs of the Emperor, crowded neighborhoods where more than a hundred people shared a latrine, and small stores where babies crabbed across wooden floors, moonfaced children ate pink gelatin candies, and families sat in circles eating rice and clicking dice and dominoes. They smelled incense, fish, and soiled baby, and heard firecrackers and gongs from Buddhist temples. And after hearing, seeing, and smelling all that, they can perhaps be forgiven for wondering if Japanese living this way might feel more loyalty to Japan than to the United States, for worrying that people displaying photographs of the Emperor might pass information about American ship movements to one of the many Japanese consular representatives in Hawaii, and for succumbing to the fear of servants, a common feature of colonial societies on the eve of insurrection or war.

As it turned out, none of these fears came close to describing what happened on December 7 when, instead of charging into haole neighborhoods waving samurai swords, or slinking toward piers and bridges with satchels of dynamite, the Japanese of Hawaii began to dismantle their former lives so determinedly and completely that within two days many signs of their culture and influence had vanished as if sucked into a tornado.

What might have seemed still more fantastic to the submariners' wives on the evening of December 6 was that they would have to wait until they were grandmothers before they could again walk down a Honolulu street and see signs written only in Japanese, restaurants and shops catering almost exclusively to Japanese patrons—although this time the patrons were tourists from Japan—and again find visual evidence to support fears and prejudices common in Honolulu on the eve of Pearl Harbor.

CHAPTER 7

ALERTED FOR SABOTAGE

Hawaii's military commanders believed that if war broke out in Asia, Oahu's Japanese shopkeepers, maids, and gardeners would attack civilian and military installations with guns and dynamite, destroying aircraft on the ground, slapping mines to the hulls of warships, and blowing bridges and electric lines. Walter Dillingham, Senior, told the Army Pearl Harbor Board "that the most serious thing that could happen to us [Army and Navy officers] in the event of war would be what the [local] Japanese would do, whether we would be knifed in bed."

The military believed in this scenario even though there had not been a single instance of sabotage in the Islands, and despite the repeated insistence of Colonel George Bicknell of Army intelligence that there were no indications of any widespread plans involving sabotage or subversive activities. They believed in it because they were certain the Japanese had a race loyalty superseding their citizenship, place of birth, or residence, and for the same reasons their wives did—because of Honolulu's Japanese atmosphere, and because, according to chief of military intelligence Kendall Fielder,

"Just the mere fact of approximately 160,000 people of Japanese extraction would lead us to believe that a certain number of them would be loyal to the Japanese empire." They believed it because of racism and the American obsession with subversion, and because they were convinced that a direct Japanese attack on Hawaii was so patently foolhardy and suicidal that sabotage seemed the only realistic threat.

The commander of the Hawaiian Department, General Walter Short, was so preoccupied with sabotage that when he received Message No. 472 from the War Department in Washington on November 27, informing him, "Negotiations with Japan appear to be terminated to all practical purposes. . . . Japanese future action unpredictable but hostile action possible at any moment," and ordering him to "undertake such reconnaissance and other measures as you deem necessary," he took it solely as a warning against sabotage. He immediately called a Number 1 Alert, described as "a defense against sabotage, espionage, and subversive activities without any threat from the outside." He could have called a Number 2 Alert, which included a defense against air, surface, and submarine attack, or a Number 3, a defense against an all-out attack.

Within an hour of receiving the War Department warning, Short replied that he was "alerted to prevent sabotage." This same message crossed the desks of numerous Washington staff officers, including Army Chief of Staff General George C. Marshall and Secretary of War Henry Stimson, none of whom thought to inform Short that his sabotage alert was not what they intended. Even worse, subsequent communications from General Marshall's adjutant reinforced Short's concern with sabotage. The failure of Washington officials to inform Short that he was misinterpreting the warning message was justifiably seized upon by Short and his defenders as mitigating his responsibility for Pearl Harbor, and Marshall later admitted, "That was my opportunity to intervene and I did not do it." Stimson, however, made the telling point that Short's reply "certainly gave me no intimation that . . . being 'alerted to prevent sabotage' was in any way an express or implied denial of being alert against an attack by Japan's armed forces. The very purpose of a fortress such as Hawaii is to repel such an attack, and Short was the commander of that fortress."

A month after Pearl Harbor, Short still believed his sabotage alert had been justified. A member of the Roberts Commission asked him, "In other words, there were no troops in your command ready for war at that moment?" He answered, "No, sir. They were ready for uprisings. They were—we were definitely organized to meet any uprising or any act of sabotage."

During the 1945 congressional hearings Short testified that, "We can't tell what would have happened if we hadn't held a tight rein over them [Hawaii's Japanese residents]. I think the feeling was that if there had been any real success to the Japanese plans, that anything might have happened."

A senator asked him what he called a "success" if December 7, 1941, had not been one for Japan.

Short replied, "A landing on the island of Oahu. They immediately would have had an army of thousands, a fifth column of thousands, ready to support them."

Many officers on Short's staff agreed with his assessment. The commander of the Army Air Forces on Hawaii, Major General Frederick Martin, told the Army Pearl Harbor Board that he had been confident there would be no Japanese strike, "because if it failed, it meant such a reduction in their striking power they would be confined to their home islands from then on." Instead, he had believed the most probable danger came from "the Japanese population of the islands."

Martin's attitude is all the more surprising because he was co-author of a widely circulated March 1941 report predicting the Japanese attack. In it, he and Rear Admiral Patrick Bellinger had warned that, "A successful, sudden raid against our ships and naval installations on Oahu might prevent effective offensive action by our forces in the Western Pacific for a long period." They foresaw that, "A declaration of war might be preceded by: 1. A surprise submarine attack. . . . 2. A surprise attack on Oahu including ships and installations in Pearl Harbor," adding that, "such an attack would most likely be launched from one or more carriers which would probably approach inside of three hundred miles," and that "in a dawn air attack there is a high probability that it could be delivered as a complete surprise . . ." But despite his own prediction, Martin was so confident Japan was intimidated by American military power, and so concerned with local saboteurs, he did not believe a surprise Japanese air raid was a realistic probability in late 1941.

Because the Army was alerted only against sabotage on the evening of December 6, ammunition was boxed and locked to prevent its theft by local Japanese, and the commanders of Wheeler and Hickman Fields had moved their warplanes out of protective revetments, disarming them and massing them closely together in the middle of the apron, making them easy to guard against Japanese saboteurs, but excellent targets in case of an air raid. Dispersing these planes would require at least thirty minutes, with even more time needed to arm and launch them. And so it would turn out that if anyone sabotaged Oahu's defense, it was General Short himself, and the only subversion occurring on December 7 involved American military commanders subverting their own defenses.

The Navy was equally sabotage-conscious, holding frequent antisabotage drills and posting guards on ships. On November 27, Admiral Kimmel received a warning from the Navy Department that was sent to naval commands across the Pacific, and was couched in even stronger terms than the message to Short. It began, "This dispatch is to be considered a war warning. Negotiations with Japan looking toward stabilization of conditions in the Pacific have ceased and an aggressive move by Japan is expected within the next few days." It went on to report that Japanese movements indicated "an amphibious expedition against either Philippines, Thai or Kra Peninsula or possibly Borneo," and ordered "an appropriate defensive deployment."

But because this message did not specifically mention Hawaii, because the Navy Department had not provided Kimmel with the decrypts of the radio intelligence data, including Yoshikawa's "bomb plot" message identifying Hawaii as a possible target, and because Kimmel believed, in his words, that "an air attack on Pearl Harbor . . . was most improbable," he failed to make the most "appropriate defensive deployment"—long-range aerial reconnaissance.

Afterward, Kimmel and his supporters argued that a shortage of planes and spare parts made it impossible for the Navy, which had the responsibility for long-range patrols, to mount a full 360-degree sweep of the waters surrounding Hawaii. But that was no excuse for sending out no long-range patrols at all. The Martin-Bellinger report had identified the waters northeast of the island as the most likely avenue of attack because of favorable prevailing winds. With the planes available to him, Kimmel could have sent patrols over those likely areas. He neglected to do so because, though he and his staff could imagine a Japanese air raid on Hawaii as a theoretical possibility, they were so confident that Japan had been intimidated by America's military superiority they did not really believe it would happen. And this is why, despite the Navy's "war warning," and despite the Army warning of "hostile action possible at any moment," all the extraordinary military measures taken on Oahu on December 6 were directed at potential civilian saboteurs.

The first military event of December 6 occurred at 2:00 A.M., when Captain James Shoemaker, commander of the Ford Island Naval Air Station, woke his men to repel a simulated sabotage attack. He had planned this drill two days earlier, after attending a meeting that Rear Admiral Claude Bloch, commandant of the 14th Naval District, had called to discuss measures for defeating sabotage attacks. Several hours later, during morning inspection at the Kaneohe Naval Air Station, Commander Harold Martin said, "Men, I have called you together here this morning to tell you to keep your eyes and ears open and be on the alert every moment. You are probably the nearest into a war that you will ever be without actually being in it." He added that the possibilities of sabotage were "unusually imminent."

The destroyer *Helm* had returned from escort duty on December 5 and was moored alone in the west loch of Pearl Harbor. One of its officers, Victor Dybdal, told me, "We came here for rest and relaxation and considered ourselves safe, and protected by the Army. We very seldom even manned our guns in port . . . but everyone was thinking sabotage; everyone was suspicious of the local Japs. We saw Army sentries on all the bridges and we had sentries posted on our ships, usually on the fantails to look out for swimmers. It was slightly ridiculous, because our sentries didn't know how to fire rifles. Finally, we had so many false alarms that we took guns away from our sentries and gave them whistles. On other ships they gave the sentries unloaded rifles and locked the ammunition behind a pane of glass on the quarterdeck. Once they were sure saboteurs were approaching, they could break the glass and load their rifles."

The Army antiaircraft unit assigned to protect Ford Island from an enemy air attack was based fifteen miles away at Camp Malakole on Barbers Point. Every day its men trucked their guns to Pearl Harbor, stopping to pick up ammunition locked in an arsenal to prevent its theft by local Japanese. After reaching Ford Island by ferry they reassembled their guns and set them in emplacements. December 6 was the first Saturday in months they had not performed this laborious exercise. Instead, they remained at Camp Malakole with their guns broken down and unloaded. On December 6, a guard at Camp Malakole saw two Japanese fishermen swimming near a boat anchored fifty yards offshore. He unholstered his .45 and warned he would shoot if they came closer. The fishermen retreated and a machine gun was hurriedly assembled and mounted on the beach to repel other fifth columnists.

At Hickam Field soldiers dug slit trenches to repel a land-based attack by saboteurs, but did nothing to protect the base against an aerial attack. On the morning of December 6, Hickam's commander, William Farthing, called a staff meeting to discuss ways to protect the aircraft against sabotage. One man attending it recalls that, "By this time security against sabotage was almost an obsession."

Wheeler Field had 125 U-shaped revetments meant to protect

its fighters from an air raid. Before General Short's November 27 antisabotage alert, its planes had been routinely parked in them and dispersed along the length of the runway. Afterward, they were gathered on the apron and fitted nose to tail in a reverse T formation, so that a single rifleman could guard them. Gus Ahola, a Wheeler Field pursuit pilot who still lives on Oahu, remembers jokes in the officers' club about how one guy could take a pass and get thirty planes in our squadron with a single bullet. But the bullets everyone feared would be shot by Japanese civilians hiding in the underbrush and pineapple fields. "We never imagined that Japanese planes would attack us," he says. "No way."

On December 6, Wheeler Field's commander ordered further antisabotage precautions, and ammunition was removed from planes and locked in hangars. Regulations requiring controls in unattended planes to be left locked continued in force. (In number 2 or 3 alerts against an enemy air raid planes were left unlocked.) The locks were cumbersome metal collars that fitted over the joystick. Four cables ending in S-hooks attached them to a seat. A pilot locked his plane by adjusting his seat until the cables were taut, and he unlocked it by easing his seat forward while at the same time pulling the rudder pedals forward to provide slack. Ahola remembers that "even on a bright sunny day, with no urgency and no one looking over your shoulder it was difficult to unlock those goddamn things."

I had assumed Ahola was a native Hawaiian because not only does his name sound Hawaiian, but it is "aloha" spelled backwards. The Army Air Force made the same mistake. When he arrived from the mainland an official military greeter gave him a VIP welcome on the assumption he belonged to the former Hawaiian royal family—because what other native Hawaiian could have become an officer? Instead, Ahola is a second-generation Finn from Minnesota who enlisted to see the world and escape northern winters. He made a career of the Air Force, retiring as a colonel and returning to live in Hawaii, where his white hair, mahogany skin, and laconic but intelligent manner make it easy to mistake him for a native Hawaiian.

The only highway from Honolulu to Wheeler Field in 1941 was the Kamehameha Highway, a narrow, two-lane road dipping like a roller coaster into canyons and gullies that the bored pilots turned into a racetrack. "You'd recognize another guy on that road, toot your horn, and away you'd go," Ahola told me.

He and I drove to Wheeler Field on that road. It had since become an ugly, but patriotic, stretch of six-lane divided highway, bordered by the outposts of mainland fast-food franchises, all flying American flags that would dwarf the ones flapping over Fifth Avenue or the Capitol. We skirted Pearl Harbor and passed the Pearl Harbor Tavern, a barnlike bar and restaurant popular with enlisted men in 1941 and owned by Japanese nationals. (In the mid-1990s, it became a Dodge showroom.) We passed high wooden fences holding back housing developments as if they were landslides. "In 1941, this was all country," Ahola said, "just sugar mills, plantation towns, and pineapple fields."

As we entered the base he told me that on the evening of December 6 he and his roommate had been playing cards, drinking coffee, and showing home movies to their girlfriends. "My God, what a way to spend that evening," he said, slapping his forehead, amazed at the innocence of those pleasures.

He remembered driving his girl home, then passing Pearl Harbor and being dazzled by the sight of its warships. They sat moored in ponds of yellow light, lit up like Christmas trees. Another pilot passed him, tooting his horn as a challenge. They raced back in their convertibles, screaming around corners and falling into dips, their headlights sweeping across empty cane fields.

Before turning in, he stopped at the runway. He saw the fighter planes, grouped in a tight antisabotage square and illuminated by searchlights as if they were in prison, and thought, "We must be the best squadron in the Pacific, with the best training, the best pilots, and the best planes."

CHAPTER 8

THE SUPREME OVERCONFIDENCE OF A GREAT ATHLETE

At 8:00 P.M. on December 6, the *Advertiser*'s presses broke while printing the December 7 edition. The following morning, its employees viewed this as a catastrophe, since it allowed the rival *Star-Bulletin* to publish the first War Extra. Sabotage, of course, was blamed, and the wife of one newspaperman wrote, "Details of the [sabotage] were given to my husband a few days afterwards by an employee of the newspaper who described it as an act of revenge for the paper's bold stand on the situation in the Orient."

But there were compensations. Not finding their paper in its accustomed place the next morning, its subscribers spent several minutes peering into hedges and walking to the ends of driveways, and saw the columns of black smoke and aerial acrobatics, sights they might otherwise have missed. More importantly, *Advertiser* subscribers would be spared reading the December 7 front-page story, headlined U.S. SURE PACIFIC WAR IS NOT LIKELY, and beginning, "Official Washington believes that the tension over the Far Eastern crisis has been eased slightly, and that now there is a fairly good reason to hope that there will be no major conflict in the Pacific, at least for the next few weeks."

They would also be spared the front-page news that Secretary of the Navy Knox had released a report declaring that, "The United States already is the world's greatest naval power as a result of the greatest program of expansion attempted by any navy in world history." Or from reading, at the same moment Japanese carrier-based planes were pounding Pearl Harbor, a magazine supplement feature titled "AIRCRAFT CARRIER—Hard-Hitting Weapon for Uncle Sam in the Pacific" that began, "By sea and by air the Navy is in fighting trim. Carrier-based aviation, which has undergone wide development in tactical scope and strategic concept, is destined to play a major role when the signal comes."

The appearance of this article on December 7 was not that extraordinary a coincidence. The feature the week before, "Nothing Can Stop the Army Air Corps," had its lead paragraph set over a photograph of Lieutenant Joe Glick and his fighter (probably destroyed on the ground on December 7), and began, "And why? Because it's men like Joe Glick, typical red blooded American youth who comes from the coal mines, the corn fields, from all America, to learn to fly by the seat of his pants. Fair weather and foul, good or bad breaks, the thousands of Joes keep-em flying!" And a few weeks before that, you could have read in the *Advertiser* about how Pearl Harbor's destroyers "proved unquestionably in their war games that they are ready for what may come. Ready with the latest battle equipment— and ready with men who are trained to know it'll be a short fight but a hot one—and victory and death are the only rewards."

Overconfidence is often mentioned as one of many failings contributing to the Pearl Harbor catastrophe, but the more you examine the attitude of the civilians and military, on Hawaii and the mainland, the more it appears that calling this state of mind "overconfidence" is a kindness, and it is better described as deluded or arrogant. Examples of it make for painful reading because its proponents were so totally wrong, one feels embarrassed for them. They also make for unsettling reading, because you may begin wondering if Pearl Harbor was not divine retribution for such hubris.

Listen to Army Chief of Staff General George C. Marshall, who told President Roosevelt in May 1941, "Pearl Harbor is the strongest fortress in the world . . . a major attack is impractical"; or to Melvin J. Mass, a congressman from Minnesota and colonel in the Marine Corps Reserves who, upon returning from active duty in Hawaii, told his colleagues in Washington, D.C., on September 3, 1941, "Japan is deathly afraid of the American fleet," and that American air and sea forces in Hawaii could defend themselves "against any combination of forces that might challenge our interest." Or to Andrew J. May of Kentucky, chairman of the House Military Affairs Committee, who released a press statement on December 1 (reported in the Honolulu newspapers the following day), urging President Roosevelt to warn the Japanese that unless they renounced their ambitions for an empire in Southeast Asia, "The United States will blast them off the land and blow them out of the water." Or to Secretary of the Navy Frank Knox, who told a private gathering in Washington on the evening of December 4, "But I want you to know that no matter what happens, the United States Navy is ready! Every man is at his post, every ship is at its station. . . . Whatever happens, the Navy is not going to be caught napping."

Journalists were equally guilty. The *New York Times Magazine* pronounced Oahu "Our Gibraltar in the Pacific," the "hub of our strategic universe," and boasted of its planes swinging "far and wide to seaward searching, searching," and "men beside the Army's 16-inchers, half hidden in the jungle growth near Barbers Point." (Barbers Point is more desert than jungle, and its ammunition was locked up on December 7.)

A June 1941 article in *Collier's* titled "Impregnable Pearl Harbor" reported that military exercises in Hawaii had demonstrated "how quickly the billion-dollar fist that America has built in the Pacific could deliver a smash." The author assured readers that, "The Army's Hawaiian division . . . can be at their posts within thirty minutes, if they're not there already. The Pacific Fleet . . . [is] always within a few minutes of clearing for action," and that "to the extent that we know how many fighting ships and planes Japan has, we're kept pretty well informed where they are and what they're up to . . . In the continental United States there may be some doubt about our readiness to fight, but none exists in Hawaii. Battleships . . . plow the ocean practicing gunnery, wary as lions on the prowl."

The blackest humor can be found in *Our Billion Dollar Rock*, in which the author described "what this mighty defense base would look like and act like if it were called on to repel an attack." He then explained, "Although this was to have been a 'surprise' attack, listeners and sound amplifiers in mountain recesses have heralded the enemy. The word is hurried from observation posts. Curtiss pursuit hawks whip into the air . . . Meanwhile, anti-aircraft guns from a dozen emplacements have found the range and are knocking enemy planes out of the sky . . . Promptly, our battleships would wheel into action against the enemy . . . Whatever the strength of the invading enemy, he would soon know he had been in a battle. For Oahu is ready."

You cannot dismiss such boasting as yellow journalism, or the result of mainland fantasies. It was repeated in wire-service dispatches and printed in the Honolulu papers, and believed there as well. It created a closed system, in which mainland delusions reinforced those of the Islands, which in turn magnified those of the mainland. As December 7 approached, the arrogance grew exponentially, reaching a peak on December 6 in a speech delivered by Senator Ralph Brewster of Maine, who claimed, "The United States Navy can defeat the Japanese navy, any place and at any time," and in a report on the state of the U.S. Navy by Secretary of the Navy Knox stating that, "The American people may feel fully confident in their Navy . . . on any comparable basis the United States Navy is second to none."

You might think the military and civilian residents of Hawaii would have known better, but in 1940 the commander of the Hawaiian Department, Major General Charles Herron, had announced that, "Oahu will never be exposed to a blitzkrieg attack. This is why: we are more than two thousand miles away from land whichever way you look, which is a long way for an enemy force to steam. And besides, it would have to smash through our Navy."

Honolulu's own magazine, *Paradise of the Pacific*, boasted in its May 1941 edition that, "The island of Oahu is so thoroughly ringed with defenses, it would be impossible for hostile planes to come over the island. Their approach would be detected long before they were in striking distance, and if they ever got over the city, the army and navy would make quick work of them before they returned to their bases—presumably ships at sea."

An editorial the same month in the *Star-Bulletin* said, "This week a high officer of the U.S. Army remarked that he knows of no place under the American flag safer than Hawaii—more secure from the onslaught of actual war." And on September 6, an article in the *Star-Bulletin* by journalist Clark Beach declared that, "A Japanese attack on Hawaii is regarded as the most unlikely thing in the world, with one chance in a million of being successful."

Hawaii's Japanese-Americans were also confident. They feared an American-Japanese war in Asia, but believed Hawaii was too strong and distant to be menaced by Japan. Seiyei Wakukawa, who for many years had traveled to China to cover the Sino-Japanese War for the local Japanese newspaper, *Nippu Jiji*, admitted to me that, "I never imagined [the Japanese] would be so stupid as to attack America directly." And on December 4, George Akita led a discussion at his high school on the topic "Can Hawaii Be Attacked?" reporting afterward in his diary, "The answers were mostly no's. They say that our navy is too strong. The distance too much. Japan can't even conquer China."

A Japanese raid was considered so improbable and suicidal it had become a long-standing joke.

One kamaaina woman told me, "My father and I would stand outside on the lanai and whenever we saw a funny boat offshore we'd say, 'Here come the Japanese,' in the same way you'd say to a child, 'Here comes the bogeyman.' "

A Marine bugler on the *West Virginia* recalled eating dinner several days before December 7 with his father, a chief petty officer based in Pearl Harbor, and having his father warn him, with a smile, "If you see any of these local Japanese fellows wearing gas masks, you be careful."

A tongue-in-cheek *Paradise of the Pacific* editorial declared, "Says one 'school of guessing' the Japanese might get a number of airplane carriers within a few hundred miles of Honolulu, then swoop over the city (from an 'unexpected' angle) and drop bombs on forts, barracks, government buildings . . . unavoidably smiting, here and there, a hospital, a hotel or two, shipping, a few private homes (mansions and 'little grass shacks'), and possibly the headquarters of the Hawaii Visitors Bureau . . . and even the Japanese consulate itself. Possibly! . . . Not too probable!"

On December 6, no one on Oahu was more overconfident than the military. Richard Sutton, a young ensign who on the following morning would witness the attack from Admiral Bloch's veranda, remembers, "We had the supreme overconfidence a great athlete has who has never been beaten—we all thought we were invincible."

Bob Kinzler, a former soldier at Schofield Barracks, says the Japanese were taken so lightly that when General Short put the base on alert against sabotage, "We changed from khaki-colored to olive-colored shirts, and spent the week lying on the ground and squeezing the triggers of our empty rifles in preparation for our marksmanship tests the following week. That was our alert."

Naval intelligence officer Don Woodrum admits, "Like everyone else I thought they'd go into Southeast Asia. Japan is so far away it never occurred to me they'd hit us here." And in an article published on one of the Pearl anniversaries, he wrote, "What never crossed the threshold of consciousness was the possibility of a hit-and-run attack on the fleet at Pearl Harbor."

Bernard Clarey, executive officer on the submarine *Blowfin*, which returned to Pearl Harbor from patrol on December 5, remembers, "We expected to relax in Hawaii, and we always thought that the real danger came during our patrols."

Bud Cooper says that on his submarine, "We believed [the Japanese] couldn't really sail a ship without going aground. We had a very low regard for their ability." A Navy commander who was hitching a ride to Hawaii from the West Coast was aboard his sub when news of the attack came over their radio. He stood as if in a trance saying, "I just can't believe it . . . I just can't believe it . . . I just can't believe the Japanese could do it."

At a staff meeting ten days before the attack, Admiral Kimmel asked Captain Charles McMorris, his fleet war plans officer, "What do you think about the prospects of a Japanese air attack?" McMorris replied, "None, absolutely none." And on December 6, when Joseph C. Harsch asked Kimmel, "Is there going to be a war out here?" Kimmel answered he was confident there would be no war because the Germans had failed to take Moscow, and "that means that the Japanese cannot attack us in the Pacific without running the risk of a two-front war. The Japanese are too smart to run that risk."

Fleet intelligence officer Edwin Layton wrote that when he admitted to Admiral Kimmel on December 2 that he was unsure of the location of two Japanese carrier divisions, "The admiral then looked at me, as sometimes he would, with a stern countenance and an icy twinkle in his penetrating blue eyes. 'Do you mean to say they could be rounding Diamond Head and you wouldn't know it?' "

On the morning of December 6, Admiral Pye, the battle force commander in Pearl Harbor, told Layton, who had just raised the possibility of a Japanese move against the Philippines, "Oh, no. The Japanese won't attack us. We're too strong and powerful." Layton rightly believed the attack on the Philippines would come the next day, although he admits, "Even if Kimmel was inclined to share my fears about an attack on the Philippines, any thought that the Japanese might also hit Pearl Harbor at the same time was far from our minds."

The best summary of Oahu's overconfidence can be found in a report written after the war by Colonel George Bicknell of Army Intelligence, in which he said, "Practically every person on the island of Oahu had been lulled into a sense of false security through the constant reiteration of the belief that the defenses of the island made it practically impregnable. In addition, it had been constantly stated that Japan, as a military and naval power, amounted to nothing when pitted against the superior equipment, personnel and tactics of our own army and navy. Our own naval personnel had made it a common practice of belittling the Japanese navy. Many times it had been stated that the Japanese fleet would be simply and easily annihilated if we started an offensive against them . . .

"Little was actually known about Japanese air power although, again, there were many stories about the poor quality of Japanese aircraft, the lack of proper equipment, and the alleged fact that the Japanese made poor aviators and would never be as good as occidentals in this field. Stories of Japanese having such poor vision that their flying ability was hampered, and tales of other physical characteristics which prevented them from ever becoming truly proficient in handling aircraft were common and many times retold."

There is a connection between the arrogance of December 6, and the search for scapegoats that began on December 8, and has continued to the present day. The preattack hubris of the military magnified the postattack humiliation because, as any "great athlete who has never been beaten" knows, there is no greater disgrace than to be defeated by an opponent you have publicly and frequently denigrated. This is one reason why the psychological wounds of Pearl Harbor have cut so deeply, and the healing skin is so thin and easily punctured. It also explains why the rumors of sabotage by local Japanese-Americans, and allegations that Roosevelt conspired to withhold crucial intelligence from Kimmel and Short continue to be widely accepted, despite convincing evidence and arguments to the contrary. They are, after all, excuses and explanations for a defeat that is otherwise inexplicable, and humiliating.

CHAPTER 9

MRS. MORI TALKS
TO TOKYO

The FBI recorded every radiophone call between Honolulu and Tokyo. On the afternoon of December 5, Thomas Flynn, the most junior Honolulu agent, sat in a cubicle in the FBI office in the Dillingham Building monitoring these calls. Flynn could not understand Japanese so what he remembers most about the soon-to-be-famous Mori call is not its content, but copying it onto a brittle 78 rpm record, and the byplay between the Honolulu and Tokyo operators.

"Good morning, Honolulu. Good morning, Honolulu. . . . I have two tickets [calls]," the Tokyo operator announced in a tinkly voice.

"Good afternoon," the Honolulu operator corrected her coldly, because the time zones were different and "she didn't like Japs," adds Flynn, who has lived most of his life in Hawaii and regards this prejudice as outdated as the 78 rpm record.

A Mr. Ogawa, a reporter at the Tokyo newspaper *Yomiuri Shinbun*, had placed the call to Mrs. Ishiko Mori, a Japanese alien who was married to Dr. Motokazu Mori, a prominent Japanese-American dentist. Mrs. Mori was a stringer for *Yomiuri* and Ogawa had cabled her several days earlier to ask for her help in recruiting influential members of the Japanese-American community willing to submit to an interview. But everyone Mrs. Mori approached refused to speak to a Tokyo reporter so she was forced to answer Ogawa's questions herself on December 5.

"Are airplanes flying daily?" he asked her.

"Yes, lots of them fly around."

"Are they large planes?"

"Yes, they are quite big," she said, an answer George Bicknell of Army Intelligence would soon consider highly significant because "big planes" indicated long-range reconnaissance missions during daylight hours.

Many of Ogawa's questions concerned Oahu's defenses. He asked: "Do they put searchlights on when planes fly about at night?" "I hear there are many sailors there, is that right?" "Do you know anything about the U.S. fleet?"

Mrs. Mori answered with information readily available to anyone in Honolulu, including diplomats at the Japanese consulate.

He asked, "What kind of flowers are in bloom in Hawaii at present?"

"The hibiscus and poinsettias are in bloom now," she replied.

American counterintelligence agents reading the transcript suspected this was a code, and that Mrs. Mori was reporting on the movement of specific battleships. After the attack, she and her husband were interned as a security measure, but never charged with espionage. Their loyalties, however, are tangential to a call that was less important for what it might or might not have communicated to Tokyo than for the warning it should have delivered to Oahu's defenders.

FBI Agent-in-Charge Robert Shivers read a transcript on the morning of December 6 and immediately judged it suspicious. He telephoned Captain Mayfield and Colonel Bicknell. Mayfield was out, but later that day his assistant described the call to him. Mayfield concluded it was "interesting," but not urgent.

Bicknell was more alarmed. The day before, he had learned that Japanese consular officials were burning their papers. The Mori call confirmed his suspicion that something was about to happen. "The general tone of the conversation, when considered in the light of recent events, filled my mind with dread," he later explained. In 1945, he told congressional investigators, "I still feel it was highly significant . . . putting it together with the information that we already had, that the Japanese consul was burning papers . . . a message of this type did, and still does, seem highly significant to me."

Bicknell called his superior, Lieutenant Colonel Kendall Fielder, and requested an audience with General Short. At 7:00 P.M. on the eve of the attack, Bicknell, Fielder, and Short met on the porch of Short's residence at Fort Shafter. Bicknell argued the call was highly suspicious, and indicated that "something was in the wind."

Fielder and Short were impatient. They were late for a party at Schofield Barracks, and their wives sat in a nearby car, wearing formal dresses and upset at the delay.

Short argued that the conversation seemed ordinary and, he said, "presented quite a true depiction of present-day life in Hawaii which a newspaperman would require for an article." He handed the transcript back to Bicknell, leaving him with the impression that he was perhaps too "intelligence-conscious."

Bicknell returned to his office and studied the transcript for another hour. His widow's most vivid memory of December 6 is his frustration at being unable to persuade Short and Fielder that the Mori call was an ominous portent. At the very least, it indicated someone in Tokyo was interested enough in Hawaii's defenses to invent a flower code and pay two hundred dollars for a fifteen-minute call.

Her most vivid memory of December 7 is of her husband standing on their terrace in Aiac Heights and mumbling about "poinsettias" and "hibiscus" as battleships burst into flames.

After the attack, the Mori call was important for the Moris, who spent four years in an internment camp because of it, and for an army of Pearl Harbor investigators, who considered it more damning evidence of the shortcomings of the Hawaii Command. The 1946 congressional investigation concluded that, "The Mori call pointed directly at Hawaii," and described Short's failure to take it seriously as "inexcusable." It did not matter if the call had been an attempt at espionage, it should still have been "of greatest significance to responsible commanders in Hawaii."

When I came across the story, I believed the Moris had been wronged and interned on flimsy evidence. It seemed too fantastic that the Japanese high command would risk revealing its intentions by asking questions like these over an open line, and no evidence was ever found in the archives in Tokyo, or in interviews conducted by occupation authorities, to indicate either of the Moris had been spies. I was also persuaded of their innocence by Don Woodrum, a junior Army intelligence officer in Honolulu at the time, who believes it might have been an attempt by the Japanese military to ascertain if there were any signs of alarm in Honolulu, or perhaps an attempt by the reporter to gather background for a story about Honolulu, which did appear several days later in *Yomiuri Shinbun*. "Perhaps someone at the paper heard a rumor of an attack on Hawaii and thought it would be cute to have a background story ready to go," he said.

I was also impressed by Mrs. Mori's replies in a 1957 newspaper interview. "I'm sure now that he [Ogawa] knew something big was going to happen here," she said. "He was laying the groundwork for a big scoop, feature and color copy when it happened."

Her explanation for her involvement with the Japanese newspaper was poignant. She had traveled to Honolulu from Japan in 1929 to stay with a family friend, Dr. Iga Mori, and fallen in love with his son. They married and had children but American immigration laws prevented her from becoming a citizen so she had to travel to Japan every two years, staying there for a year before returning to American territory. After several heartbreaking separations, she discovered she could remain in the United States if she became a diplomat, missionary, international merchant, or journalist.

It must have taken courage to leave Japan and marry knowing she would be separated from her family every two years. I also liked her honesty. In 1957, she admitted she had not yet become an American citizen because, "Gradually I am learning to love America the most and when my heart tells me I am sincere, I will become a citizen."

When asked if she had spied for Japan, she laughed. "Of course not. I loved Japan, I still do, but I was never disloyal to the United States," she said, which is as true an expression of the conflicted emotions of Japanese aliens in Honolulu as you could want.

But the more I wanted to believe the Mori call had been innocent, the more I doubted it. There was the matter of the transcript, which was, indeed, as Colonel Bicknell had described it, "very irregular and highly suspicious."

Mrs. Mori had said, "It seems that the fleet has left here." (Actually only the aircraft carrier task forces had left.)

"Is that so?" Ogawa asked, adding in the same breath, "What kind of flowers are in bloom in Hawaii at present?"

Bicknell believed their exchange might be an open code, a common method of passing information. He saw it as suspicious that only two of the many flowers blooming in Hawaii in December then were mentioned, and that Ogawa appeared to become confused when Mrs. Mori mentioned poinsettias, an indication their code may not have been working properly.

It would be easier to dismiss Bicknell's suspicions if he had been one of those mainland officers who considered every Japanese resident a potential spy or saboteur. But he was a longtime resident of Hawaii who repeatedly defended the Japanese community against charges of disloyalty or sabotage.

There is also the troubling question of who actually spoke with Ogawa on December 5. Mrs. Mori later claimed to have persuaded her husband to be interviewed, and the transcript appears to confirm this. At the end of the call Ogawa says, "Best regards to your wife," and Mori replies, "Wait a moment please?" Then he hangs up. Both Shivers and Bicknell testified that the speaker was Mrs. Mori, not her husband, and that perhaps Ogawa had said, "Best regards to your wife" because heavy static on the line misled him into thinking he was speaking to a man. Bicknell told the joint congressional investigation, "As I remember the original record, it was a woman's voice. We may be mistaken. It may have been Dr. Mori himself. But he denied that he had the conversation and said it was his wife who did the talking when we examined him." If you examine the transcript closely, it points to Mrs. Mori. Ogawa opens by saying, "I received your telegram and was able to grasp the essential points." The voice identified as "H" for Honolulu does not dispute this, and since Mrs. Mori was the correspondent for *Yomiuri*, it makes sense that she would have sent the telegram. But why would she later lie about taking the call, shifting suspicion onto her husband? And why would he lie, placing his wife in danger?

The Moris were not listed in the Honolulu phone directory and I was told they had both died. I went to their former address, 702 Wylie Street, hoping its current residents might have known them.

Wylie Street ran through a predominantly Chinese and Japanese neighborhood of modest bungalows. The Moris' former home was an exception, a rambling white elephant set on a corner lot and distinguished by its circular driveway and a porte cochère. Three rusting commercial vans parked outside proclaimed, "DRAIN BRAIN—A. Breitinstein, Sewer and Drain Cleaning Service."

After twenty years in Honolulu, Mr. and Mrs. Breitinstein were preparing to retire to Oklahoma, and packing crates, files, and plumbing tools jammed their downstairs rooms. But I could see the Moris' legacy in the circular Oriental window, teak dining-room table, huge Japanese bathtub, built-in curio cabinets, and in the spacious parlor where they held receptions for visiting Japanese dignitaries. "We often feel as if we are living with the Moris' ghosts," Mr. Breitinstein told me.

"We have *definitely* had ghosts," Mrs. Breitinstein added. The house was haunted by a lady, perhaps Mrs. Mori, or her daughter. The spirit had appeared while her own daughter and Japanese son-in-law were visiting from Japan, and their half-Japanese granddaughter had seen a "lady" in her room. Their grandson saw her

A view of Diamond Head as seen from the Royal Hawaiian Hotel in 1941. (USS *Arizona* Memorial, National Park Service)

The USS *California* moored in Honolulu Harbor by Aloha Tower. (USS *Arizona* Memorial, National Park Service)

Adm. Husband E. Kimmel (*center*), Commander in Chief of the U.S. Pacific Fleet in 1941, conferring with his chief of staff, Capt. William Smith (*right*), and his operations officer, Capt. W. S. DeLany. (USS *Arizona* Memorial, National Park Service)

Above left: Lt. Col. George W. Bicknell, the intelligence officer who was suspicious of the Mori call. (Courtesy of Dorothy Bicknell)

Above right: Sterling Cale on his twentieth birthday, November 29, 1941. (Courtesy of Sterling Cale)

Left: Lt. Donald Woodrum, a young naval intelligence officer, on December 7, 1941. (Courtesy of Donald Woodrum)

Sailors posing with a native girl at a Honolulu photo studio in 1940. (USS *Arizona* Memorial, National Park Service)

Below: Pvt. Bob Kinzler at the Schofield Barracks in 1941. (Courtesy of Bob Kinzler)

Visitors aboard the USS *Arizona* in the late 1930s. (USS *Arizona* Memorial, National Park Service)

Sailors on a Honolulu street, Liberty Cross, before the war. (USS *Arizona* Memorial, National Park Service)

Left: Sue Isonaga, who still reveres the memory of FBI agent Robert Shivers. (Courtesy of Sue Isonaga)

Below: Tadeo Fuchikami, the RCA messenger who delivered the belated telegram warning of a possible Japanese attack, poses on his motorcycle several years after the war. (Courtesy of Tadeo Fuchikami)

A decoded version of the famous "Silk Ad" that ran in the December 3, 1941, *Honolulu Star-Bulletin* and was widely believed to be a coded warning to Japanese agents and sympathizers in Honolulu. (Reprinted by permission of the *Honolulu Star-Bulletin*)

Aerial view of a peaceful Pearl Harbor in October 1941, six weeks before the attack. (USS *Arizona* Memorial, National Park Service)

View of "Battleship Row" taken by a Japanese plane at the start of the attack. Notice the shock waves in the water caused by exploding depth charges. (USS *Arizona* Memorial, National Park Service)

next. Then their daughter complained of waking up paralyzed, unable to move her hand and telephone for help. The experience lasted twenty minutes and repeated itself two weeks later. The Breitinsteins hired a Japanese priest from the Buddhist temple to perform an exorcism. He spent an hour upstairs, laying out plates of rice and fruit, lighting candles, and praying. The ghost reappeared five years later, again during a visit from their daughter and Japanese son-in-law. This time the priest performed an exorcism throughout the entire house.

It made sense for Mrs. Mori to haunt the Breitinsteins. They were Japanophiles who had lived in that country for many years and had chosen to move to Honolulu because of its Japanese atmosphere. They had never met Mrs. Mori, yet even they believed she had been a Japanese agent, or at least an active sympathizer. Their late neighbor, Mrs. Wan, a Chinese schoolteacher, insisted the Moris had been spies, and claimed to have seen them rushing into the street on December 7, shouting "Banzai!" and waving on the Japanese planes.

I was suspicious of Mrs. Wan. I had no doubt that a few of the forty thousand Japanese aliens in Hawaii on December 7 must have secretly rejoiced at the attack, or at least had conflicting emotions about it, but few could have been foolish enough to make such a public display. The Japanese invasion of China created tensions between Japanese and Chinese communities in Hawaii that survived the war, and I had already come across other "Banzai!" stories. In one version, an elderly Japanese man dressed in a kimono stood on his rooftop waving at the planes. In another, he waved a Japanese flag, or a samurai sword, then threw off his kimono to reveal the dress uniform of a Japanese naval officer.

Mr. Breitinstein had more convincing evidence, he said. While running speaker cables for his music system underneath the house he had discovered antenna wire leading to more wire, and more, three hundred feet in all, a ground bounce for transmitting shortwave signals. "And on that much wire you can bounce your signals a long way," he said.

While searching for a plumbing leak, he found more wire in what he called the Moris' "secret room." He showed me how the ceiling of a kitchen passageway had been dropped to create a small, secret room reached via a sliding panel. Inside, he had discovered the kind of electrical connections necessary for a shortwave radio.

But did that prove anything? Perhaps Dr. Mori or his son had been ham radio enthusiasts, a common passion in the thirties and forties among Japanese, who used shortwave sets to communicate with friends and relatives in Japan.

Short and Bicknell discussed the Mori call again after Pearl Harbor. Short, nervous about his cavalier dismissal of it, said, "Well, Bicknell, you couldn't prove anything by that, that it meant anything."

Bicknell answered, "Well, I still can't prove anything by it, and we never will be able to."

I felt the same way. Were the Moris Japanese agents, or the innocent dupes of a reporter attempting to collect background for a scoop? But why had one of them lied about who had taken the call, and why the secret room?

The Mori call was like other Pearl Harbor mysteries—the more you learned, the more difficult it became to prove anything. Mysteries such as "Why did a Navy commander disappear while walking in the hills overlooking Pearl Harbor several months before December 7?" and "Did a Japanese pilot land on a golf course during the attack just feet from Admiral Kimmel's Japanese caddy?" (as this caddy claimed until his death) will never be solved. And these mysteries, and the unresolved Pearl Harbor disputes over who was responsible for the catastrophe, and who mishandled which intelligence, is the kind of atmosphere that encourages ghosts.

CHAPTER 10

ENSIGN YOSHIKAWA'S
LAST CABLE

Takeo Yoshikawa drove to Aiea Heights to spy on the fleet again on the morning of December 6. Then he returned to the Japanese consulate on Nuuanu Avenue and locked himself in the telegraph room. At 1:00 P.M., he responded to Tokyo's urgent request for information about "observation balloons" and "anti-mine nets," cabling back, "In my opinion the battleships do not have torpedo nets . . . At the present time there are no signs of barrage balloon equipment." Then he added a final and reckless sentence that could have changed the course of history. He did not know if or when Japan would attack Pearl Harbor, but the urgency and nature of Tokyo's requests for information in early December certainly indicated it was a possibility, and so, perhaps elated by the casual attitude of Oahu's defenders, he made a breathtaking error, adding the gratuitous comment that, "I imagine that in all probability there is considerable opportunity left to take advantage for a surprise attack against these places."

His cable was intercepted by monitoring stations in Hawaii and on the West Coast and sent to Washington for decoding by Magic.

A copy was also passed to Navy Intelligence by the RCA office in Honolulu. Nowhere was it decoded and translated in time.

That afternoon, Yoshikawa visited Pearl City and Aiea Heights again to count warships. At 9:00 P.M. he sat alone in a darkened consulate and, with the sky outside illuminated by the reflected glare of Pearl Harbor's lights, dispatched his final ship-movement report. It ended, "It appears that no air reconnaissance is being conducted by the fleet air arm."

Nineteen years later, Yoshikawa remembered that evening in romantic and heroic terms, recalling a clear tropical night, taro fronds stirring gently in the breeze, and the coral rock in the consulate's drive shimmering in the moonlight. "In truth, if only for a moment in time, I held history in the palm of my hand," he said.

After being repatriated with other interned Japanese diplomats, Yoshikawa was ignored and served out the war at the same rank. He feared prosecution by American occupation authorities as a war criminal and panicked when seven naval officers involved in spying on America were sentenced to long jail sentences. He hid in a forest, risking starvation, became an apprentice Buddhist monk, and supported himself by making candy. After two years, he surfaced to open a filling station. He discovered, he said, that "people who knew of my past said I was a very great patriot, or they avoided me." He complained that no one trusted a spy, not even his own countrymen.

His anonymity ended in 1960 when he wrote a book about his experiences in Honolulu and promoted it on television. He advertised himself as the Pearl Harbor "master spy" and negotiated lucrative contracts to teach industrial espionage to Japanese executives. He returned to Honolulu in 1961 to appear on a Walter Cronkite documentary. The Japanese government, however, never rewarded or acknowledged his exploits, and his request for a pension was denied by an official who told him, "You must be some kind of child to think that we will ever acknowledge your activities in Honolulu. The government of Japan never spied on anyone."

Whenever Yoshikawa reminisced about his life in Honolulu and his return to the city in 1961, he described his residence there as the happiest time of his life. "I found Hawaii a most beautiful place," he told one American reporter. "It also made me want to see the rest of the United States. Do you think I would be received favorably in the United States? Do you think I could obtain a good job there?"

In 1981, he owned a plumbing business and was still hoping to revisit Hawaii. He told a journalist from the *Star-Bulletin* he would come in 1982 for his seventieth birthday, but poor health forced him to cancel the trip and he later suffered a fatal stroke.

Had Yoshikawa returned to Hawaii, he would have found most of his former haunts substantially changed. The Japanese consulate has been remodeled and expanded from the original two-story concrete block, and trees planted to honor postwar visits by the imperial family have altered the garden where Japanese diplomats burned their codes.

Had Yoshikawa taken his favorite drive down the Kamehameha Highway to Pearl City, he would have seen strip malls, shopping centers, and the vast, asphalt-and-concrete precincts of the Pearl City Mall. Pearl City peninsula is now a restricted area of naval housing, and self-service gas stations where clerks sit mute in plastic boxes, gesturing for payment in advance before turning on the pumps. A Funway Rental office offering "Samurai jeeps," and car dealerships with acres of Nissans and Toyotas now block the views of Pearl Harbor Yoshikawa once found so revealing.

The Shuncho-Ro teahouse has become the Natsunoya teahouse, but it occupies the same sprawling two-story wooden house sitting on a bluff overlooking Honolulu, and its employees know all about Yoshikawa. The shabby, cream-colored dining rooms have worn linoleum and tatami mats smelling faintly of dirty socks. All but one of its 1941 geishas has been pensioned; the balcony from which Yoshikawa observed Pearl Harbor has been enclosed in glass, and the surrounding trees have grown taller, blocking the view of the harbor.

I also notice that Pearl Harbor is too distant to be clearly observed even through a strong telescope. Spying was a pretext; evidently, Yoshikawa had frequented the Shuncho-Ro for drink and romance.

The Natsunoya still promotes its view, though, promising Japanese visitors "a spectacular panorama." Instead of Pearl Harbor, its patrons see the Japanese-owned office buildings of downtown Honolulu and the Japanese-owned hotels of Waikiki. This view is also featured in the Natsunoya's handsome but unsettling brochure, which shows lines of black Japanese characters poised like lines of falling bombs above Honolulu's skyline.

I am given a tour by a headwaiter who complains that ever since Japanese companies purchased so many Waikiki hotels and equipped them with Japanese restaurants, fewer groups make the twenty-minute drive to the Natsunoya. The teahouse depends on "deluxe kinds of tourists," who arrive by taxi and know about its history. They want to know where Yoshikawa sat, and where his telescope was sited. Here at the Natsunoya, at least, he is famous, a hero to his countrymen.

CHAPTER 11

A WHITE RIVER FLOWS DOWN HOTEL STREET

The evening of December 6, 1941, is often described as "still" or "peaceful," words evoking Christmas Eve, and implying a world catching its breath before a great event.

Honolulu was then a city of deep shadows and soft light. Campfires flickered at beach picnics, and bare lightbulbs swung from backyard trees. At dusk, the ocean turned purple, the surf became luminescent, and one saw the lanterns of Japanese sampans, the glowing portholes of moored freighters, and luau torches flickering at parties.

Drive around Honolulu on a Saturday night now and you smell exhaust and hear the steady hum of traffic. But on December 6, 1941, Honolulu hummed to music—to swing bands on jukeboxes, fox-trots played by orchestras at the Ala Moana and Royal Hawaiian, and slushy Hawaiian music coming from the radios of partying sailors and lonely guards.

At Pearl Harbor's Bloch Arena there was a "Battle of Music" at which battleship bands competed in playing "I Don't Want to Set the World on Fire" and "Take the A Train." The band of the

U.S.S. *Arizona* had won second place in a contest held on November 22 and most of its members, who were scheduled to compete in the finals on December 20, were attending the concert to cheer on friends from Navy band school. A now-famous photograph had been taken of the *Arizona* band two weeks before. While most military group photographs of that time show a blur of khaki or white, in this one, the musicians have removed their hats and are sitting near the camera, making it impossible not to notice their innocent high-school faces. Perhaps I am unsettled by their *Arizona* shipmates, sitting behind them in dress whites and already a ghostly presence, or the proud way they hold up their trombones and clarinets, or the knowledge that not a single member of this band would be alive after 8:02 the next morning, but if I had to choose the most heart-wrenching Pearl Harbor photograph, this would be it.

The *Star-Bulletin* of December 6 carried a front-page story by Lawrence Nakatsuka titled "Baby Boom Hits Hawaii, Stork Calls Every Hour." Nakatsuka quoted a medical expert as saying, "There is . . . a natural urge to produce offspring before being shot to pieces." This desire to live for the moment and enjoy what might be a last weekend of peace perhaps explains why people appear to have been restless on December 6, attending numerous dances and parties, and determinedly searching for fun. At the Japanese consulate, Kita was hosting one of his frequent stag parties for Honolulu's leading citizens. Admiral Kimmel had been invited, and although he had attended such parties before, this time he refused, one of few decisions he made on December 6 for which he would later be thankful. Colonel Bicknell also declined, perhaps because he remembered Kita's earlier functions as "really wet parties, [with] a bottle of scotch at each place and a geisha girl pouring it out." One such party had ended with the geishas using blankets to toss local businessmen into the air.

At the University of Hawaii there was a party for the Willamette football team and a junior-class dance, attended by many of the young niseis who would return the next day to defend the Manoa campus against enemy paratroopers. Many prominent islanders at-

tended an engagement party for the son of former Governor Lawrence Judd, others were at a belated harvest moon festival at Waikiki's Lau Yee Chai, whose mahogany screens, carp pools, and
miniature backyard mountain made it "the most beautiful Chinese
restaurant in the world."

Pilots from Wheeler and Hickam Fields danced at the Hickam
officers' club, the men dressed in white dinner jackets and their
wives in long dresses in accordance with the base rule that officers
and wives wear formal clothes after 5:00 P.M. Dorothy Anthony and
her husband, a prominent Honolulu attorney, hosted a party at the
Pacific Club for two of his Harvard Law School friends who had
been posted to Hawaii with the military. "We all knew war might
break out in Asia, because all the big newspapermen stopped here
on their way back and forth," she remembers. "But that night you
couldn't have gotten anyone at our party to say war would come to
Hawaii."

On the sixth day of every month for the six months preceding
December 6 a young lieutenant from the *Arizona* and his wife, Jim
and Jinny Dare, had thrown a champagne party to celebrate their
monthly wedding anniversary. Ruth Flynn, personal secretary to
FBI Agent-in-Charge Robert Shivers, recalls the Dares' December 6 party as being their gayest yet, with young officers from the
Arizona and several other warships filling their cottage on the
grounds of the Halekulani Hotel. The next day Flynn would feel
the FBI office in the Dillingham Building sway from nearby explosions, but it is the Dares' party she remembers the most vividly, perhaps because she knew so many men from the *Arizona*. She and her
friends often went to the *Arizona* in the evenings when she was in
port to watch movies on her fantail, and usually attended the
monthly *Arizona* dances at the Ala Moana. By December 6 she knew
so many *Arizona* sailors that she could not walk down Waikiki's
Kalakaua Avenue without having someone from the ship say hello.

Earlier that evening she had eaten a supper of Chinese food
washed down with zombies with a man she disliked. After returning
home she received phone calls every five minutes from an officer on

the *Arizona*, Lt. Bucky Walsh. He threatened to continue calling until she agreed to attend the Dares' party. Finally, she gave in and went with him. "There were lots of women, but not enough," she remembers. "This mob of young officers had been at sea for weeks, and when they saw Bucky walking up the path with a female, one of them grabbed me and flung me over his shoulder like a sack of potatoes. That was how I made my entrance." She began feeling ill, and Walsh walked her home. They made a date to attend the nine o'clock mass at St. Augustine's in Waikiki. He told her he was going back to the *Arizona* but changed his mind and returned to the party. "When it ended," Flynn says, "the Dares insisted he spend the night in their cottage, and that's why he survived." Most officers returned to the *Arizona*. Now when friends from the mainland visit Flynn she cannot bear to take them to the *Arizona* Memorial. "It's gotten to be too much, looking at that list of names and seeing so many people I knew," she says. And this may be why she and others remember December 6 so clearly, because it was the last time they saw their friends alive.

While officers danced in hotel ballrooms and drank at private parties, enlisted men entertained themselves in the taverns, shooting galleries, and pool halls lining Hotel Street, a narrow thoroughfare running through the commercial center of Honolulu into Chinatown. Throughout the afternoon and evening of December 6, buses and rattletrap taxis raced down the two-lane highway connecting Pearl Harbor and Honolulu, past the wrecks of similar taxis, and by sunset, a white river of sailors was flowing down Hotel Street.

The men squinted into the falling sun and slouched under stuttering fluorescent bulbs, smoking and laughing, cartoon sailors with flapping pant legs and caps pulled over one eye. They bought silver daggers, fringed satin pillows saying "I Love You Mother o' Mine," photographs of bare-breasted women holding up patriotic slogans, and monkey-pod carvings that today bring two hundred dollars in

Honolulu curio stores. They squandered money on Skee-Ball and pinball, on throwing baseballs at milk cans, and at shooting galleries run by White Russian émigrés pushed out of Manchuria by the Japanese. They sat bare-chested under naked bulbs as Filipino tattoo artists pricked their skin, and crowded barbershops where Japanese girls cut their hair. They drank too much and sobered up with coffee at the Swanky Franky, which made so much money selling hot dogs to servicemen that it became the foundation of the Spencecliff chain, purchased by Japanese interests forty years later.

Most of all, they wanted women and, finding none, they paid for them. Honolulu has always been a city of lonely men: first the New England whalers who brought the venereal diseases that decimated the native population, then Chinese laborers who sent back photographs that were pasted onto those of their families (the only way they could be reunited), then Japanese plantation workers who chose picture brides from photograph albums, then Filipino cane cutters who patronized the taxi-dance halls because they were forbidden to marry, and finally, the American servicemen who flocked to Hotel Street on December 6.

Even though Hawaii is considered paradise now, in 1941 many servicemen loathed the Islands. Some had not seen their families for almost two years, and they pursued the lonely-man pastimes of beer drinking and card playing, fighting with local youths they called "gooks," and sitting on shoreline rocks, heads in hands, staring toward San Francisco. Their suicide rate was higher than on mainland bases, and in October 1941, one despondent soldier the newspapers called a "human bomb" threw himself from the roof of the University Cinema onto the orchestra seats.

You might expect someone like Bob Kinzler to have fond memories of his Army days at Schofield Barracks, particularly since he settled in Hawaii after the war, served in the Army Reserves, and sent a daughter to West Point. Instead, he remembers the "pathetic sight" of soldiers lining up outside whorehouses. "We had no contact with the Asian population except through the Japanese lady barbers," he told me, "and civilians thought we were just a bunch of bums who had enlisted in the military because we couldn't get real jobs."

The lonely soldiers paid to embrace Filipino taxi dancers whose heavy eye shadow melted down their faces like tears, and patronized the Hotel Street photographic studios where they paid handsomely for the pleasure of wrapping their arms around girls in grass skirts who clicked on smiles and ignored their whispered pleas for a date. They joined the double lines stretching around the block from houses of prostitution that advertised on matchbooks ("The Bell Rooms—Give the Bell a Ring!") and were so efficient that nearby taverns sold tokens good for a screw. Yet, despite the prostitution, then quaintly known as "white-slave traffic," and despite neighborhoods with forbidding names like Tin Can Alley, Blood Town, Mosquito Flats, and Hell's Half Acre, and despite the sneak thieves and pimps, there was a certain innocence to Hotel Street, a sense of order and propriety that later vanished from the place. "Wholesome fun for the lads and a place to spend their money without too much exploitation," said the magazine *Paradise of the Pacific*, and that was not too far wrong. Most Hotel Street blocks also had lei shops with Hawaiian women stringing flowers. The taxi-dance halls were heavily varnished, barnlike rooms reminiscent of church halls, where liquor was prohibited and dancers forbidden to leave until their mothers or husbands collected them. In his memoir of prewar duty aboard the U.S.S. *California*, Theodore Mason describes a December 5, 1941, liberty on Hotel Street, writing, "There was a boisterous innocence about it all in the Honolulu of 1941, a brash and blind naivete which assumed without question that the necessary steps were being taken to ensure all would be well. Children of the Great Depression, most of us yet trusted and believed in our leaders."

Hotel Street runs through a Honolulu neighborhood that resembles its 1941 photographs, a bowling-alley narrow street fronted by low stucco and granite buildings, and shaded by tin awnings. But go closer and you can see it has changed. Antique stores and boutiques, and markets catering to an exploding Chinese and Vietnamese population coexist with a few holdout bars still exhaling their timeless halitosis of cigarettes and stale beer. Inside are lizardy men with fading tattoos, Filipino toughs with needle tracks, and prostitutes wearing splotches of heavy pancake makeup to camouflage their AIDS blemishes. Every patron seems cursed by an ugly cough, a limp, a damaged eye, or a scar. Hotel Street is in its death throes, a place for bottom-of-the-barrel fun and as nasty as a run-over dog, thrashing, snarling, and snapping its jaws, a place that would shock the December 6 sailors.

Although December 6 appeared to be a Saturday night like any other on Hotel Street, of course it was not. For some men, a Swanky Franky would be their last meal, a beer at the Pantheon tavern their last drink, throwing a baseball at three milk cans their last fun, and a taxi dancer the last woman they would touch. In wartime, men understand this. But the tragedy of December 6 is precisely that because it seemed an evening like any other, these lonely men did not drink more, screw more, or throw more baseballs.

Although Honolulu's civilians did little to entertain enlisted men, some nonetheless disapproved of their attempts to entertain themselves, and would later argue that the real tragedy of December 6 was that these servicemen drank or whored at all.

At nine o'clock that evening, Mr. Chris Benny, executive secretary of the Temperance League of Hawaii, and two other members of this league, Mr. Sanbourne and Mr. Castle, the head of one of Hawaii's wealthiest families and a director of Castle & Cook, all met at the Army and Navy YMCA near the eastern end of Hotel Street for the purpose of investigating the alcoholic debauchery of a typical Saturday night. They walked down Hotel Street, up River Street to Beretania, over to Nuuanu, then back to the YMCA, passing the most notorious dives. "We noticed a number of drunken Army and Navy men and a great many sitting at the tables in the taverns drinking beer and hard liquor," Mr. Benny would later report. "We loitered on the streets, standing outside some of these places . . . to observe whether the men were going up and down to the entrances to houses of prostitution."

Benny's delegation never counted inebriated sailors, nor witnessed anyone being arrested, yet on January 3, he wrote a letter to the Roberts Commission charging the timing of the Japanese attack had been "based on the well known but grim and awful fact that we have only half a Navy, half an Army, on Saturday night and Sunday morning." That was an exaggeration common to rumors promoted by temperance organizations after the attack, with one prohibitionist tract claiming that "the free flow of alcohol was a fifth column working for the Japanese" and that "prohibition *before* Pearl Harbor might have saved us from the worst defeat our nation has ever undergone." In truth, servicemen behaved rather well on December 6. The Honolulu Police arrested only four men for public intoxication and the records of the Military Police and Shore Patrol show a similarly quiet evening.

At midnight on December 6, as on every Saturday night on an island still dominated by the descendants of missionaries who had banned the hula and dressed native women in shapeless gingham dresses, bars closed and dancing stopped. Orchestras played the national anthem and men in uniform snapped to attention. Sailors poured from bars and shooting arcades, and Hotel Street again became a swollen river of white uniforms, this time flowing east toward the YMCA, where buses waited to return sailors to Pearl Harbor. Back at the docks, the men engaged in a Saturday night ritual of fighting for places aboard the last liberty ships, laughing and falling into the water.

In less than eight hours, some would become heroes, diving into burning water to rescue shipmates. But the heroes on Oahu that night were the defense workers laboring on the night shift at the Pearl Harbor dry dock, repairing the battleship *Pennsylvania* and several destroyers. No blame for the defeat would attach to them, and they would be given the task of rebuilding the fortifications the military had misused, and salvaging the ships they had lost. These defense workers (soon to be called "war workers") were the kind of confident, muscular young men newsreels idealized for building New Deal public works. But their grimy clothes and grease-smeared faces were an uncomfortable reproach to Hawaii's languid workday, and I was told that no one extended them much of an aloha, that they wore their aloha shirts "badly," and that even Oriental girls scorned them. Enlisted men resented them because they had more money. The Caucasian establishment suspected their ranks concealed professional agitators planning to organize the plantation workers. Everyone blamed them for Honolulu's crowding, traffic, and crime, and it was feared they were another in a long line of the single white men—the whalers, beachcombers, and traders—who had left Hawaii the worse for their presence.

The military parades that often filled Honolulu's streets before Pearl Harbor now appear to have been exercises in bombast, but the 1941 Honolulu Labor Day parade still strikes me as stirring. Eight thousand defense workers turned out, rank after rank of lathers, plumbers, and plasterers, and boilermakers, painters, carpenters, ironworkers, and hod carriers, the men wearing white shirts and ties or matching coveralls, the women in gingham dresses. They rode floats showing riveters and machinists at work, and carried banners saying, "Ironworkers 101% for Defense—Are You?" The sight of them was so impressive that spectators fell silent and, according to one newspaper account, no wisecracks were heard from those witnessing the "men who will build the air and navy bases which must someday protect Hawaii from a foe that will strike without warning."

Ed Sheehan, who was working at Pearl Harbor on the night of December 6, recalls putting new steel plates on the destroyer *Downes* while listening to "Moonlight Serenade" and "Moonglow" played over loudspeakers, and the contrast between the dry-dock lights and the darkness outside, and how the lights sent great shadows dancing upon the walls.

Nearby in the shipyard dispensary, Pharmacist's Mate Sterling Cale worked alone to bandage the cuts and scrapes of night-shift workers like Ed Sheehan. Like many Pearl Harbor sailors, he was a Depression-battered teenager, the son of a former Illinois sharecropper who was relieved to have found a secure job in the Navy. He had made Eagle Scout in high school and approached his naval service as if it was a chance to earn more merit badges. He graduated second in his class at Hospital Corps School, and once in Hawaii took courses at the submarine base in order to become a frogman. Unlike most enlisted men, he thought Oahu was magic. He went picnicking and dancing with civilian nurses and became friends with the tobacco heiress Doris Duke, sometimes attending parties on her four-masted schooner and driving around Honolulu in her convertible, mesmerized by the sight of her golden hair flowing in the tropical breeze.

At 11:00 P.M., shortly before Japanese mother ship submarines launched five two-man midget submarines, their crewmen noticed the lights of Honolulu twinkling in their periscopes. Perhaps they saw the neon lights of Waikiki, the flashing lights of the Aloha Tower, the headlights of Gus Ahola's speeding jalopy, the aircraft warning lights on the Hickam water tower, the bright lights of Sterling Cale's dispensary, or, burning brightest of all, the dry-dock spotlights illuminating the work of men who would ultimately prove more dangerous to Japan than the slumbering battleships.

Earlier that evening the Army had ordered Honolulu radio station KGMB to broadcast all night in order to provide a beacon for a flight of unarmed B-17s arriving early the next morning from the mainland. Japanese pilots also picked up KGMB, hearing *Plantation Melodies* and *Swing Nocturne*. The station provided them with a beacon, too, and there is a photograph of Japanese flight crews in the carrier briefing rooms on December 6, laughing and performing crude hulas to music that appeared to prove America was just as they had hoped, hedonistic and unprepared.

PART THREE

DECEMBER 7, 1941

CHAPTER 12

HAWAII TAKES
A DEEP BREATH

Early in the morning of December 7, the two-man crews of the Japanese midget submarines boarded their craft, carrying warm sweaters and bottles of sake, and shouting "On to Pearl Harbor!" Steel clamps released the midgets from their mother ships and they headed toward Oahu. The submariners had been ordered to lie on the bottom of Pearl Harbor until morning, then launch their torpedoes at the American battleships.

The first midget reached the Pearl Harbor channel at 0330. A sliver of moon lit a sky with scattered trade-wind clouds. The eighty-six ships of the Pacific Fleet sat moored at docks or anchored singly or in pairs, dark silhouettes lit only by their anchor lights. Only a quarter of their gun batteries were manned, and even their ammunition was locked in boxes. Three warships were under steam as the midgets approached Pearl Harbor. The minesweepers *Condor* and *Crossbill* were checking for mines, while the *Ward*, an obsolete World War I destroyer staffed with naval reservists from Minnesota, was patrolling the channel entrance to Pearl Harbor.

At 0342, the *Condor* sighted what appeared to be the wake of a submarine two miles from the entrance buoys to Pearl Harbor. The *Ward* went on the alert and for the next hour used its sonar to search for the submarine. The captains of the *Condor* and *Ward* did not relate information about this possible sighting to the headquarters of the 14th Naval District at Pearl Harbor. The *Condor*'s skipper believed that the identification was "not positive enough" to justify a wider alert.

At 0630, the supply ship *Antares* sighted what its log called a "suspicious object" attempting to follow its wake into the harbor and alerted the *Ward*. Seven minutes later, just as dawn was breaking, the *Ward*'s watch officer spotted what appeared to be a submarine conning tower trailing the *Antares*. Captain William Outerbridge of the *Ward* appeared on deck wearing a kimono over his pajamas. A gunner asked him, "Captain, what are we going to do?" and Outerbridge, showing a decisiveness lacking in other officers during this final hour, responded, "We are going to shoot." At 0645, the *Ward*'s number three gun hit the midget, sinking it in twelve hundred feet of water and winning the first engagement of the Pacific War.

At 0653, Outerbridge radioed the 14th Naval District headquarters in Pearl Harbor and reported, "Attacked, fired upon, depth bombed and sunk submarine operating in defensive sea area. Stand by for further messages."

Instead of electrifying its recipients, causing sirens to sound, pilots to dash to their planes, and warships to put to sea, Outerbridge's message touched off a round of telephone calls first between the watch officer receiving it and Captain Earle, the staff officer to Admiral Bloch, commander of the 14th Naval District, then between Admiral Kimmel's duty officer, Admiral Bloch, and Kimmel himself, who had risen at seven for a round of golf with General Short. Because of telephone busy signals, and because Earle and Bloch discussed Outerbridge's message for ten minutes, a half hour passed without a decision.

Earle argued it might be "just another of those false reports." Kimmel decided to wait for verification. Meanwhile, Bloch neglected to call Fort Shafter and inform the Army that a hostile submarine might have been sunk off Pearl Harbor, a call that might at last have put General Short on an alert not directed solely against local saboteurs. Instead, Bloch decided to "wait further developments."

At last, at 0751, four minutes before the attack, and an hour after Outerbridge's report, the naval command sent the destroyer *Monaghan* out to join the *Ward* and provide "verification." The delay cost the *Ward* the honor of becoming perhaps the most celebrated United States naval vessel of the century. Instead, her decisive action became a footnote, her crewmen formed a little-known organization called the First Shot Naval Vets of St. Paul, Minnesota, and her number three gun, instead of being displayed in the Smithsonian, sits on the grounds of the Minnesota State Capitol.

A second missed chance to sound an alarm came at 0706, when Privates Joseph Lockhard and George Elliott, the operators of the Opana Mobile Radar station at Kahuku Point on the northernmost tip of Oahu picked up an enormous blip on their oscilloscope. They correctly interpreted this as a large incoming flight that Lockhard decided was "probably more than fifty planes" located 132 miles northeast of the island.

The Opana station was one of six established along Oahu's coastline at the end of November. But General Short was unconvinced of the value of radar, did not understand it, and used it, as he later admitted, "for training more than any idea that it [an attack] would be real." This attitude explains why radar stations on Oahu only operated between 0400 and 0700 on Sundays, and sporadically during the week, why the Army failed to establish approach lanes enabling friendly aircraft to be separated from enemy ones, and why the Hawaiian Department's fighters were on a four-hour alert, meaning it would take that long to arm and scramble them, even though mobile radar units like the one at Opana only picked up aircraft when they were about an hour offshore.

Lockhard and Elliott only detected the first wave of 175 Japanese planes because the truck sent to collect them from Kahuku

Point at 0700 was several minutes late. Elliott called the Fort Shafter Information Center and reported to Private Joseph McDonald he was seeing a blip on his screen that was "very big . . . very noticeable" and "out of the ordinary."

At the time Elliott made this call, there were only two men on duty in the Information Center. The Pursuit Officer in charge was a Lt. Kermit Tyler, a pilot who had only filled this role once before and had only recently learned that radar existed. He was supposed to help more experienced officers assign planes to intercept enemy aircraft reported by the radar stations, but these officers were not on duty on Sunday morning, and the enlisted men who plotted aircraft positions on a huge board had finished their shift at 7:00 A.M., leaving Tyler and McDonald alone.

McDonald wrote down Elliott's report and read it aloud to Tyler: "Large numbers of planes coming in from the north, three points east." McDonald added this was the first time he had received such a report, and it looked "kind of strange." He called the Opana Station back, spoke to Private Lockhard, and persuaded Tyler to pick up the telephone.

Lockhard told Tyler he was seeing "an unusually large flight . . . coming from almost due north at some 130 miles," but neglected to tell him the sighting appeared to consist of more than fifty planes. This proved a crucial omission because Tyler had heard that a flight of B-17 bombers were expected to arrive this morning from the West Coast. He assumed Lockhard's radar had picked up this much smaller flight of planes, and offered a five-word reply that would haunt him for the rest of his life, "Well, don't worry about it."

It has been said in Tyler's defense that he had no training as Pursuit Officer and only a single day of experience, that the radarscopes then were incapable of distinguishing friend from foe, that Lockhard erred by not estimating the number of planes, and that Fort Shafter's communications system was so rudimentary that he could not have instantly contacted the airfields and scrambled the planes in time to meet the Japanese. Nevertheless, he has been criticized by historians, ridiculed by journalists, and portrayed as a drunken slob in the film,

Tora! Tora! Tora! The Army was more understanding, and the 1944 congressional investigation fixed most of the blame on senior Army and Navy officers in Hawaii, concluding that, "If the Army command at Hawaii had been adequately alerted, Lieutenant Tyler's position would be indefensible. The fact that Lieutenant Tyler took the step he did merely tends to demonstrate how thoroughly unprepared and how completely lacking in readiness the Army command really was on the morning of December 7."

Tyler retired in 1961 as a lieutenant colonel and returned to Hawaii for the fiftieth anniversary of the attack, where he spoke at a symposium including Lockhard and Elliott. Some survivors still blamed him for ignoring the radar warning and grumbled about his presence on the symposium, but left the meeting in tears after meeting Tyler. He returned to Hawaii again in 1999 to deliver the keynote speech at the fifty-eighth anniversary, during which he insisted, as he has since 1941, that he had only done what was logical, in light of his training. He admitted being a reluctant participant in the ceremonies, but had come, he explained, because "I am a part of history, and I have an obligation."

Elliott had been the first to pick up the Japanese planes, but because Lockhard was more experienced, and had the fateful conversation with Tyler, he became the postattack celebrity. He was awarded the Distinguished Service Medal, promoted to staff sergeant, portrayed as a hero in wartime song, and became the subject of a profile in *True* magazine that neglected even to mention Elliott. In 1994, the Opana Radar Site was named a National Historic Landmark, and in 2000, the Institute of Electrical Engineers identified it as the site of an "electrical engineering milestone." Commemorative plaques and a large interpretive sign have been erected on the grounds of the Turtle Bay Hilton, a concrete monstrosity squatting beneath Opana ridge where, because of its excellent situation, the Navy maintains a top-secret telecommunications station surrounded by a high security fence.

Senior military leaders in Washington also missed several opportunities to send a last warning to Admiral Kimmel and General Short. The first thirteen parts of a fourteen-part Japanese ultimatum to the American government had been decoded on December 6, but an ominous fourteenth part, a so-called "trigger" message instructing Japanese diplomats to deliver the entire message before 1:00 P.M. on December 7 and then destroy their code machine, was not decoded and translated until early on the morning of December 7. The Chief of Naval Operations, Admiral Harold Stark, received it at 10:30 A.M. He calculated that 1:00 P.M. in Washington would be early in the morning in the Far East, and concluded the delivery of the Japanese ultimatum must be timed to coincide with operations in the Far East, and possibly Hawaii.

Stark's director of naval intelligence, Captain Theodore Wilkinson, suggested sending an additional warning to Pearl Harbor. He asked Stark, "Why don't you pick up the telephone and call Kimmel?"

Stark lifted the receiver, then shook his head. "No, I think I will call the president," he said.

The moment was lost. The White House switchboard was engaged, and Stark, believing Kimmel had been adequately alerted by the "war warning" message of November 27, decided that the Army Chief of Staff, General George C. Marshall, should transmit an alert to General Short, instructing him to inform the Navy.

Marshall was horseback riding that morning and did not see the "trigger" message until 1125, two hours after its decoding, at about the time Japanese carriers were preparing to launch the first wave. He agreed it appeared to indicate a Japanese attack on an American installation shortly after 1:00 P.M. Washington time and drafted a warning in longhand on a piece of scrap paper that said, "Japanese are presenting at 1:00 P.M. eastern standard time today what amounts to an ultimatum. Also they are under orders to destroy their code machine immediately. Just what significance the hour set may have we do not know but be on the alert accordingly. Inform naval authorities of this communication."

Marshall did not telephone this final warning because he believed his scrambler telephone was not secure enough. Instead, he ordered it sent by the "fastest safe means possible" to the Army's Pacific bases. It was further delayed because War Department clerks needed several minutes to decipher his hasty scrawl, then delayed again by poor atmospheric conditions over the Pacific. Finally, at 1217 Washington time, 0647 Honolulu time, an officer at the War Department Signal Center decided to send it to Hawaii via commercial cable. It arrived at the RCA cable office in Honolulu at 0733. Five minutes later, RCA messenger Tadeo Fuchikami collected it from the Kahili pigeonhole, but because the envelope was not marked "urgent," he did not immediately jump on his motorcycle and race to Fort Shafter.

These last, heartbreaking chances to put Oahu on alert have the slow-motion inevitability of a nightmare. I wish I had been there, telling Stark not to put down that telephone but to complete his call to Kimmel, warning Marshall not to trust the vagaries of his signal center, urging Fuchikami to race to Fort Shafter, persuading Tyler to alert Wheeler Field, and arguing Kimmel out of dismissing the Ward's encounter as a possible false alarm. "How could it be," I want to shout, when Outerbridge has reported "firing on" a submarine, meaning he used his deck guns, meaning he had *seen* it!

There were other missed clues and missed opportunities to go on the alert, such as Mrs. Edgers's ignored translation of the "lights" message, and the Japanese scout planes that flew undetected over Maui and Pearl Harbor an hour before the attack, too many to be explained as "bad luck," so many that no one should doubt the thick carapace of overconfidence cloaking Washington and Honolulu.

But even had this prompted a last-minute alert, an American victory was not assured. Oahu would have had less than an hour's warning, not enough time to wheel every antiaircraft gun into place or untangle and arm the Wheeler Field fighters, but enough time to unlock the ammunition, man ships' batteries, break up the Japanese formations, and blunt the attack. The American pilots who saw action on December 7 recorded an impressive ratio of kills, four each for Second Lieutenants Ken Taylor and George Welsh. The fact that the Japanese inflicted the most serious damage during the first twenty minutes, and relatively little during the following hour and a half, when they met serious resistance, indicates what might have happened had Oahu's defenders had thirty minutes' warning. Warships would have still been damaged, lives lost, and planes destroyed, but the United States would have salvaged some honor from the engagement, lessening the humiliation and anger.

The blips appearing on Lockhard and Elliott's screen represented forty torpedo bombers, forty-three Zeros, and one-hundred dive-bombers and level bombers launched from a Japanese battle fleet 230 miles north of the Opana station (the same patch of ocean where the Apollo 15 astronauts splashed down after their mission to the moon). This first wave of planes crossed the north shore of Oahu at 0740, flying undetected by military command centers as their speeding shadows flickered across checkerboard fields of pineapples and sugarcane, but heard and seen by civilians and servicemen.

There were approximately a hundred thousand servicemen based on Oahu on December 7, so it is not surprising that many Americans live near a Pearl Harbor survivor. For many years, the survivor living closest to me was Lyle Lawrence, who until his recent death lived about ten miles from my home in upstate New York. He had been the crew chief of a two-man radar unit charged with guarding the Opana station after Lockhard and Elliott shut it down for the morning. He and another off-duty radar operator stood outside their tents at Haleiwa on Oahu's north shore that morning, shielding their eyes from the bright dawnlight with one hand and counting the first wave of Japanese planes with the other. He had reached 138 by the time he left for the Opana station. As he arrived there he could hear the thump of distant explosions. Lockhard and Elliott showed him the dozens of planes they had mapped on their plotting board. They were impressed the Army Air Force could launch so many aircraft at once, and excited by the size and realism of the exercise.

Large flights of aircraft were so common over Oahu that most of the servicemen, fishermen, surfers, churchgoers, and golfers who glanced up and saw the first Japanese planes believed they were American, and soon returned to their Sunday morning routines. Years later, they recalled this morning as beautiful, but strangely quiet. They remembered the green Koolaus standing sharp against sheets of blue sky, Pearl Harbor calm as a millpond, and the normal early-morning sounds of whistling kettles, clinking plates, and crying babies. They remembered wives or husbands across a breakfast table, and silvery, dragonfly planes shooting between puffy clouds. Then, at 0754, the wind dropped, clouds froze, and an eerie stillness descended on Oahu, as if the world was pausing for a deep breath.

Private pilots in the air over Oahu, sailors on duty in the Pearl Harbor signal tower, and the Japanese pilots had the best views of this last minute of peace.

Every morning at 0755 a signalman in the Pearl Harbor tower raised a white-and-blue flag standing for the letter *P*, known in the international flag code as "Prep." It told color guards assembled on warships to raise the Stars and Stripes in precisely five minutes so that their ceremonies would occur in smart concert.

On December 7, the Pearl Harbor signalman watched color guards assembling on the eight battleships, eight Cruisers, twenty-nine destroyers, and assorted submarines, minecraft, tenders, and auxiliaries of the Pacific Fleet. The battleship *Pennsylvania* was nearest the tower, resting in dry dock number one alongside destroyers *Cassin* and *Downes*. The destroyer *Shaw* sat in floating dry dock number two, and just north of them were the light cruiser *Helena* and minelayer *Oglala*. Farther northeast, the shipyard berths held over a dozen cruisers and destroyers. Seven battleships were tied to mooring blocks lining the eastern shore of Ford Island. The *Tennessee* and *West Virginia* and the *Maryland* and *Oklahoma* were moored in pairs. The *Nevada* and *California* sat alone. The *Arizona* was tied to the repair ship *Vestal*. Beyond the runways, hangars, and fuel tanks of the Ford Island Naval Air Station, more warships sat anchored, moored to blocks, and tied together in groups of two to six.

On smaller vessels, a single sailor and boatswain with whistle prepared to raise an ensign. Cruisers had turned out a bugler and four-man Marine honor guard. On some battleships the entire ship's band had assembled.

The signalman raised the Prep flag at 0755, seconds before other men in the tower detachment noticed one line of planes approaching from the southeast, and another from the northeast. Another line suddenly appeared out of the sun to the east, and another still from the south. The air vibrated with their droning and buzzing. A line of bombers dived toward the hangars and parked seaplanes of Ford Island and a string of low-flying torpedo bombers headed for Battleship Row. Color guards, ship's bands, and men gathered on decks for religious services scattered. A petty officer in the signal tower grabbed a telephone and called Admiral Kimmel's headquarters. On Ford Island, Lieutenant Commander Logan Ramsey sent his famous message: "AIR RAID, PEARL HARBOR, THIS IS NOT A DRILL."

The pilots of five small private planes flying over Oahu that morning also had a spectacular view of the attack. Two parties of Army pilots had rented two-seater Aeroncas and were two miles off the west coast of Oahu. The Japanese immediately shot them down. Flying instructor Cornelia Fort was circling the John Rodgers civilian airport when she noticed a bomber heading for her at the same altitude. She grabbed the controls and jerked the single-engine plane upward while cursing the reckless pilot. Then she saw red circles on the bomber's wings and black smoke rising from Hickam. Sticks of glistening bombs tumbled toward Pearl Harbor.

Seventeen-year-old Roy Vitousek and his father were two thousand feet over Oahu when the first Japanese bomb exploded in a Ford Island hangar. Roy thought they were witnessing a hangar fire and a flight of American P-40s. They dived to take a closer look. His father shouted, "P-40s, hell, they're Japs!" They circled above Oahu for the next thirty minutes, hanging like bats over the attack and watching falling bombs flash like mirrors as they caught the sun.

The Japanese planes appeared as well rehearsed as circus horses, as deferential to one another as the Japanese diplomats who at this moment sat in the anteroom of Secretary of State Cordell Hull's office in Washington. Zeros in V-formations patiently waited their turn at strafing. Dive-bombers flew in circles, peeling off to make an attack, screaming down, and disappearing into billowing smoke, then rising to re-form in a circle.

Japanese pilots wagged their wings in triumph and wounded planes spun out of control, crashing in cane fields and igniting fires that marched toward highways. Seaplanes burned like torches, and bombers at Hickam Field blew up in sequence, like falling dominoes. Sheets of burning oil raced across the water as warships puffed fists of black smoke. Scarlet dots of fire flashed across downtown Honolulu.

As the first wave began leaving, Vitousek's father dived for the John Rodgers airport. The rear gunner of a torpedo bomber fired on them, then a Fort Shafter antiaircraft battery opened up, mistaking them for a Japanese control plane. As they landed the Japanese were strafing hangars, hitting a civilian aircraft boarding passengers for Maui and killing Bob Tice, the popular manager of a local flying service.

The Vitouseks jumped from their plane and dived behind a bunker. When the strafing ended they taxied back to the hangar, where they encountered passengers and workers who still believed they had witnessed an American exercise gone terribly wrong. One man said, "Some goddam drunk American pilot killed Bob Tice."

CHAPTER 13

THE MANEUVERS
ARE REALISTIC

Their temperament and proximity to the battle determined the reactions of Oahu's servicemen and civilians. Most experienced denial and shock, then panic, fear, and anger. Some had a flash of disbelief, followed by hours of fear and panic. For others, the period of denial was long, and the shock has still not ended; still others had a second of panic, and a lifetime of anger. Troops in later World War II battles also came under fire suddenly and without warning, and civilians elsewhere found themselves in a battle zone, but because Pearl Harbor was such a complete surprise, it produced emotions and flashbacks of exceptional intensity.

Twelve-year-old Elwood Craddock's father managed the Waipahu Pineapple Plantation. It sat on Oahu's central plateau, a mile and a half from Wheeler Field. Craddock woke before sunrise and ate a quick breakfast before setting out to hunt pheasants and doves with his twenty-two-year-old cousin, Rufus Hough. They walked a mile through pineapple fields, shot a pheasant with Craddock's shotgun, then stopped on a ridgeline to admire the view. The land was red clay, dusty and arid—a semidesert. The ridge was the highest point for miles and had a fine view of the hangars and planes at Wheeler Field. Craddock and Hough noticed warplanes circling tightly overhead, then breaking loose one by one to dive-bomb the base.

When a hangar burst into flames Craddock shouted, "Japanese planes!"

"Nah, they're Navy planes," Hough insisted. "It's a drill."

"But look at them. We don't have planes like that!" Craddock answered. He had grown up in the shadow of the base, watching maneuvers and building balsa models of its warplanes. "They have red circles on their wings. Our planes have a smooth surface, and the Japs' are corrugated, like these."

"The insignia were painted on to make the exercise realistic. And those aren't real bombs, they're just blowing up sticks of dynamite to make it took real."

The attackers reorganized into a bombing pattern two miles in circumference, positioning themselves five hundred feet above Craddock and Hough. One plane fired its guns at them and the bullets kicked up dust. Only then did Hough believe the attack was for real.

Craddock is the only civilian witness I met in Honolulu (or read about in the narratives filling the University of Hawaii's War Records Depository) who immediately recognized the planes as being Japanese. Like his cousin, most everyone else believed it was so inconceivable for Asians to attack Caucasians, and for a Japanese fleet to have sailed so close to Hawaii without being detected, that even when they saw shell bursts and tumbling bombs, they believed it was all an elaborate drill.

The denial of the truth was so widespread, and so resistant to visual evidence to the contrary, that it bordered on mass delusion. It was caused by the same misconception about the invincibility of American forces and the inferiority of Japanese ones that had encouraged the complacency of Oahu's defenders, and it was shared by haoles, native Hawaiians, Chinese, Portuguese, and Japanese, and by civilians distant from the battle and sailors under direct attack.

Even Takeo Yoshikawa initially believed he was witnessing a drill, and General Short thought the Navy was having a battle practice and had neglected to inform him, or that it had slipped his mind.

Some officers had trouble persuading men to return to their stations. An Army Intelligence officer reported, "They did not believe that they were being correctly informed. Such a thing simply could not happen." Colonel Bicknell experienced what he called "a few seconds of absolute disbelief" while watching the attack from the lanai of his house on Aiea Heights. He became convinced when the *Arizona* exploded and a clearly marked Japanese plane burst into flames and fell into the harbor. Then he called his headquarters and had difficulty persuading the officer of the day that Oahu was under attack.

Many civilians stood in the open, staring skyward, watching the attack with no more show of emotion than witnesses to a Fourth of July fireworks display. For the first thirty minutes, Honolulu mayor Lester Petrie believed the smoke was a practice smoke screen, and the explosions, mines detonated to simulate bombs.

Mr. Yee Kam York of the Territorial Tax Office heard an explosion, saw Pearl Harbor burning, watched through field glasses as planes were hit by antiaircraft fire, and remarked to his wife, "These Americans, when they have maneuvers, they certainly make it realistic."

Ethelyn Meyhre, who lived above the city in the Manoa Valley, believed the silvery planes American bombers. When she turned on the radio and heard the truth she woke her father. He laughed, rolled over, and went back to sleep. She turned on the radio and woke him again. An announcer was saying, "All men report to your post! Calling all nurses! Proceed to Pearl Harbor!"

"It's only another practice attack," he insisted.

They heard, "Oahu is being attacked! The sign of the Rising Sun is to be seen on the wings of the attacking planes!"

"It's impossible," he said.

A woman living near the University of Hawaii watched planes dogfighting overhead, heard the calls for defense workers and physicians to report to Pearl Harbor, and concluded it was a skillfully prepared practice. Her husband said, "If the real thing should happen, people might think they were crying 'wolf' and not respond." When an announcer said planes with the Rising Sun on their wingtips were over Pearl Harbor, she wondered if the "enemy" group of our air corps had painted the emblems on their planes.

Dorothy Anthony's eleven-year-old son ran into her room shouting, "Mother, this doesn't sound like practice!" She and her husband dashed downstairs to see an antisubmarine net being stretched across the mouth of the harbor. But they refused to believe their eyes, and still convinced it was only a realistic drill, enjoyed a relaxed breakfast on their terrace.

Explosions woke correspondent Joseph C. Harsch in his room at the Royal Hawaiian Hotel. He told his wife they were "a good imitation" of what a European air raid sounded like. They then took their morning swim, assuming, like the other guests, it was all another practice maneuver by the Navy.

After seeing bursts of antiaircraft shells from his Waikiki apartment, Admiral Pye told his wife, "It seems funny that the Army would be having target practice on Sunday morning." At Wheeler Field, General Davidson believed he was hearing "those damn Navy pilots jazzing the base," and continued shaving.

To convince J. Edgar Hoover the attack was real, Robert Shivers held his telephone receiver out the window of his office so Hoover could hear the gunfire and explosions. Fred Tillman, the FBI's local Japanese expert, was driving Ruth Flynn to their office. She told him a civilian defense worker had reported Hickam "all shot to hell." Even though they could see the smoke, and hear shells bursting overhead, he replied, "Ah, this is all nonsense. It's just another maneuver."

Walter Dillingham was still wearing his rumpled tuxedo from the night before when he drove through the main gate of Hickam Field. He thought his friend and fellow pilot Jake Jenkins was dropping dummy bombs and firing machine-gun bursts to scare the Hickam pilots. *Goddammit! I bet Jakie's doing it again*, he thought, *except this time he's dropped a real bomb instead of a dummy*. When a plane strafed his car he thought, *Christ, this time Jenkins has gone crazy*. He rolled down his window and shook his fist. "You son of a bitch, that's too close," he shouted.

At the John Rodgers Airport, Dr. Homer Izuma and Dr. Harold Johnson saw a flight of warplanes wheeling and circling in a loop formation. Izuma noticed red circles on their wings. "Gee, Harold, that looks like a Japanese emblem," he remarked.

"Yeah, don't they get realistic nowadays," Johnson replied, hoisting his son onto his shoulders to get a better look. Izuma's plane for Maui was announced. Its passengers boarded, and were waving good-bye to friends through its windows when Izuma saw a man running across the field, shouting something that sent the crowd dashing for their cars.

Eleven-year-old John Smythe, the son of an Army colonel, continued riding his bicycle through Schofield Barracks during the attack because he thought the bullets and bombs falling on nearby Wheeler Field were only maneuvers. Even the sight of an officer firing his sidearm into the air did not disturb him, he said, because he was so certain of the invincibility of his father's army he could not imagine any nation being foolhardy enough to attack it.

A local Japanese teenager named Kazuma Oyama, who had been drafted into a quartermaster battalion at Schofield, was on leave and pruning his father's grape arbor when Japanese planes flew over their home. Until a misfired naval shell almost killed his sister, he dismissed the commotion as a drill and told his worried father that his drill sergeant had convinced him that no nation would dare to take on the American Army.

Former Governor Lawrence Judd heard fire engines and watched shells splashing off Waikiki from his home on Maunalani Heights, high above Diamond Head. "These maneuvers are getting too realistic," he told his wife. "Someone's going to get hurt." Black smoke rose from Pearl Harbor, and she asked, "Isn't it unusual to be burning cane on Sunday morning?"

Admiral Kimmel witnessed the initial moments of the attack

from a lawn overlooking the base. He and his neighbor, Mrs. John Earle, the wife of Admiral Bloch's Chief of Staff, watched the Japanese planes circling in figure eights before diving at battleships. Even when fierce fires began burning, Mrs. Earle said, they both found the sight "unbelievable" and "impossible."

On board the minesweeper *Oglala*, Robert Hudson stood on deck smoking a cigarette with the ship's cook. As Japanese planes fell on Ford Island and its hangars burst into flame, they laughed, thinking it was a drill gone wrong and the Army Air Forces would be in real trouble. They heard an explosion and agreed it must be accidental. A plane headed at them from forty feet above the water, dropping a torpedo. Convinced it was a dummy, they shook their heads and laughed again. They believed the red flashes flickering under a plane's wing came from a red light on a camera recording the drill. Even when bullets from this machine gun ricocheted off a bulkhead, hitting the cook in the mouth and killing him, Hudson considered it all a tragic mistake.

Lieutenant Clarence Dickinson piloted one of the eighteen scout planes sent ahead by the carrier *Enterprise* to check the waters near Pearl Harbor. He was approaching Ford Island for a landing as the attack began. He thought the smoke came from cane fires, and that a rain of big shell splashes in the water were coastal artillery batteries gone "stark mad." He told his tail gunner, "Just wait! Tomorrow the Army will certainly catch hell for that!"

Marine bugler Richard Fiske was standing on the deck of the *West Virginia*. His father, a chief petty officer, had been serving aboard the U.S. Navy gunboat *Panay* in China when it was attacked by Japanese planes in 1937. After returning home he urged his sons to join the Navy because he believed that when the inevitable war with Japan came, the other services would be doing the heavy fighting and suffering the heaviest casualties. But Fiske thought that would be glorious, so he and his best friends from high school, Charles Jones and William Finley, joined the Marines and put in for sea school and battleships. Fiske had been assigned to the *West Virginia* and Finley and Jones got the *Arizona*. They were moored a hundred yards away. When the first Japanese planes appeared, Fiske believed they were from Wheeler Field, and told his shipmate Stanley Bukowski, "I guess we're going to have an exercise." When bombers with torpedoes visible beneath their wings circled Ford Island, then peeled off to make a bombing run, he said, "Well, there goes the Army. We'd better get to our battle stations."

"No, wait," Bukowski answered, "They're going to drop some dummy torpedoes. Let's go over to the port side and see them." So the two men remained on the bridge as four airplanes flew at them fifteen feet above the water, dropping torpedoes. One exploded, throwing up a wall of water that washed Fiske through a passageway to the starboard side. Yet, like Annapolis ensigns, twenty-year veterans, fighter pilots, and rear admirals, he persisted in believing this was an exercise, only accepting the truth when a Marine sergeant yelled, "Goddammit, get to your battle stations, it's the Japs!"

From his battle station on the bridge, Fiske watched five torpedo planes coming in low. Two dropped torpedoes that headed for the *Oklahoma*; the other three targeted his ship. Then the planes climbed sharply and one pilot flew within yards of the bridge. "He had his greenhouse [canopy] back and we made eye contact," Fiske told me, "and I've dreamed about that son of a gun for more than fifty years."

Sterling Cale was walking home from the dispensary when he noticed a half dozen planes performing maneuvers over the shipyard. He dismissed it as another training exercise for National Guard and Reserve pilots, and assumed the rattling guns were firing blanks and the puffs of smoke were fireworks. Then a bomb exploded, a plane banked overhead, and he saw the Rising Sun painted on a wing. He and some other sailors broke the locks at the receiving station armory and handed out Springfield rifles. Some men tried hitting the low-flying planes with these single-shot antiques. More planes dropped torpedoes. When several slammed into the *Oklahoma*, Cale ran to the nearest landing and persuaded two sailors manning an officers' barge to take him out to the crippled battleship so he could tend to its wounded.

The destroyer *Helm* had just left her anchorage near the mouth of West Loch and was steaming into the harbor to be demagnetized, a process intended to prevent her from attracting magnetic mines. Lieutenant Victor Dybdal, who was standing watch on the stern, thought the planes were American ones returning from the *Enterprise*. He changed his mind when one dropped a bomb and dive-bombers strafed the *Helm*. Afterward, he remembers, their pilots smiled and waved and, for some inexplicable reason, perhaps because no one yet believed the attack was real, sailors on the *Helm* waved back.

Retired Rear Admiral Dybdal suggested we visit Pearl Harbor together on one of the cruise boats, since they crossed the waters at the mouth of the harbor where the *Helm* had been attacked. I would have spotted Dybdal even if we had not been among the few Caucasians boarding the cruise at Kewalo Basin. Like Gus Ahola, he had the mahogany tan and laconic manner that are the hallmarks of military officers who have retired to Hawaii.

We sat at a table on the ship's upper deck, surrounded by Japanese tourists who had arrived in a convoy of buses. The men wore loose white shirts and golf hats, and heavy cameras and telephoto lenses dangled from their necks, giving them a stooped walk. They were middle-aged or elderly, old enough to know about Pearl Harbor. A brochure placed on our seats showed a map of the harbor printed in Japanese, and there was something disturbing about seeing the names and locations of the Pearl Harbor warships written in this language. Admiral Dybdal demanded a map in English, and looking around at our fellow Japanese passengers, said, "When I took my grandchildren on this cruise it wasn't, well, it wasn't this crowded."

At least I think he said that, because I was having trouble hearing him. The Japanese at our table were loud, the crew frequently interrupted to hawk drinks and souvenir booklets, and an account of the attack in Japanese and English boomed from loudspeakers. As we steamed past Honolulu Harbor, Sand Island, Honolulu International

Airport, and Hickam Field, I heard Dybdal's narrative in fragments, interrupted by bursts of Japanese and a departing Japan Airlines 747, which caused some Japanese passengers to shout in excitement and lean across us to take photographs.

The American narrator referred to the attack as "brilliantly conceived and executed," adding, "it would be a glorious victory for Japan."

"That's why they like to come here," Dybdal said without a trace of bitterness, "and why they like to take these tours and see the *Arizona*. For them this was a great victory, one of the greatest in their history."

The narrator said, "It was an old Japanese custom to begin wars with a sneak attack," as if this were a quaint national trait. He added that American economic sanctions had put Japanese "backs to the wall," but omitted mentioning Japanese militarism, or the atrocities against the Chinese, who really did have their backs put to the wall.

Dybdal looked pained, and said, "Claiming we forced them into the war is a lot of crap. We didn't start the damned war, they did. And those Japanese militarists were as crazy as Hitler. They wanted to take over all those Asian countries." The narration reminded him of the documentary film that until 1992 was shown to visitors to the *Arizona* Memorial. He condemned it as a "damned movie that gives the impression it was all our fault." He insisted he was not upset at Japanese tourists for visiting Pearl Harbor—it was only understandable they should be interested in this battlefield. When his mainland friends complained about the Japanese at the *Arizona* Memorial he told them, "It's a free country."

But slanting the causes of Pearl Harbor to avoid offending Japanese sensibilities did upset him, and has always upset me, too. Arguing that the United States "forced" Japan to attack Pearl Harbor because of its embargo of oil and raw materials implies the United States had a moral obligation to supply Japan with the resources necessary to attack China, and that total warfare is a justifiable response to economic sanctions. The Japanese advanced similar arguments after the war, with a former chief of their Military Affairs

Bureau once claiming that, "The only place where Japan could continue to get oil and other raw materials had to be from the United States. If this failed, Japan, as a nation, could not survive, especially the industries and the navy . . . Japan felt the United States was under obligation to furnish oil and raw materials as it meant the future existence of Japan."

As we entered the harbor we passed near the *Helm*'s December 7 anchorage. Dybdal said the landscape had changed very little since 1941. Cane fields still surrounded West Loch, and Hickam's water tower and hangars dominated views to the east. The main difference was the smell. A sweet, pungent odor of sugarcane had once enveloped the harbor; now you smelled jet fuel.

Pearl Harbor's shape has been likened to a fleur-de-lys, a three-fingered hand, or a flower. Its most important characteristics are a long, narrow entrance, calm waters, and three extensive bays, called lochs by the original Scottish surveyors. It is an unusual anchorage for the Pacific, and an ideal harbor for the peacetime Navy because of its size and the protection it offers. But its narrow entrance channel makes it treacherous in wartime since a single disabled ship can trap the fleet for hours, and a sunken one can bottle up the harbor for days.

We circled Ford Island clockwise, passing the wreck of the *Utah* and lawns where dying sailors once lay in rows. Shell fragments pockmarked mooring blocks still carrying the names of their December 7 battleships in black letters. As we neared the *Arizona* Memorial, it was announced that our captain would lead us in a "brief ceremony of remembrance" by throwing a flower lei onto this "altar of freedom." Taps played over the loudspeakers and Admiral Dybdal shot out of his chair, his right hand over his heart, his eyes watering. The Japanese whispered and looked confused. The announcer said, "We must all pray that this terrible sacrifice shall not have been in vain." Then, after a pause so brief it was easy to miss, and without changing his tone of voice, he recommended a souvenir booklet—"Makes an excellent gift. The only booklet of its kind printed in color," and, I noticed, printed in Japan.

As he sat down, Dybdal admitted he had never considered the possibility of a sneak attack, adding, "I thought you had to declare war, that there'd be a big buildup. To attack a warship without notice seemed basically unfair and against the rules, like shooting a policeman on the beat."

The *Helm* had been the first warship to sortie from Pearl Harbor and had inflicted considerable damage on the enemy. Her guns sent a plane crashing into Hickam and shelled Ensign Sakamaki's midget sub, disabling its steering. But after two Japanese bombs shorted her electric systems she spent the rest of the day zigzagging off Waikiki, hunting submarines and preparing to repel an invasion.

We were also steaming in circles off Waikiki. "We're waiting for the photographs," a crewman explained. They had been taken as we boarded and a motorboat was rushing out the prints. When they arrived, pandemonium ensued as the crew tried to match each enormous, wedding-portrait-sized photograph with the correct Japanese passenger.

Admiral Dybdal turned his back and stared back toward Pearl Harbor. "December 7 taught me you never know," he said. "You can never be sure something bad won't happen. When I was in the South Pacific during the war, dolphins used to be attracted to my ship. I'd see them and think it was a torpedo wake. I'd wonder, 'What should I do? Turn the ship and head into it? Or what?' For years after Pearl Harbor I never slept well. I felt as if someone had wound something up in the middle of my stomach that was taking years to unwind."

CHAPTER 14

THE WARM AIR OF AN UNENDING SUMMER LAND

Oahu's sensational beauty left some Japanese pilots almost regretting their mission, and others remembering the battle as a poetic event. Later, they spoke of "four bombs in perfect pattern" becoming "as small as poppy seeds" before disappearing, and graceful waterspouts splashing over the smokestacks of destroyers, then collapsing like exhausted geysers. They saw American planes, "the color of gold dust, in tidy rows," and "beautiful clouds colored by the rising sun." A plane dropping a torpedo resembled "a dragonfly laying an egg on the water." From above, the ships of the Pacific fleet resembled "toys on a child's floor—something that should not be attacked at all."

One pilot thought, "This island is too peaceful to attack!" Another flew so low his plane sent the sugarcane rustling, and he felt "the warm air of an unending summer land."

Only a few dozen of the 609 Japanese airmen who attacked Pearl Harbor were believed to be alive twenty-five years later. What is startling is not how few survived the war and death by natural causes, but how many of the few who did have returned to this unending summer land. The Japanese pilots, too, appear to have been "wound up" by Pearl Harbor. "That moment changed my life," Zero pilot Yoshio Shiga said on the fortieth anniversary. "It was forever burned in my memory."

After the war, the Japanese officer who had planned the attack, Commander Minoru Genda, became a member of the Japanese House of Councillors (Senate), and persuaded Japan to accept U.S. bases and visits by nuclear-powered submarines. Despite his pro-American positions, when he lectured at Annapolis the Pearl Harbor Survivors Association (PHSA) and relatives of men killed on December 7 mounted a spirited protest. Genda's speech there was remarkably honest. He admitted that if Japan had developed the atom bomb it would have used it, and if he was planning the attack again, he would have invaded Hawaii.

When Zero pilot Makato Bando attended the fortieth anniversary ceremonies he brought his own Japanese television crew and hired a launch so they could film him at December 7 sites around the harbor. He turned up at the *Arizona* Memorial and met Fred Garbuschewski, who had been tuning up his clarinet for the Sunday call to colors aboard the *California* and remembered a pilot flying so close to the battleship he "could have hit him with a baseball bat." Journalists described Mr. Bando as "robust and animated."

Six other Japanese pilots and their wives attended the forty-fifth anniversary. National Park Service officials at the *Arizona* Memorial interviewed them, and the videotape showed a line of elderly men wearing dark suits so similar they could have been uniforms. Their bald foreheads glistened and they appeared ill at ease. The sound was poor and I caught only fragments of sentences. Mr. Yamamato, who had attacked the *Nevada*, said, "We were so close, so low to the ground." As Mr. Goto made a planing motion with one hand, an interpreter said, "His wish was that he not be hit until he released his bomb. *That* was the only thing he was praying for." The pilots swooped their hands like seagulls, then threw their arms over their heads to depict clouds of billowing smoke.

There was something unsettling about these men coming on an organized junket and so cheerfully visiting a city they once saw through bombsights and memorials to people they had killed. I wondered if the British pilots who destroyed Dresden returned there on group holidays, bringing wives and followed by cameramen as they visited buildings built on the ruins of the city they had destroyed. And did the German pilots who destroyed Coventry, or Warsaw, return on package tours, announcing themselves to local authorities? I know that for years veterans have been visiting one another's countries, and meeting at battlefields. German and British pilots have traded stories about the Battle of Britain, and Americans and Japanese have embraced on Pacific islands. But what was most striking about these Japanese pilots was their youthful enthusiasm as they relived what had been, after all, no ordinary battle, but a surprise raid leading to three and a half years of horrific slaughter.

The most notorious airman ever to return to Hawaii was the attack's commander, Mitsuo Fuchida. He had commanded the first wave, fired flares signaling the order of attack, ordered his radioman to give the famous "*To, to, to*" signal (the first syllable of *totsugekiseyo*, Japanese for "charge"), and led a bombing run on the *Maryland*. He remained overhead throughout most of the attack, flying over Hickam and Wheeler to assess the damage, then circling Pearl Harbor to take the photographs illustrating so many Pearl Harbor books. He had begged Admiral Nagumo to launch a third wave against the submarine base and fuel tanks, and had his advice been taken, the American fleet would have had to retreat to California.

Fuchida was shot down and rescued during the Battle of the Java Sea. He crashed in Borneo and spent days walking out of the jungle. Six days before the Battle of Midway he suffered appendicitis aboard his carrier and the man replacing him was killed. During Midway, a bomb blew him off the flight deck and broke his legs. He volunteered for a kamikaze mission that was canceled at the last minute. He was in Hiroshima one day before the bomb was dropped. Afterward, he visited Hiroshima with eleven other officers to evaluate the effects of the bomb, and was the only one not to die from radiation poisoning. In the early postwar years, he became a farmer and complained that, "My days passed in loneliness . . . I was like a star that had fallen. At one moment I was Captain Mitsuo Fuchida, and the next, I was nobody!"

He attached religious significance to his narrow escapes and in 1950 became a Christian. Like everything in Fuchida's life, his conversion was dramatic. He jumped into the speaker van of evangelical American missionaries preaching in Osaka, grabbed their microphone, and shouted, "I am Mitsuo Fuchida who led the air raid on Pearl Harbor. I have now surrendered my heart and my life to Jesus Christ."

Headlines proclaimed, "FROM A SOLDIER OF FAME TO A SOLDIER OF LOVE," and Fuchida became a "general" in Sky Pilots International, an organization of former World War II pilots who had become evangelical Christians.

He visited the United States in 1953, traveling thirty-five thousand miles on a cross-country speaking engagement, and met Billy Graham. (He would later describe himself as a "small-scale Billy Graham.") The American missionaries accompanying him dismissed as "small-minded" the war veterans protesting his visit. His last stop was Honolulu, where he planned to place a wreath on the *Arizona*, and claimed to be surprised that this should provoke any protest. Then he moved to Seattle and considered applying for U.S. citizenship. His daughter became an interior designer in California and his son a Manhattan architect. He visited Oahu in 1956, 1958, and 1966. A supporter referred to the twenty-fifth anniversary ceremonies as "a good backdrop" for a Fuchida documentary and Fuchida's presence in Honolulu became a major event. He was, at last, no longer a "star that had fallen," no longer a "nobody," and his photograph accompanied the Pearl Harbor story on the front page of the *New York Times* in 1966.

On December 6, 1966, Fuchida attended a dinner party at the home of Bud Smyser, editor of the *Star-Bulletin*. Among the guests were Kendall Fielder, chief of Army Intelligence in Hawaii in 1941, and his former deputy, George Bicknell. I read an account of the occasion in a newspaper clipping and noticed that Fielder, unable to manage the customary "all is forgiven" statement, had said, "You try to forgive and forget." He was described as pausing for a moment before adding, "I lost a lot of friends that day."

Bud Smyser told me Fuchida stood in the middle of the room. At first, he was nervous and the conversation was stilted. The atmosphere changed when Smyser's six-year-old son asked, "How big were the bombs you dropped?" Smyser produced photographs of the attack taken by Japanese planes, perhaps by Fuchida himself, and Fuchida immediately "lightened up." He moved a finger back and forth across the photographs, naming every ship.

Bicknell's widow told me, "Fuchida's eyes were glowing, you could see he was still thrilled. As he made those zooming motions with his hands, I thought, 'He's still in the air bombing Pearl Harbor. It was the high point of his life, and he's still there.' "

At sunrise on December 7, 1966, Fuchida and his camera crew motored out to the *Arizona* Memorial, arriving two hours before the official ceremony. There he met twelve *Arizona* survivors who were returning for the first time since 1941. Fuchida's entourage encouraged the American veterans to stand next to him for a group photograph. Most refused, including veteran Don Stratton, who said, "They just killed so many people who never had a chance." It had apparently not occurred to Fuchida that Pearl Harbor survivors who had traveled thousands of miles to stand over the grave of their shipmates might be unsettled to find, waiting for them there, the man who had directed the attack.

Fuchida next attended the official memorial services at Punchbowl. In one news photograph he is making a point of consulting his watch at exactly 7:55 A.M. Afterward he drove to Aiea Heights and posed for photographers on a hill overlooking Pearl Harbor. One onlooker praised his ability to describe the precise location of the ships that were in harbor on December 7.

The more I learned about Fuchida, the less I liked him. He admitted in his 1952 pamphlet *From Pearl Harbor to Golgotha*, "My heart was ablaze with joy for my success in getting the whole main forces of the Pacific Fleet in hand." But when he sought permission to lay a wreath on the *Arizona* in 1953, just a year later, he told a reporter that "There was no real joy in my heart at the time of the attack."

I also disliked his breezy assumption that he would be welcome everywhere on the twenty-fifth anniversary of the attack, and his 1967 trip to Hawaii was truly odious. For ten days, he spoke in churches and military bases, and during those sermons and lectures, the man who led the attack that had started the Pacific War, and who had said upon becoming a Christian, "I believe no war could be righteous and pave the way for peace," now proclaimed himself eager for Americans of my generation to die in Vietnam. He insisted that "the spread of Communism must be stopped," and often expressed his irritation with "those protesting against the Vietnam War."

Far more appealing have been the efforts of Zenji Abe, a dive-bomber squadron leader who attacked the *West Virginia*. During the late 1980s, Abe spent months traveling across Japan, tracking down the surviving pilots who had attacked Pearl Harbor and persuading them to sign a letter of apology to American survivors. He flew to the United States alone and unannounced, without an entourage of journalists, camera crews, and interpreters. (He is a retired businessman who speaks excellent English.) After landing in Atlanta he hired a taxi to drive him two hours into the countryside to the home of a senior official in the Pearl Harbor Survivors Association. He rang the bell and introduced himself as one of the pilots who had attacked Pearl Harbor. Then he presented the signed apology of the surviving Japanese pilots. The survivor told him he could shove his apology up his ass, and slammed the door.

Abe was devastated and immediately flew back to Japan. Despite this shattering experience, he organized a small group of Pearl Harbor pilots to travel to Oahu and participate in a seminar during the fiftieth anniversary ceremonies. There Abe met a more tolerant group of survivors, and returned home encouraged enough to organize a group with the improbable name, "The Japan Friends of Pearl Harbor."

CHAPTER 15

A VOICE FROM THE
BOTTOM OF THE SEA

As Fuchida's planes bombed and strafed Pearl Harbor, the seaplane tender *Curtiss* sighted the periscope of a Japanese midget submarine and attacked with its artillery and machine guns. The submarine, Midget B, launched a torpedo that exploded harmlessly onshore. The destroyer *Monaghan* rammed her and dropped depth charges, decapitating her captain. Two weeks later, the Navy raised the sub from the harbor and used it as fill for a pier at the submarine base. A military funeral was held for the Japanese crewmen before a crane dropped their sub into a hole near the present-day officers' club, where it is still entombed.

On Midget C, Captain Kazuo Sakamaki had to navigate with his periscope because of a defective gyroscope. Destroyers spotted him and dropped depth charges. Sakamaki was knocked unconscious and woke to see smoke rising from Pearl Harbor. Two destroyers pursued him as he raced for the harbor channel. He hit a coral reef, extricated himself, then made a final attempt to enter the harbor. His steering was so badly damaged that the midget swung in circles and began filling with fumes. Sakamaki and his crewman, Kiyoshi Inagaki, passed out and drifted toward Oahu's windward coast. When he regained consciousness, he assumed he had reached the rendezvous point with his mother sub off Lanai. Then his batteries died and his sub slid onto another reef. He lit a scuttling charge and swam for shore. The charge failed to ignite and crewman Inagaki disappeared in heavy surf. When Sakamaki regained consciousness he was lying on Waimanalo beach, guarded by a Japanese-American sergeant, and about to become America's first World War II POW.

The military repaired his submarine and outfitted it with two mannequins dressed as Japanese sailors. It was shipped to the mainland, mounted on a trailer, and hauled across forty-one states as the featured attraction of war-bond drives, once stopping in a town near the Wisconsin POW camp where Sakamaki was held prisoner. After the war, it ended up at the United States Navy submarine base in Key West, and is currently an exhibit at a Key West museum.

Sakamaki initially begged his captors to take him to a hill overlooking Pearl Harbor and shoot him. Instead, they imprisoned him on Honolulu's Sand Island. He refused to answer questions and disfigured his face with cigarettes, methodically burning himself with an inverted triangle of scars to symbolize his disgrace. At mainland POW camps he punished himself by taking cold showers and wearing thin cotton pajamas. But after several months of captivity he had a change of heart and disavowed suicide because, he wrote later in his book, he was impressed by his humane treatment and the beauty of the American countryside.

Sakamaki was repatriated to Japan after the war and quickly became a celebrity, POW # 1. Men wrote demanding he commit harakiri to atone for his capture. Women sent love letters. He married, took a job at Toyota, and became production chief of its export division and then president of Toyota in Brazil, causing rumors to circulate among American Pearl Harbor survivors that the disgrace of his capture had forced him to emigrate.

When he returned to Hawaii for the twentieth anniversary he asked reporters meeting him at the airport how to find Kaneohe, a windward coast town near Waimanalo. He returned again four years later and complained of being "attacked with strange impressions" while on a Pearl Harbor sight-seeing cruise. He came back several more times during the 1970s, and again in 1981. For a former POW to return to the battlefield where he was captured is not unusual, but there was something obsessive about Sakamaki's frequent visits.

The former curator of the Pacific Submarine Museum at Pearl Harbor, Ray de Yarmin, told me Sakamaki had come in 1981 hoping to find where his crewman, Kiyoshi Inagaki, was buried and make sure it was properly marked and maintained. De Yarmin spent several days with him checking death certificates, visiting cemeteries, pursuing rumors of a headless torso washing ashore near Bellows Field, and interviewing elderly Japanese-Americans, on the chance that local Japanese had secretly buried Inagaki. Sakamaki still felt a need to explain his capture, telling de Yarmin he had not drowned himself because he believed Japan was about to occupy Hawaii, and insisting that "The only thing I ever wanted to do was return to the Japanese Navy and fight."

Sakamaki retired from Toyota in Brazil in 1993 and returned to Japan. He refused an invitation to travel to Honolulu in 1995 for the fiftieth anniversary of the signing of the Japanese surrender and has rebuffed journalists seeking interviews. A survivor who became friendly with Zenji Abe in 1991 asked Abe if he would speak with Sakamaki, should Sakamaki attend one of the Pearl Harbor anniversaries. Abe, who had been so determined to make amends with the American veterans, replied coldly, "Do not ever mention Sakamaki's name in my presence again."

Four American destroyers reported firing on enemy submarines and it is believed that between them they were responsible for sinking Japanese Midgets D and E. In 1960, Navy divers practicing near the mouth of Pearl Harbor found Midget D. She lay two thousand yards offshore, submerged in seventy-six feet of water, crusted with coral, and badly warped, indicating damage from a depth charge. The Navy raised the midget and brought her to Pearl Harbor. The naval officer who inspected the interior found bent piping, shattered glass, and a motor torn from its mounting. The fuse of a scuttling charge had been lit, but the charge had failed to detonate. There were no maps, charts, or human remains. In the official report of the recovery a naval doctor asserted that "even if human remains had disintegrated through the years, the victim's teeth would have resisted the water's corrosive effects. No teeth or evidence of bodies were found."

An article about the midget in the *Naval Institute Proceedings* concluded, "Little doubt exists that her two-man crew left the submarine. Whether or not they survived remains a mystery. . . . If they were able to swim the mile to shore across placid Keehi Lagoon, they could have easily melted into the local populace of Hawaii with its many Orientals. . . . Their devotion to Japanese ideology would likely have caused them to reveal to no one, either during or after the war, that they had failed in their mission. Therefore, it is a remote possibility that one or both may be alive today."

Ray de Yarmin was cagey when I asked about this theory, saying, "It's not impossible that they're alive, because the dishonor of having survived would have kept them hidden." He added that, "The truth will never be known, but there are things people have overlooked."

In 1967, a Japanese man in suburban Baltimore claimed to be Okino Sasaki, one of the Midget E crewmen. (The crewman of one midget is recorded in Japanese archives as Naokichi Sasaki, and Okino is presumably a shortened form of this first name.) His story, "A Voice from the Bottom of the Sea," appeared with his photograph in the December 1967 issue of *Our Navy*, a monthly magazine for retired and serving U.S. Navy personnel that has long since ceased publication. The author, former Navy officer Ellsworth Boyd, claimed to have met Sasaki by chance at the Jade East Chinese restaurant in Towson, Maryland. Sasaki said he owned the restaurant and was tending bar because his regular bartender was ill.

Boyd described Sasaki as "a small, cordial, slightly balding forty-three-year-old Japanese gentleman." He told Boyd he had been drafted into the Japanese navy in 1941 and assigned to the submarine service, then chosen by lot to be a ballastman in one of the two-man midgets. He claimed to have been captured on December 8 and spent the war in a POW camp. After the war, he worked on a tramp steamer. When it called at Baltimore he met and married a Japanese-American girl, working in her father's restaurant until he had saved enough money to open the Jade East.

Boyd did not identify Sasaki's prison camp, nor explain why the U.S. government had publicized Sakamaki's capture, but kept Sasaki's capture a secret, or why Sasaki had chosen to reveal his story now. Instead, most of his article was devoted to Sasaki's account of his experiences before and during the attack. He remembered that as he and his commander, Lieutenant Sakamoto, were readying to board the midget on December 6, one of the crewmen thrust a small duffel bag into his hands. This crewman had originally been assigned to the Kaiten command. (*Kaiten*, "a turn toward heaven," was the undersea equivalent of the kamikazes—human torpedoes, or "Impact submarines," fitted with a tiny compartment in which the pilot rode on his one-way mission.) "Anticipating the cold he knew I would confront in the little sub, he had wrapped a bottle of sake in one of his heavy woolen sweaters and stuffed it in the duffel bag," Sasaki said.

Sasaki described how the midget malfunctioned during the attack, finally sinking in ninety feet of water at the harbor entrance, its power off but its torpedoes intact. He and Lieutenant Sakamoto remained submerged for nine hours, first listening to faint thumping sounds from the battle above, then feeling violent undersea explosions that rocked the ship like a cradle. That night, Sakamoto lit a fuse attached to the scuttling charge. Then they flooded the conning tower and escaped through the hatch. "When I reached the surface, I swam like hell for shore," Sasaki told Boyd. "Fires raged everywhere. People were scurrying as sirens wailed in the night. When I reached the beach I collapsed. That's all I remember. When I awoke I was in a prison camp."

Sasaki's story is made more credible by details such as the sake bottle wrapped in the sweater, and his explanation of the midget's technical problems. The official Navy salvage report confirms an attempt to scuttle the sub, saying, "Demolition experts removed an explosive charge from the submarine that was designed to blow it apart. The fuse of the charge had been lit but the charge had not detonated. This factor, coupled with the discovery that the conning-tower hatch was unlocked from the inside, led us to believe that the two crewmen escaped." This report also supports Sasaki's description of the duffel bag he left behind. "Some shoes and a pair of unmarked coveralls were found in the sub along with a small canvas bag. The bag contained a full bottle of sake and a woolen sweater. The sweater had Japanese writing on it which has been translated as 'Kaiten.' "

If Sasaki's story is a hoax, it is a puzzling one. Why would Boyd concoct this story, only to sell it to an obscure magazine? And if Sasaki had gone to the trouble of obtaining the salvage report from Navy archives and making himself an expert on the midget subs, then why not seek more publicity? But if he had been a POW, why did the military not report his capture as it had Sakamaki's? Another explanation is that on the night of December 8 Sasaki swam across the Keehi Lagoon, slipped ashore, and waited out the war camouflaged by Honolulu's large community of Japanese aliens. Keehi Lagoon is near densely populated Kalihi, a neighborhood that in 1941 contained many aliens speaking only Japanese.

The Jade East restaurant closed in the early 1980s but I tracked down one of its previous owners, Jimmy Han. He swore it was the only restaurant of that name in the Baltimore area, and that he had never heard of Okino Sasaki, although after the *Our Navy* article he had received inquiries about Sasaki.

Perhaps Boyd changed the restaurant's name to protect Sasaki, perhaps Sasaki was merely a customer at the restaurant, or the story *was* a hoax. But we are still left with a 1967 photograph of Sasaki that bears a strong resemblance to the one of Sasaki on a Japanese mural of the midget crews. We are also left with Sasaki's accurate and detailed account of December 7, with a sake bottle wrapped in a Kaiten sweater, and with the suspicion that one of the legacies of Pearl Harbor may be a now elderly Japanese gentleman who swam ashore from Midget E, lived incognito in Honolulu throughout the war, then moved to the mainland and remained hidden until one evening in 1967 when he told his story, then vanished again.

CHAPTER 16

THE ARIZONA OPENS
LIKE A FLOWER

Trace the paths of the Japanese fighters and bombers over a map of Oahu and the island begins to resemble an insect caught in a dense spiderweb of lines and arrows, and you can appreciate how confusing the attack must have been for American forces on the ground. The most chaotic and damaging period was the first half hour, from 0755 until 0825, when more than twenty ships were attacked by 183 Japanese fighters and torpedo, dive-, and high bombers. This was when Oahu's defenders suffered the heaviest material losses and casualties, when great battleships capsized and sank in flames, and Japanese pilots destroyed or damaged most of the 188 Army and Navy planes lost on December 7.

There was a lull from 0825 until 0840, punctuated by sporadic strafing and bombing. Then a second wave of 171 planes crossed Oahu's northern coast at 0840. Joined by high-level bombers from the first wave, they struck Pearl Harbor and the airfields between 0915 and 0945. During this final phase, Zeros engaged American fighters and strafed automobiles and residential areas. American resistance was stronger, and the Japanese suffered more losses and inflicted less damage.

Eyewitness memories are less chronological and ordered, and reflect the chaos of that morning. People are often unsure about when certain ships were hit or planes destroyed, or if they were themselves victims of bombs or torpedoes. But everyone remembers how the great battleships and their crews looked in their death throes, and the sight of the *Oklahoma* capsizing, and the explosion that destroyed the *Arizona* in a matter of seconds.

The *Oklahoma* turned over before Sterling Cale could go aboard. He immediately dove into the burning waters of Pearl Harbor and, putting his frogman training to use, swam underwater to the nearest wounded sailor. He splashed the water as he surfaced, making a hole in the flames before hoisting the victim onto the officers' barge. He spent the next six hours in the water and rescued forty men. Most were severely wounded, with blood running down their faces and deep gashes in their bodies. A few screamed, but most had been stunned into silence. Every time the barge filled, Cale climbed aboard and they raced to the landing at the Naval Hospital, where the dead lay stacked like cordwood.

At 0810, fifteen minutes into the attack, an eighteen-hundred-pound armor-piercing bomb dropped by Lt. Shojiro Kondo struck the *Arizona* forward and to the right of its number two gun turret, passing through four decks in less than seven seconds and exploding in a powder magazine. The hot gas from that explosion hit a bulkhead and was deflected upward. A half second later the *Arizona*'s other magazines exploded. A fountain of flame and black smoke shot skyward and the ship appeared to leap from the water. Its foremast pitched forward, and its deck opened like a flower.

According to Theodore Mason, a sailor on the *California*, "a red fireball shot up and spread into a mushroom of death nearly a thousand feet high," and "a mighty thunderclap of sound, deep and terrible, rode over the cacophony of planes and bombs, and now-awakening guns."

Mitsuo Fuchida, who had an excellent view of the explosion, remembered that, "The smoke and flames erupted together. It was a hateful, mean-looking red flame, the kind that powder produces." As

Fuchida's plane shuddered from the shock wave of the explosion his heart filled with "joy and gratification."

From his station on the bridge of the *West Virginia*, Richard Fiske watched the descent of the bomb that killed his high school buddies Finley and Jones. At first he thought it would hit the *West Virginia*. Then it changed direction and fell into the *Arizona*. As with many Pearl Harbor accounts, Fiske's conveys a sense of the attack unfolding in slow motion. Bombs take ages to tumble to the ground; torpedoes move so slowly sailors have time to comment on their direction; witnesses stand frozen as bullets stitch holes in pavement; and planes appear to hang suspended in midair, enabling witnesses to notice the expressions on pilots' faces, see their scarves and goggles, make eye contact, and exchange waves and obscene gestures.

The shock wave from the explosion of the *Arizona* blew Fiske backward. Flaming men and body parts flew upward from the *Arizona*. Body parts, naked corpses, and letters from home landed on nearby ships or were snagged by trees on Ford Island. Men stumbled across the deck, burning like torches. Their helmets were on, but their clothes had been seared off. The men who jumped into the harbor were heard to "sizzle." The body of the *Arizona*'s captain, Franklin Van Valkenburgh, was never found, although after the ship cooled a boarding party found his Naval Academy ring in a pile of ashes.

Shrapnel killed Mervyn Bennion, the captain of the *West Virginia*. Richard Fiske was standing next to him when he was mortally wounded. Then seven torpedoes slammed into the *West Virginia* and she settled onto the shallow bottom, her decks awash. Fiske grabbed a fire hose and sprayed water on his shipmates as they staggered from belowdecks in flames. After the order was given to abandon ship, he swam to Ford Island through burning oil.

On Ford Island, thousands of survivors from the *Arizona* and other wounded battleships wandered through clouds of smoke. Theodore Mason said their skin was "black and crusted," as if exposed to blow torches. Some were naked, dripping oil, skin, and blood, screaming in agony. "The only thing I could see were their eyes, lips, and mouths," one survivor said. "Their mouths were reddish; their eyes looked watery. Everything else was black."

The dead lay in lines on the lawns of the Ford Island officers' bungalows, their blood soaking the ground and blackening the grass. Burial parties gathered dismembered arms and legs from roofs and trees. Many hung in the branches of a banyan tree near the water.

The more I read about sailors turned into ashes, the more I found myself thinking about Hiroshima. The *Arizona*'s sailors had been cut down in a single, searing blast, by an explosion sounding to witnesses like a powerful and heavy wind blowing through thick foliage. Then a fireball mushroomed into the air leaving a great mushroom cloud hanging over the battleship. No wonder some Honolulu residents later claimed that newsreels of Hiroshima reminded them of Pearl Harbor.

Sixty times as many people died at Hiroshima as at Pearl Harbor, and most were civilians. But in 1941, when the United States was at peace, to lose over a thousand sailors in seconds, on a single battleship and to a single bomb, was an unprecedented catastrophe. It represented more sailors than had been lost in action in the Spanish-American War and World War I combined, the most lost in the sinking of a single vessel in U.S. naval history, and the greatest number of human beings killed in a single explosion in the history of warfare, a record broken only by Hiroshima.

Both bombings were, in a way, "sneak attacks." Hiroshima occurred during a declared war in which civilians had become frequent victims, but its sneak-attack quality lay in the fact that the Japanese were unaware of the atom bomb, and for the first time in history the total destruction of a city was the sole purpose of an air raid. In that brief moment separating the explosion and annihilation, Hiroshima's inhabitants must have been as stunned as sailors on the *Arizona*, who had several seconds between the muffled thud of the bomb hitting the first magazine and the final thundering explosion to ponder their fate.

These similarities provide context for what might otherwise be dismissed as coincidental. The banyan tree facing the *Arizona* is known as the Hiroshima Banyan, presumably because its shape resembles a mushroom cloud, but it is really no more mushroom-shaped than any other banyan. Both Honolulu and Hiroshima have built memorials around ruins surviving their respective explosions, and each is the most visited memorial in the country. At Hiroshima, the memorial is at the ruined dome of the Industrial Promotion Hall, a structure marking the epicenter of the explosion, just as the *Arizona* symbolizes the epicenter of Pearl Harbor. There is also an official "sister city" relationship between Honolulu and Hiroshima, based on their similar climate, size, and positions as Pacific port cities, but nurtured by similar experiences and populations. Many Japanese living in Hawaii in 1941 had come from Hiroshima prefecture and had relatives killed there. There are Japanese-Americans in Hawaii who witnessed Pearl Harbor, enlisted in the Army, were posted to the occupation forces after the war, and returned to Hiroshima in American uniforms to search for members of their families.

The prewar photographs of the *Arizona*'s stainless-steel galleys, brass caldrons, and lines of hammocks echo the ghostly ones of prewar Hiroshima, with its busy train station, packed streets, and trolley cars. Both depict an innocent and doomed population. The fact that both sets of victims were so unsuspecting reveals that their most powerful connection is that they were killed by attacks that were at the time outside the boundaries of traditional warfare, ones perhaps better characterized as mass murder.

Sterling Cale was placed in charge of a six-man graves registration and burial detail that went aboard the *Arizona* on December 11. It was the first time Cale had ever been aboard a battleship, and he had no idea what he would find. He wore hip waders so he could descend to the second deck, and black leather gloves up to his elbows, so he could handle the body parts.

He saw little piles of ashes surrounding the anti-aircraft guns, and more ashes blowing across the open deck, and swirling around his ankles. He thought, *My God, these were human beings!* He swept some ashes into sea bags, but the tradewinds blew others over the side.

He found torsos without heads, and heads without torsos. In the fire control tower there was a three-foot-long mass of charred bodies fused together so tightly he could not make out a single individual sailor. As he tried separating the bodies, a head, or an arm, or a leg, or some other body part came off in his hands, or fell from the mass. Several times he stopped to vomit.

Cale spent a week on the *Arizona*, working every day until dusk, putting remains into sea bags. He saved and tagged any personal items—a knife, a watch, anything that might help identify a victim. He meticulously recorded in a notebook the precise location of every item and body part, reasoning that if a sailor had been at his normal duty station at the time of the explosion, then this information could help identify him. But shortly afterward, the Master of Arms confiscated and destroyed the notebook on the grounds that it was an illegal war diary. This is one reason why, sixty years later, so many *Arizona* casualties buried at the National Memorial Cemetery of the Pacific at Punchbowl, a volcanic crater overlooking Honolulu, are identified by markers saying simply, UNKNOWN.

The known and unknown Pearl Harbor dead lay in temporary cemeteries at Halawa and Nuuanu until 1949, when they were moved to Punchbowl. At these temporary cemeteries the grave markers for the 653 Pearl Harbor Unknowns identified their death date (December 7, 1941) and the ship where their remains were collected, information also available on official burial records. Yet, inexplicably, when the Unknowns were reburied at Punchbowl, many of the new 1-by-2–foot granite markers failed to carry their date of death or location of the remains.

This omission angered Ray Emory, who had been a seaman first class on the cruiser *Honolulu* at the time of the attack. Shortly before the fiftieth anniversary Emory had driven up to Punchbowl to place flowers and flags on the graves of the Pearl Harbor Unknowns. He was appalled to find so many markers lacked any identifying information. He returned with a clipboard and spent weeks walking through the cemetery, consulting burial records, taking notes and photographs, and discovering that of the 265 markers identifying the comingled remains of 653 Pearl Harbor Unknowns, not one carried the place of recovery, and 107 carried no date whatsoever, meaning the victim could theoretically have died at any time during the war.

During the 1990s, Emory succeeded in matching the grave numbers of all 265 Unknown markers with the original burial records from the temporary cemeteries, making it possible to provide each with a date of death and ship. When he presented his findings to officials at the Office of Veterans Affairs, which manages Punchbowl, and to the U.S. Army, the official next-of-kin for all Unknowns, they both refused to make any alterations on the markers, citing their belief in the sanctity of the word *unknown*, and claiming that such changes would set a dangerous precedent. The Army replied that not only were the current inscriptions appropriate, but it had also "expended more than enough manpower and hours in researching and responding to your many inquiries."

"You could say I'm a real thorn in the side of the people who run this place," Emory told me with considerable satisfaction when we met at Punchbowl on the day before the 59th anniversary of the attack. "I guess they never imagined that fifty years later some seaman first class would come along with a computer and expose their screw-ups."

He had brought albums filled with original burial records and photographs of the markers. He led me first to marker Q-1. It read UNKNOWN, and DEC 7, 1941. Then he opened an album and pointed out a burial record indicating that Q-1 had been X-219 at the Halawa cemetery in 1949, where it had been identified as containing six unknown seamen from the *Oklahoma*.

Emory was pleased that due to the assistance of Hawaii congresswoman Patsy Mink he had won a significant victory. On October 30, 2000, President Clinton signed a defense appropriations bill containing a provision inserted by Mink stipulating that the name of the ship and date should be added to the seventy-four markers of the *Arizona*

Unknowns at Punchbowl, graves that probably include the remains of Richard Fiske's high school friends William Finley and Charles Jones. It was a start, Emory said, but he would not rest until every Pearl Harbor Unknown received a similar honor. "These kids gave up their lives and each of these stones costs just sixty-eight dollars. That's all they got, and you're telling me we can't do a better job of saying when and where they died?" he asked. "It's a matter of simple justice."

He believed that once these graves were properly marked, then the Unknowns' former *Arizona* shipmates might visit them to lay flowers and pay their respects. But I suspect he had also embarked on this crusade for the same reason that Sterling Cale had finally written down his Pearl Harbor experiences after fifty-nine years of silence, and that Dick Fiske later became friends with the Japanese pilots who had bombed the *West Virginia*: They were all trying, in their different ways, to exorcise their own Pearl Harbor ghosts.

The rest of the *Arizona*'s dead, a total of 1,102 crewmen, remain at Pearl Harbor, entombed in her wreckage. In 1942, pockets of gas killed two divers attempting to recover their remains. After two more divers engaged in a similar mission perished in 1947, the Navy abandoned all efforts to recover the dead. What this means is that beyond the *Arizona*'s open hatches and unbroken glass portholes, behind her fourteen-inch armor plating curled like lettuce leaves by the explosion, beneath a deck strewn with firehoses and the poles that once anchored awnings, and mixed in among shards of crockery and silverware from the mess, are the human remains most likely to survive fifty years of submersion—hundreds of sets of teeth.

The *Arizona* Memorial now feels like a cemetery. There is a heavy silence, broken only by the chug of a tour boat or ferry, and the calm waters surrounding it are flat and green, like a graveyard lawn. The white mooring blocks once anchoring the doomed battleships resemble old tombstones. Nearby are other buried remains: the wreck of a midget submarine, the crash sites of Japanese planes, and urns containing the ashes of *Arizona* veterans that over the years have been lowered onto the wreckage in a stainless-steel cylinder the Navy has built for that purpose. And there is the *Arizona*'s oil. A droplet escapes from her broken tanks every nine seconds, then floats along passageways, up ladders, and through a small crack in the deck, spreading a rainbowed film on the water, a process park rangers describe as "bleeding."

After the war, the *Arizona*'s twisted superstructure was dismantled for scrap, but the oval outline of its deck remained visible beneath the waters of Pearl Harbor, a rust-brown corpse. Tucker Gratz, a Honolulu businessman, first conceived of building a memorial over this wreckage on December 7, 1946, when he laid a wreath on the *Arizona* to commemorate the fifth anniversary of the attack and found there, undisturbed, the same wreath he had laid in 1945. Five years later, the Navy erected a flagstaff, although it did so reluctantly because many officers agreed with Admiral Nimitz, who was opposed to memorializing Pearl Harbor because it had been, he said, "a great defeat for us." After the flagstaff came a wood platform, a commemorative plaque, and a stone obelisk. On Memorial Day 1962, the Pacific War Memorial Commission, headed by the indefatigable Tucker Gratz, dedicated the *Arizona* Memorial, a stark white rectangular structure spanning the *Arizona* and appearing to hover over the water. Besides being the most important World War II memorial in the country, it defies the customary pattern that as wars become more distant, their visitors shrink to an elderly trickle. Instead it has attracted progressively larger crowds, becoming the most popular cemetery on earth.

The *Arizona* Memorial is a striking and beautiful structure, but lacks a necessary morbidity. It does not immediately tell you, as does the Vietnam Memorial or those rows of crosses in Normandy, that the ground has been drenched by the blood of heroes. It was designed by Alfred Preis, an Austrian refugee who fled Hitler's Vienna as a young man and arrived in Honolulu with his wife in 1939. When I called him he said he had a twitchy guard dog and suggested we meet at a Burger King near the University of Hawaii. As we sat at a Formica table drinking iced tea from plastic cups, Preis told me his original design for the *Arizona* Memorial called for it to echo the jewel-encrusted crypts of the Hapsburg emperors. From his boyhood in Vienna he remembered how these crypts made death seem close and imminent, and the wreckage of the *Arizona* bore certain similarities to them, although its hull was encrusted with barnacles rather than jewels.

Preis had first proposed an underwater chamber next to the *Arizona*; he imagined this would make a powerful antiwar statement. It would be open to the sky and be entered down a flight of stairs from a boat landing. Visitors would face the ship, viewing it through portholes cut in a wall, standing opposite the remains of the crew, and reminded of the horror of being trapped underwater. But the Navy and his partners rejected that plan as too morbid, the same charge that would later be made against the Vietnam Memorial, and one reflecting an understandable military discomfort with memorials connecting war and death.

After his first concept was rejected, Preis reconsidered the Navy's original suggestion for an open bridge over the wreckage, and designed the soaring white rectangle now spanning the *Arizona*. The floor and ceiling sag in the center, reflecting the despair of December 7, then rise at both ends to symbolize victory. Stained-glass windows light a shrine room, and the effect is reminiscent of Coventry Cathedral and other European churches rebuilt after the war. Preis describes it as a serene and friendly space, and although it fails to make the antiwar statement he had intended, he hopes visitors "contemplate personal responses," and imagine the attack.

CHAPTER 17

THE "LITTLE YELLOW BASTARDS" DESTROY THE ARMY AIR FORCE

Gus Ahola had just woken and was lying in bed in his Wheeler Field quarters, debating whether to spend the morning playing golf or washing his car when he heard the distant whine of a plane. He assumed it was having engine trouble, but then it kept coming closer and closer, getting louder and louder, and he said to himself, *Jesus, pull out of it, pull out of it!*

There was a loud explosion. The building shook, and he thought, *Oh hell, oh hell, that poor fellow's bought the farm.*

He spread open a crack in the Venetian blinds and looked outside, hoping to see a parachute. Instead, plumes of smoke rose from the far end of the runway. His roommate woke next, and despite weeks of alerts and headlines about a possible war with Japan, neither man considered the possibility that the planes might be Japanese.

Perhaps it was the "damned Navy," Ahola suggested, staging another mock raid and dropping sacks of flour. He rolled to the edge of his bed and again peered through the blinds. This time he saw a line of bombers painted with the Japanese meatball. "Navy, hell!" he shouted. "Those are the goddam Nips!"

As he pulled his uniform on over his pajamas and jammed his

bare feet into shoes, he remembered how his squadron was parked in a tight antisabotage formation, and thought, *Boy, they're going to clobber us!*

He reached the flight line as the first bombing run ended. Flames shot from hangars and the enlisted men's barracks. Over a hundred aircraft, parked wingtip-to-wingtip to deter saboteurs, had already been damaged. Bullets had ignited fuel tanks, and a river of burning gas flowed across the tarmac. A circle of Japanese warplanes formed overhead, then peeled off for a strafing run, flying so low they later found telephone wires wrapped around their landing gear, and so slow Wheeler's commander saw pilots lean out of their planes and smile, and claimed to have seen the gold fillings sparkling in their teeth.

There were no antiaircraft batteries at Wheeler because they would have been useless against saboteurs. There was little small-arms or rifle fire from Wheeler's defenders at first because to prevent ammunition being stolen by fifth columnists it had been locked in one of the hangars now in flames. The unarmed airmen died in their beds and washrooms, while attempting to disentangle their planes, or while huddling in hangars and taking cover behind bunkers because the base lacked air-raid shelters. Thirty-nine airmen were killed and fifty-nine were wounded. The heaviest casualties occurred among men sleeping in tents and barracks along the runway.

Newsreels and photographs avoided showing the American dead on the grounds it would damage morale, picturing instead the injured recuperating in hospitals. Early eyewitness accounts of Pearl Harbor made the wounds sound clean and the deaths painless. According to Private Charles Legshock of Monroe, Louisiana, "The men, most of them kids like myself, were really something to see while under fire. They all reacted well, and many died with smiles on their faces."

My earliest images of Pearl Harbor all came from documentaries, histories, and movies, and none were morbid. When I thought of Pearl Harbor, I imagined bravery, treachery, tactics, and surprise, but not of over a thousand men killed in seconds on the *Arizona,* or of 2,403 dead in under two hours. I pictured American pilots battling swarms of Zeros, wounded ships puffing smoke, and Japanese diplomats arriving at the State Department in baggy suits. I saw serene maritime deaths and captains going down with their ships. I had not known about men trapped in pockets of air in the *Oklahoma* who survived underwater for two weeks, chalking off the days with X's on overturned cabin walls before dying, or about the antipersonnel bomb that hit a busy mess hall at Hickam Field, sending sharp and jagged masses of steel tearing into five hundred men, leaving horrific wounds. Nor had I known about the corpses stacked up to the windowsills at the Hickam Field hospital, men dying under flowering trees on lush lawns while awaiting hospital beds, the forty garbage cans filled with amputated limbs outside the Tripler Army Hospital, or the amputation saw that was used and sterilized so often that all day it remained hot to the touch, or that the airmen at Wheeler Field had been so terrified some had attempted to escape the strafing by digging through their wooden tent floors with their bare hands, and that the hands of the dead were found to be lacerated, with their fingernails torn away.

When I visited Wheeler Field with Gus Ahola, I was surprised at how closely it resembled its 1941 photographs. There were the same louvered windows, Art Deco streetlamps, and barracks constructed in a Southwestern mission style of thick walls, deep verandas, and high ceilings; the same runway, hangars, and views west to pineapple fields and the Waianae Mountains. The blue star insignia of the Army Air Corps decorated the hangars, Japanese bullets scarred their steel beams. According to Ahola, the biggest change from 1941 was that palms, bougainvillea, and mangoes had grown taller, and there were so many mangoes the officers could not even give them away.

In 1941, Wheeler, Hickam, and Pearl Harbor had been busy little military cities surrounded by deserted beaches and cane and pineapple fields. They were impossible to miss from the ground or air. Bases like Wheeler are still impossible to miss, but only because they are oases of space and calm amid Oahu's sprawl. Simply by not changing they have become among the most attractive and un-spoiled communities on the island. Outside their gates, you find flimsy houses on an eighth of an acre, meadows of asphalt, and scrubby transplanted palms; within are plantation mansions and adobe houses surrounded by parklands of graceful palms and flow-ering trees.

Communications and engineering units occupy Wheeler's bun-galows now, and its short runways, unsuited to modern warplanes, can only accommodate army helicopters. From the bachelor offi-cers' quarters where he had lived on December 7, Ahola stared down Wheeler's silent streets to the empty runway. He said the day's weather was like that on December 7, trades from the northeast, scattered clouds, and brief showers. (Wheeler's weather is often dif-ferent from Pearl Harbor's.)

We drove to the runway, following the same route he had taken on December 7, and found the overgrown bunker where he had taken cover. As he described the attack I caught him flicking his eyes to the horizon.

When the first wave of Japanese planes departed he had raced down the flight line and jumped into one of the few planes looking airworthy. He taxied it away from the others. Its tail section was burned out, its controls damaged, and its guns had no ammunition. He planned to take off and ram an enemy aircraft, cutting off its tail with his propeller, and thereby become America's first kamikaze. In-stead, the plane spun in a huge ground loop. "God, what a disap-pointment," he said. "There we were, the best pilots, fully trained, gung ho, with the best planes, and we never had a chance to fight. If we'd had twenty minutes warning, only twenty minutes!" Then they could have untangled a few planes and lessened the devastation at Pearl Harbor, "although a lot of us probably would have been killed."

"Including you," I suggested.

He shrugged. "Perhaps."

I did not doubt that if he could change history, he would ask for that twenty-minute warning, preferring to exchange the certainty of fifty years of life for the chance to shoot down a Zero on December 7.

An Army sergeant tending the helicopters came over to check out why an elderly man was standing on the apron making planing motions with his hands. When Ahola explained he was a Pearl Harbor survivor, the sergeant insisted on shaking his hand and showing us the scars from Japanese bullets. He asked us about the yellow bumps on the apron. Ahola explained they were part of the old refueling system. As we left, he stiffened, and said, "Honored to have met you, sir. Yeah, that sure was something . . . December 7, 1944 [sic]."

Ahola flashed a pained smile and we started back to Honolulu in silence. As Pearl Harbor came into view, he said, "You know, by midafternoon we had some planes in service and I flew two missions. Fighter command told us to climb as high and fast as we could. Only three made it up to twenty-six thousand feet. That night the city was blacked out, but fires still burned in Pearl Harbor. Our flight commander, Charlie McDonald, asked what we were supposed to be going after. Fighter command said a bogey had been reported over Diamond Head. We climbed to thirty thousand feet but saw nothing. Finally Charlie radioed back, 'Doesn't anyone there have an astronomy table? Don't you know that Venus is bright this time of year?' There was a long embarrassed pause before someone said, 'Okay. Come in and land.' "

The Japanese attacked Hickam Field without being challenged by fighters from Wheeler or antiaircraft fire. They bombed hangars, ammunition storehouses, and the Hale Makai Barracks, killing thirty-five men who were eating breakfast. They destroyed or damaged most of Hickam's sixty-four bombers, which had been parked on the aprons with their wingtips ten feet apart so they could be guarded by soldiers armed with revolvers. The only Hickam bomber that became airborne was the one blown through the roof of its hangar.

When Hickam opened in 1939 it was the most modern and self-contained of any overseas American base. After seeing its Moorish water tower, Art Deco offices, and lawns and four-lane parkways, a *Star-Bulletin* reporter compared it to "the heart of Palm Beach or any of the resort centers of the southland." An Army publication depicted it as "laid out like an exclusive residential park," adding that "its streets wind and curve in an easy, carefree manner, and with a leisurely Hawaiian indifference to the Euclidean maxim."

Hickam's Hale Makai Barracks were the largest in the world, an octopus of a building whose ten wings contained bunks for three thousand soldiers, and mess hall could feed two thousand at a sitting. It has since become offices for the headquarters of the U.S. Air Force in the Pacific, but its exterior remains untouched. Lines of bullet holes run up walls, stopping at windows, and bomb fragments scar courtyards. When a base commander ordered the holes filled, a protest by veterans resulted and the building became a National Historic Monument.

Glass cases in its lobby display a rusty part from a P-40, a bullet taken from a hangar door, the Protestant chaplain's communion set, and the flag that was the centerpiece of a famous and stirring photograph that shows it flying from a tower over the burning barracks. Machine-gun fire has ripped its middle and shredded its end, and below palm trees are bent backward and smoke drifts across a parking lot of beetle-backed cars. The uncanny way this photograph illustrates the lyrics of the "Star-Spangled Banner" led to captions like, "The Flag Was Still There," and until the 1945 picture of Marines raising the Stars and Stripes over Iwo Jima it was the war's most stirring flag photograph.

At Schofield Army Barracks, Private Bob Kinzler believed a mess-hall oven had exploded when the bombing began. Outside, a plane was circling the headquarters building. Its fuselage was marked by a red circle and its canopy was black. Kinzler noticed the two airmen wore fur-lined helmets. That Japan would attack Hawaii was so inconceivable that he went to breakfast convinced the explosion had been accidental, and the strange planes belonged to the Navy. Suddenly, buglers trumpeted an alert and the mess hall emptied. Kinzler and the others dashed into the quadrangle, some grabbing rifles and firing from rooftops at the planes attacking Wheeler.

At 0930, while the second wave was still overhead, Kinzler's company climbed into a truck and headed for defensive positions along the shoreline, from where they expected to repel a Japanese invasion. As they came over a rise in the Kamehameha Highway, they saw ships burning in Pearl Harbor. "We wore World War I pie-plate hats, were lightly armed, and our average age was nineteen," he remembers. "We all thought we were going to die."

His buddies began speculating on how much it would hurt to be hit by a Japanese bullet. One boy said, "Hey, I've heard the Japs only have .25-caliber ammo. Do you think that would hurt as much as being hit by a .30-caliber?" Another agreed it would hurt less. But how much less?

Kinzler fought throughout the war and became an officer. He returned to Hawaii after the Japanese surrender to manage a sugar mill on Aiea Heights. In 1941, there had been cane fields just below his house, then houses scattered through forests of bamboo. Since then, he has watched construction crews creeping toward him up the hill, leaving curving streets and suburban homes on the former cane fields. A neighbor's roof has partially blocked what was once an uninterrupted view of Pearl Harbor, although from an angle he can make out the *Arizona* Memorial.

I was puzzled that Kinzler could not recall any casualties from Schofield, or any bombing or strafing. According to a popular book of Pearl Harbor photographs published in 1981 and reprinted fourteen times, "Schofield was attacked as well. Building 1492 on the west end of the barracks was one of the first structures hit. Quad C, one of the main barracks, was strafed, as well as the post library." In the film version of *From Here to Eternity*, Japanese planes swoop over the barracks while soldiers scatter across a quadrangle, some pitching forward dead. I had assumed that because author James Jones was at Schofield his portrayal in his novel of events on December 7 had been factual. He wrote about three planes coming from the southeast "firing full blast," a strafing attack continuing fitfully for over an hour, a boy being killed—"The red-haired boy lay sprawled out floppy-haired, wild-eyed and silent, in the middle of the pavement"—and a Japanese pilot flying so low soldiers saw "the helmeted head with the square goggles over the slant eyes and the long scarf rippling behind it and the grin on the face as he waved."

Hundreds of official photographs show planes attacking Oahu's other bases, yet the only one I saw of Schofield Barracks on December 7 was captioned, "C Quad at Schofield Barracks under mock attack. This photo depicts a dramatization of the attack done for the movie *From Here to Eternity*."

Herb Garcia, a retired Army colonel who is curator of the base museum, believed the Japanese never attacked Schofield. He could find no mention of casualties or enemy action in official military police reports, duty rosters, or the journal of the 25th Infantry Regiment. He showed me this last document, an impressively detailed, minute-by-minute account of that day that includes the attack on Wheeler and rumors of paratroopers and saboteurs, but makes no mention of any bombs or bullets hitting Schofield. Garcia has also checked the Army engineers' reports of home repairs for December 1941 on the theory that if the post suffered damage, it would have to be mentioned there. He read instead of clogged toilets and broken screens, and the journal of the base hospital's chaplain spoke of him attending to casualties from Wheeler Field, but not from Schofield.

Garcia conceded that a dud naval shell from Pearl Harbor fell into a barrel of flour in the kitchen, that a Japanese pilot might have squeezed off some rounds while heading for Wheeler, and that empty shell casings might have fallen into the quadrangles and been mistaken for live ammunition. He said, "Remember, the soldiers who witnessed this were not trained observers, just excitable Depression-era kids. Then rumors got bigger in the telling and were reinforced by *From Here to Eternity*. Now, 90 percent of the veterans who return here say, 'Yeah, I was bombed, I was strafed.' If I argue, they say, 'Look, buddy, I was here and you weren't.'"

Garcia almost wished he *had* been here. "Those guys in the Schofield battalions lived together for several years in the peacetime Army, making a miserable twenty-one dollars a month. When the war came they fought together, surviving terrible combat for four years as their numbers dwindled. As they got fewer and fewer, they became closer." He, on the other hand, had commanded a battalion in Vietnam, where officers quickly revolved through commands, a tour of duty was a year, and the intense bonding common to World War II was missing.

Garcia was obviously a man of great enthusiasms, but I thought he took too much delight in deflating the earlier generation's war stories. When I mentioned the shell hole in the base library that Kinzler believed was evidence Schofield had come under attack he laughed, and said, "Three holes, and more likely made by a drill than a bullet. See for yourself."

They were on the north wall of the stone building housing his office and museum. Someone had painted a red bull's-eye around them, but they were the wrong size for a Japanese .50 caliber shell, and angled in the wrong direction. To make them, Garcia pointed out, a Japanese pilot would have had to be flying four feet above the ground.

Had someone drilled them on purpose, or were they made by a workman, then mislabeled as Pearl Harbor relics by someone upset the Japanese had not considered Schofield an important enough target? If nothing else, they were more evidence of how tightly braided Pearl Harbor fact and myth have become.

At a reunion of the 25th Infantry Association, Herb Garcia had met a Mr. Welden, who claimed to have been the model for Sergeant Warden in *From Here to Eternity*, and a Robert E. Lee Stuart who, like the Robert E. Lee Prewitt in the book, came from West Virginia and was a bugler and a boxer who had once blinded an opponent. According to Garcia, Stuart had printed up business cards identifying him as Prewitt and had blown taps at the drop of a hat, and preferred being called "Prew" to "Stu," his real Army nickname. Garcia considered this evidence of how closely Jones modeled his characters on real people. I thought it also showed how readily people will adjust their real lives to conform to fictional ones, and how easily fictional and factual memories of historical events can become confused. This happened to Jones when he returned to Schofield in 1973 and tried to remember being ordered to march to the Kolekole Pass carrying a full pack. "I had used the incident on Prewitt in the novel, and it had been reproduced in the film version," he wrote. "Now I no longer knew whether Prewitt had done it, or I had."

I asked Garcia to point out the Kolekole Pass that Japanese planes had used on their way to Wheeler Field.

"Another myth!" he said, delighted I had mentioned it. "Not one plane ever came through that pass."

But *Tora! Tora! Tora!*, acclaimed as a meticulously accurate recreation of Pearl Harbor, showed planes flying through Kolekole, and magazine and newspaper accounts had Japanese pilots "barreling" or "screaming" through it. In *Day of Infamy*, Walter Lord wrote of a staff sergeant seeing "a line of six to ten planes come through the Kolekole Pass to the west." My book of December 7 photographs included a picture captioned "Kolekole Pass looking east out into the Leilehua Plain. This was the view the Japanese pilots had as they came out of the pass. Wheeler Field and Schofield Barracks were dead ahead."

Garcia explained that although from the vantage point of Schofield and Wheeler Kolekole appeared to be a clear gap in the Waianae Range, from the air you could see that a mountain rose in its middle on the western side, making it impossible to fly through. On December 7, Japanese pilots had followed the eastern side of the Waianaes, turning near the Kolekole to launch their attack on

Wheeler. When soldiers at Schofield saw the planes silhouetted against an open sky, they assumed they had come through the pass. I checked the official Japanese and American maps and saw Garcia was right, not a single plane had used this pass.

He drove me up to Kolekole where a plaque announced, "It was through the Kolikoli [sic] Pass and through this valley that some Japanese aircraft flew on their way to Pearl Harbor on December 7, 1941." Just beyond, a small hill filled the center of the pass.

The next day I returned to Wheeler and Schofield on my own, looking up at the Kolekole from every angle, and deciding the myth was so appealing because it reinforced the idea that Japanese planes had only appeared seconds before they attacked. This made the failure to detect them sooner more excusable, and it confirmed the treacherous nature of the Japanese.

For Americans, there has always been something despicable about hiding behind a ridge and then swooping down on unsuspecting victims. The other enemy famous for using this technique were the American Indians, and the Waianaes are stark and red, like the hills concealing an Indian ambush in a Hollywood Western. Americans have fought two enemies they considered subhuman, the Indians and the Japanese, and it is perhaps only natural that the second should assume some of the characteristics of the first. The Indians, too, were supposedly treacherous and sneaky, and lacking any respect for human life or the rules of war. They, too, lay in wait behind pink desert ridges, ready to ambush unsuspecting white men, and perhaps this parallel not only explains the Kolekole Pass myth, but also why after December 7 the expression "The only good injun is a dead injun," became "The only good Jap is a dead Jap."

Lieutenant Cy Gillette was taking a shower in his home at nearby Kailua as Japanese planes attacked Kaneohe Naval Air Station. His wife shouted over the sound of water that his duty officer had called to order him back to base. He dismissed it as another war game and took time to shave. It took a second call, reporting that planes were on fire, to send him racing to Kaneohe in his convertible.

He found the base in chaos. Hangars were burning and sailors were running down the runway, chased by Japanese bullets, their pajama legs poking from under their uniforms. Only three of Kaneohe's thirty-six PBY seaplanes were on patrol. The rest were riding at anchor, sitting in hangars, or parked on the apron. Kaneohe had no fixed gun emplacements and its mobile antiaircraft guns had been rolled away for the weekend. Even its rifles and machine guns were under lock.

Gillette followed a crowd of sailors to the armory, where they smashed the locks. He grabbed a Thompson submachine gun and sprinted across the runway, followed by bullets from a Zero. An ensign next to him fell over dead, and Gillette describes this moment as if he still cannot believe it, "One moment we were running next to each other, and the next he was down on the tarmac."

After the war, Gillette settled in windward Oahu, living in a house on Kailua Beach with a view across the water to Mokapu Point and the Naval Air Station. He later moved to a condominium overlooking Kaneohe Bay and the base. When I visited him there, he showed me where the seaplanes taxied and turned around, and where they had been moored on December 7. I asked how living within sight of the battlefield where he was almost killed had affected him. "I rarely think about it," he insisted, explaining he had chosen Kaneohe because there was excellent sailing in the bay.

He took me outside to his lanai, which had an even better view of the base, and said, "After the Japanese left, we heard rumors of paratroopers landing on Barbers Point. We moved cars and trucks onto the runway to prevent their planes from landing. Then we took machine guns, blankets, and water to a hill overlooking the base, where we planned making a last-ditch stand against a Japanese invasion." This hill, known as Kansas Hill, rises sharply from the water and dominates Kaneohe, and is the kind of natural feature that, like Bunker Hill, seems ideal for making a last stand.

Gillette and his buddies stayed there throughout the afternoon and evening, camouflaging and darkening their uniforms by dipping them in coffee, and listening to panicky Army units shooting at shadows. They believed an invasion had begun and by tomorrow they would either be dead or seeing a Japanese flag flying over Kaneohe. "Instead, at eight the next morning, we saw the Stars and Stripes being raised on the base flagpole," he said. "Then we broke down and cried because . . ." He stopped to wipe his eyes, then broke into deep sobs. Tears ran down his cheeks. "Because it looked like those words from the Star-Spangled Banner—'Our flag was still there'—and we were so proud, so emotional, and, I suppose, so glad to be alive."

When a second wave of Japanese bombers attacked Kaneohe at 0915, its defenders fired back with pistols, rifles, and makeshift machine guns mounted on pipes the sailors had pounded into the ground with sledgehammers. The bombers retreated and the Zeros descended, flying at rooftop level and strafing.

Duels became personal, and one sailor remembers a pilot laughing, and seeing his teeth and open lips. Among the pilots was Lt. Iyozo Fujita, who would survive December 7 and the war to become a Japan Air Lines pilot. He sometimes flew the popular Tokyo-Honolulu run, and admitted that each landing in Hawaii triggered "uneasy memories."

One Japanese pilot crashed into the ocean, another, Lt. Fujita Iida, lagged behind as his comrades re-formed to return to the carriers. He decided to make a final suicidal strafing run, then guide his crippled plane into the Kaneohe armory. As he came in low and alone, he became a target for every gun on the base. His Zero took numerous hits and slammed into Kansas Hill. A Chinese civilian worker, Sam Chun, pulled his mangled body from the wreckage. He was still wearing his "belt of a thousand stitches," a good-luck charm sewn by his fiancée. His head had been mangled and his feet amputated. Someone stole his flight boots (nine years later, his mother received them in the mail, accompanied by an apology), and Chun kept his fur-lined helmet.

Iida's corpse was stuffed into a galvanized garbage can that sat on a sidewalk near the sick bay. He was buried the next day with full military honors.

At ceremonies at the Kaneohe Naval Air Station marking the fortieth anniversary of the attack, some of the sailors who fired at Iida met and embraced Kikuyo Iida, the Japanese woman who had become obsessed with him after reading about his glorious death. She had been only twelve years old at the time and had contacted his mother, who introduced her to Iida's cousin. They married in 1954, and through a series of coincidences and a correspondence too complicated to recount here, she made contact with Conrad Frienze of Seattle, who had fed bullets into the machine gun that his brother, Richard Frienze, fired at Iida's plane. Also present at Kaneohe in 1981 was John Finn, who won the Congressional Medal of Honor for heroism at Kaneohe on December 7 and claimed that Iida's plane had taken hits from rounds fired from his machine gun seconds before it crashed. Another former Kaneohe sailor, Guy Avery, credited an aviation ordnanceman named Sands with the kill, saying Sands had emptied his rifle at a Zero that was coming in on a constantly decreasing line of flight, as if the pilot intended to crash at the sailor's feet.

All three men had probably contributed to Iida's death, and forty years later the first two felt haunted by it. Finn was reported to be nearly overcome with emotion as he visited the monument marking where Iida's plane had crashed. He told journalists he respected Iida, and had since learned he had been, "real cheerful, a jolly little guy who was much liked."

Frienze praised Iida for dying like a Samurai, adding, "he intended to draw as much fire as possible so the other Japanese planes would have a better chance to get away. He served his nation and his Emperor as well as any man could, and I'm proud that I've gotten to 'know' him." This is a generous interpretation of Iida's last strafing run. Other eyewitness accounts indicate his plane was already badly damaged and he was presumably fulfilling a pledge he made before the attack to crash into an enemy target rather than make an emergency landing. Had he succeeded, he would have killed dozens more American sailors.

Frienze and others attending the ceremonies at Kaneohe had come to "know" Iida through the efforts of Kikuyo Iida, who arrived carrying Iida's diaries, letters, photographs, and an essay, "Commander Iida Has Been My Eternal Sweetheart," describing the years she had worked "to serve the commander's grave." She also bought a cache of Lieutenant Iida memorabilia she handed out as "souvenirs" to the Kaneohe veterans. She was accompanied by Yaeko Munakata, Iida's former landlady and a repository of syrupy stories about Iida's fondness for children. Munakata said she had come to Kaneohe "to worship [the] commander's monument."

This monument, the only known one on a U.S. military base dedicated to a former enemy, is a small pile of lava rocks bonded together with concrete and topped with a stone marker proclaiming in capitals, "JAPANESE AIRCRAFT IMPACT SITE," then in smaller letters, "Pilot-Lieutenant Iida, 1. J.N. Cmdr. Third Air Control Group." It is arguable whether it is a battlefield marker or, as Mrs. Iida and Mrs. Munakata choose to believe, a memorial to Iida. On the afternoon of December 6, 1981, the two Japanese ladies burned incense in front of it, decorated it with a photograph of Iida, and anointed it with sake. Afterward, Kikuyo Iida wrote to base commander Colonel C.D. Robinson, "It was a very emotional moment to face Lieutenant Iida's memorial, for I have been dreaming [of] it during the past forty years. . . . I can see the monument in the night when I close my eyes." She added that she hoped to return for another visit soon, and in 1990 the Kaneohe public affairs officer told me Iida had indeed come back numerous times, making something of a nuisance of herself.

Some American veterans have protested Iida's marker. After the 1981 anniversary, Mr. Joseph Nemish wrote to Colonel Robinson, "As an American citizen, I take extreme offense to that marker being on property of the Government of the United States of America. With your permission I will at my own expense remove that marker and plant grass."

Robinson replied, "There seems to be a slight misunderstanding regarding the marker. It is not a monument to Lieutenant Iida, but merely a historical marker."

I thought the misunderstanding was more than slight, and concerned more than this marker. The military authorities at Kaneohe had imagined a small ceremony of Japanese-American reconciliation, with Mrs. Iida exchanging reminiscences with the men who claimed the honor of killing her husband's cousin, her hero. How could they have known she would treat the marker as his grave? Or that her visit would monopolize press coverage of the anniversary at Kaneohe?

By the time I returned to Kaneohe in 2000, it had become a Marine Corps base, and contained a new headquarters building for the commander of the U.S. Pacific Fleet Patrol and Reconnaissance Force named for John Finn. He had attended its dedication ceremonies and, according to the filmmakers accompanying him, seemed to become younger and more vigorous as he described the attack. He had unsuccessfully sought permission to search Kansas Hill with a metal detector for remains of Iida's plane.

Marine Corps Lt. Angela Judge, who escorted me to the impact site, said, "First of all, I want to make it very clear that this is a marker, *not* a memorial." But, despite her protest, and those of all the base commanders and public affairs officers before her, the fact remained that for Mrs. Iida, who had continued coming almost every December 7 to weep, anoint the marker with sake, and lay a photograph of her eternal sweetheart against it, and for the Buddhist priests and other Japanese who appeared with her, the impact site marker *was* a memorial, in fact the only one in Hawaii dedicated solely to the memory of a Japanese casualty.

On December 7, 1999, Mrs. Iida, along with thirty-one other Japanese, returned yet again. On this occasion she took possession of the brown-leather flight helmet Commander Iida had worn when he crashed. For years, Sam Chun, the Chinese-American who had extracted Iida's corpse from his shattered Zero, had been telling his family he wanted to return this object to Iida's relations. After his death in 1967, his daughter, Mrs. Elfreida Tsukayama, continued to search for them. After she presented the helmet to Mrs. Iida, the two women embraced and wept. "Only in America can we do this. Yesterday's enemy became today's friend," Mrs. Iida said.

Mrs. Tsukayama lives near the base in Kailua and I met her for lunch after visiting Kaneohe. She told me how her father had often spoken about returning the helmet but had never really done much about it. It sat in a plastic bag in her closet and when her kids were young they sometimes put it on and used it in their games. She said she had finally decided to act because she began feeling guilty, and knew her kids would never return it after she died. She contacted the Japanese consul in Honolulu, but he was no help at all, and she had almost given up when she read a newspaper article about Mrs. Iida's yearly pilgrimages to Kaneohe.

But even Mrs. Tsukayama's act of Pearl Harbor reconciliation, one staged fifty-eight years after the attack, was not without controversy. Mrs. Iida told reporters the helmet would be a featured exhibit in a museum honoring Lieutenant Iida that her husband had built in his hometown in Yamaguchi Prefecture. After the ceremony, a local reporter pointed out that Mrs. Tsukayama could have given the helmet to a local museum instead, and asked her, "This man could have killed your father, and yet you're returning his helmet to Japan. Why?" (Iida also could have killed Mrs. Tsukayama, who was eleven at the time and making poi with her grandmother and remembers bullets, perhaps ones fired by Lieutenant Iida, flying through her grandparents' banana patch.)

Mrs. Tsukayama told me she had given Mrs. Iida the helmet because she considered it a way of honoring her father's memory. But a few minutes later she admitted that her father, like many Chinese of his generation, had loathed the Japanese for the horrific atrocities they committed in China. He disliked them so passionately that in 1943 he had pitched a pan of food out the door because Tsukayama and her stepsisters had dared to cook it the Japanese way, with soy sauce. When his stepdaughters both married Japanese men, he disowned one, and the other divorced her husband to please him. He had refused to accept Mrs. Tsukayama's Japanese-American husband into the family until they gave him a grandson. Only then did the two men become close friends.

So why had Mr. Chun kept a Japanese helmet for twenty-six years? And why had he often spoken of returning it to Iida's family? And why did Mrs. Tsukayama, knowing how her father felt about the Japanese, believe returning it would somehow honor his memory?

The answer may be that for many years there has been a powerful urge, particularly in Hawaii, to find the right gesture, speech, or memorial to exorcise the Pearl Harbor ghosts, and that this urge is as mysterious, and contradictory, as the return of Lieutenant Iida's tattered helmet fifty-eight years after he last wore it.

CHAPTER 18

ONCE A JAPANESE, ALWAYS A JAPANESE

Fabulous and incredible stories explaining how bow-legged and nearsighted Japanese pilots could have scored such a magnificent triumph began circulating even before the last planes had departed. It was said Oahu's defenders had been befuddled by alcohol, stabbed in the back by fifth columnists and saboteurs, and that the Germans (another Caucasian people) had masterminded and participated in the raid.

Sailors in Pearl Harbor reported seeing swastikas painted on planes flown by blond pilots. Civilians on Aiea and Alewa Heights also saw Nazi planes, and among the "Rumors and Facts" jotted down that day by Mrs. Robert Thompson were "German shot down in Wahiawa, flying Japanese plane," and "H. K., who lives on Alewa Heights, saw the actual coming in of enemy planes from the sea; swears that those planes were German Stukas."

Harold Kay had such a superb view of the attack from his Alewa Heights home that Army Intelligence agents asked him to summarize his observations. He wrote, "The observer and his family gained the immediate conviction that the great majority of planes observed were German . . . The more experienced pilots, German in the observer's opinion, were assigned to the major objectives which were all stationary . . . The planes appeared to be operated with the skill and experience exceeding that attributable to the Japanese in general, leading to the conclusion that the attack was led by German pilots."

The *Chicago Tribune* reported on December 8 that many congressmen believed German pilots had carried out "the damaging blitzkrieg . . . in planes marked with swastikas." A December 9 *Star-Bulletin* story, headlined TALL AVIATOR OF ENEMY DOWNED; WAS HE GERMAN?, said the body of an aviator over six feet tall had been found in the wreckage of a Japanese plane and that "Reports from Hongkong quoted eye witnesses as saying a German was the pilot of one of the twenty-seven planes which raided Kowloon." The December 15 *Newsweek* carried an article by retired Admiral William Pratt asserting that, "Undoubtedly it [the attack] had its birth in Berlin, for it bears all the earmarks of the Nazi method of operation."

Even the Japanese consul general, Nagao Kita, discounted the abilities of Japan's military. He told American intelligence afterward he had not thought the attacking planes were Japanese because he did not believe Japan's navy could get so close to Hawaii undetected. Instead, he had believed a bizarre rumor that because of a deal between Japan and Nazi Germany, the pilots were Frenchmen belonging to the Vichy French air force in Vietnam. Kita was so convinced the planes were not Japanese he delayed burning his ciphers and correspondence.

A 1951 editorial in a small right-wing Chicago newspaper, *Women's Voice*, claimed the pilots attacking Pearl Harbor had been American and British, ordered into battle by Roosevelt and Churchill as part of their plot to drag the United States into the European war. Furthermore, on the evening of December 6 officers with drawn revolvers had prevented sailors boarding their ships, American soldiers had drained fuel from planes to keep them from fighting back, and a staff sergeant reported seeing "planes manned by white men, men whom I knew—British and Americans," adding that, "There seemed to be a few Japs, but the shooting was done by white men."

This is the most extreme example I have found of the revisionist fantasy that President Roosevelt orchestrated Pearl Harbor. According to this theory, Roosevelt wanted to provoke the Japanese into striking the first blow, so he instituted an oil embargo and demanded they cease their aggression against China. When he learned a Japanese task force was heading for Hawaii, he prevented Kimmel and Short from receiving the decoded Magic material that would have put them on the alert, thereby permitting the Japanese to kill 2,403 U.S. servicemen and cripple the Pacific fleet.

As delusions go, the one depicting FDR as architect of Pearl Harbor ranks with Lyndon Johnson planning the Kennedy assassination. It enjoyed its greatest popularity in the decade following the war and touched off a pamphlet war between Roosevelt's enemies and admirers. Former isolationists, implacable Roosevelt-haters, and many retired Army and Navy officers have embraced it because it absolves the armed forces and places all the blame on Roosevelt. Its propagandists have ranged from scoundrels like the author of the *Women's Voice* editorial to respected historians like John Toland, who considered it to be the most rational explanation for Washington's failures to share current intelligence with the Hawaiian commanders. It was revived in 2000 by Robert Stinnet's book *Day of Deceit— The Truth about FDR and Pearl Harbor*.

It is difficult arguing facts or logic with anyone who believes FDR was the archvillain of Pearl Harbor. The dynamics of large organizations are such that simply because on the morning of December 7 it became known at some levels in the Washington hierarchy that Japan was likely to attack some American base at 1:00 P.M. Washington time, it does not necessarily follow they all knew the base would be Pearl Harbor, or that the information was automatically available to President Roosevelt.

One can point out that even Rear Admiral Edwin Layton (Ret.), who was Kimmel's former fleet intelligence officer and is generally sympathetic to him, has written, "Our leaders in Washington *knew* by the evening of 6 December that Japan would launch into war in a matter of hours rather than days. Not a shred of evidence has been uncovered from all the declassified intelligence files to suggest that anyone suspected that Pearl Harbor would be the target."

One can argue that although Japan had to strike first, it was not necessary that this first strike result in an American catastrophe. Had Roosevelt and his advisors *really* known the location of the Japanese strike force, Kimmel and Short could easily have been alerted the day before, and inflicted serious losses on it, particularly since Admiral Nagumo had orders to press the attack even if American forces discovered his fleet within the final twenty-four hours. Furthermore, the simple fact of a Japanese task force coming so close to Hawaii would have been *casus belli* enough for most Americans.

Finally, one can argue that neither Roosevelt nor anyone else could have assumed that the Japanese attack on Pearl Harbor would result in the United States becoming involved in the European war. If anything, it made that goal more unlikely, because an aroused American public would only naturally demand that U.S. resources be concentrated on the Pacific War, and in extracting revenge for Pearl Harbor. Roosevelt's so-called "conspiracy" only worked because Hitler declared war on the United States on December 11.

One can argue all this, as I sometimes have to survivors who still blame Roosevelt rather than Kimmel and Short, and none of it matters, because underneath all the December 7 delusions is a stubborn racial and military pride, and a desperate need to explain Pearl Harbor without conceding victory to Japanese arms, or defeat to American overconfidence.

At first, Admiral Kimmel blamed himself. As he stood by a window at fleet headquarters, a spent .50-caliber machine-gun bullet flew into the room and struck him on the chest, leaving a dark splotch on his uniform. He picked it up, and said, "It would have been merciful had it killed me." Then he reached up and tore the four-star boards off his shoulders and reappeared from his office wearing his two-star boards. Later that day, he told two of his subordinates, "If I were in charge in Washington, I would relieve Kimmel at once. It doesn't make any difference why a man fails the Navy, he has failed."

The first of nine Pearl Harbor investigations was conducted by Supreme Court Justice Owen Roberts. His commission began holding hearings in Hawaii on December 22, five days after Kimmel and Short were relieved of their commands. A month later, Roberts delivered a report to President Roosevelt, placing most of the blame for Pearl Harbor on Kimmel and Short. Although the War Department was criticized for not telling Short that his antisabotage alert was not sufficient, and for emphasizing the possibility of aggressive Japanese action in the Far East, Kimmel and Short were charged with "dereliction of duty." Both men retired and reverted to their previous ranks as two-star officers, and when Congress enacted postwar legislation permitting officers to retire at their highest wartime ranks, specific exceptions were made so Kimmel and Short could not reclaim their four stars.

Kimmel soon changed his mind about his responsibility for Pearl Harbor, saying, "Since learning the definite information of the Japanese intention to attack Pearl Harbor was in the hands of the War and Navy Department and was not supplied to me, I now refuse to accept my responsibility for the catastrophe." Until his death, Kimmel waged a campaign to vindicate himself and lay responsibility for the defeat on FDR and the Navy and War Departments. At the time of the twenty-fifth anniversary, he told an interviewer, "My principal occupation—what's kept me alive—is to expose the entire Pearl Harbor affair." He maintained that Roosevelt, General Marshall, and others in Washington had made him a scapegoat, and charged that, "FDR was the architect of the whole business. He gave orders—and I can't prove this categorically—that no word about Japanese fleet movements was to be sent to Pearl Harbor except by Marshall, and then he told Marshall not to send anything." In a 1966 *Newsweek* interview published shortly before his death he declared that, "FDR and the top brass deliberately betrayed the American forces at Pearl Harbor."

In 1995 Kimmel and Short's descendants persuaded the U.S.

Senate Armed Services Committee to reexamine whether vital radio intercepts had been purposely denied to the Hawaiian commanders as part of a conspiracy to have America become involved in the war. They asked Congress to restore Kimmel and Short to their preattack ranks, thereby posthumously restoring their reputations. At the direction of the Senate, the Pentagon conducted an investigation and seven months later produced a report concluding that although blame for Pearl Harbor should be shared between Washington and Hawaii, Kimmel and Short had been guilty of serious errors of judgment warranting their demotion. In the words of the report, responsibility "should be broadly shared," but "the intelligence available to Admiral Kimmel and General Short was sufficient to justify a higher level of vigilance than they chose to maintain."

This opinion is supported by the results of nine separate Pearl Harbor investigations conducted by the Army, Navy, and Congress, and endorsed by the vast majority of reputable historians. Nevertheless, the tenacity of Short and Kimmel's descendants, combined with the current reluctance to hold individuals responsible for their errors, a predilection for bizarre conspiracy theories, right-wing resentment at Roosevelt's exalted place in twentieth-century history, and the need for a nonmilitary scapegoat for Pearl Harbor, have contributed to an attempt by the U.S. Congress in 2000 to rewrite history, and absolve Kimmel and Short of any blame for Pearl Harbor. A section of a defense appropriations bill approved on October 30, 2000, called on President Clinton to restore Kimmel and Short to their wartime ranks. Both Delaware senators, William Roth and Joseph Biden, sponsored the measure, presumably because of lobbying by Kimmel's son, Edward R. Kimmel, a retired Delaware attorney. A *New York Times* article said the bill's congressional supporters "seemed largely ignorant of the enveloping conspiracy theories and disavowed any intention of passing the buck to anyone."

The bill states that Kimmel and Short "were not provided necessary and critical intelligence that would have alerted them to prepare for the attack," which, by implication, puts the onus on the high command in Washington. It gives respectability to the theory that Pearl Harbor was the fruit of a conspiracy masterminded by FDR and his high command. It leads to the inescapable conclusion that despite having received numerous alerts in the weeks and days before the attack, the commanders responsible for having no long-reconnaissance planes in the air, leaving their warplanes parked on aprons instead of in revetments, permitting antiaircraft batteries to sit unmanned, and sending radar crews off duty at 7:00 A.M.—that these commanders, Kimmel and Short, bear no responsibility whatsoever for the resulting catastrophe.

Another hardy Pearl Harbor delusion is that a fifth column of Japanese living in Hawaii stabbed Oahu's defenders in the back. This lie began circulating during the attack and spread quickly throughout Honolulu, and is still believed by some civilian and military survivors. It was said local Japanese had cut telephone lines, signaled offshore submarines with blinker lights, used ham-radio sets to interfere with Army broadcasts, drawn large Oriental characters with a bulldozer across Sand Island, and carved arrows in cane fields to direct Japanese aviators to their targets. They had driven slowly on purpose and pretended to break down on the narrow two-lane roads leading to Pearl Harbor, in order to block traffic and prevent reinforcements and ambulances from reaching the base. It was said ammunition caches had been discovered on Japanese property, and sampans from Kewalo Basin had allegedly picked up downed flyers and provisioned Japanese submarines, explaining why a loaf of Love's bread was purportedly found on board Ensign Sakamaki's submarine, a vessel that was allegedly manufactured in Hawaii by Japanese-Americans and fueled by them from a secret depot on the remote north shore of Kauai.

The most bizarre rumor had dead Japanese fliers wearing Honolulu high-school letter sweaters under their flight jackets, and having pockets filled with dollars and Honolulu Rapid Transit tokens. Among Mrs. Robert Thompson's Rumors and Facts was that "some of the aviators who attacked that Sunday were island boys." A colonel she knew had seen a McKinley High School ring on a dead Japanese pilot, and she speculated that Kurusu (the Japanese envoy) must have given the local boys instructions when he stopped in Honolulu the month before. They had then sailed out to the carriers in sampans on December 6 and flown back the next morning.

The most vicious rumors claimed local Japanese had driven a truck down the flight line at Wheeler, disabling fighters by smashing off their tail sections. In 1943, *Collier's* reported that, "Fifteen minutes before the first bombs fell . . . a Jap dairy truck entered Hickam Field to deliver milk. After it had reached a point in front of the barracks, the driver stopped and pretended to fix his engine. As our pilots rushed out to man their planes, the sides of the truck fell off and six Japs hiding in it with machine guns were able to kill eight Americans before they themselves were shot."

Some rumors had a tenuous factual basis. The genesis of the dairy-truck story was an incident at Hickam Field in which two teenage Japanese defense workers burned their hands while feeding ammunition into a machine gun. After helping to down a plane they ripped the insignia off the uniforms of the dead crew and brought them to Naval Intelligence, boasting they had come off "the damned Jap fliers."

Traffic on the Pearl Harbor road was indeed congested on December 7, but by servicemen rushing back to their bases and civilians evacuating areas under attack. And it was congested again that evening as motorists drove home in the blackout without headlights. An experimental cane field in Ewa had recently been harvested, leaving a bare spot with a diagonal that could have been mistaken for an arrow pointing at Pearl Harbor. The rumor of poisoned drinking water started when a woman suffered an epileptic fit at a downtown drinking fountain. The Japanese voices jamming radio frequencies came from a commercial Japanese-language station in Argentina. Fires allegedly set to signal to Japanese submarines were cane fires ignited by antiaircraft shells and a downed power line. The so-called "signal lights" to Japanese submarines resulted from loose window shades, open doors, and the reflection of the moon on skylights. The story of local Japanese boys participating in the attack was later traced back to the mysterious disappearance of two young nisei boys from Honolulu in the spring of 1941. It turned out that Army Intelligence had sent them to the Philippines to infiltrate the alien Japanese community there.

The rumors seem preposterous now, but they placed every Japanese resident under suspicion. After the attack, police and military switchboards received reports of "a Japanese man who does not understand English," and "Japanese holding a meeting," who turned out to be a Japanese family buying groceries. Colonel Bicknell reported that, "In the minds of many people every local Japanese became an enemy agent or saboteur," and that "Desire for revenge upon any and all individuals of Japanese blood was frequently expressed . . . from wishing to shoot each Jap on sight to devising the most lingering form of death."

A nisei maid overheard speaking Japanese on the telephone on December 8 was dismissed by her Caucasian employer who explained, "I won't have any Jap plotting against me and my country within my own home."

On December 9, the driver of a military truck swerved to the shoulder and tried to run down a middle-aged Japanese laborer while his passengers shouted, "Kill him! Kill the dirty Jap!"

On December 10, a Filipino drove his panel truck to Pearl Harbor and told Marine Lieutenant Cornelius Smith, Jr., "Got four Japs in truck, no good man, I kill them!" Smith went outside and found them, he reported, "dead as mackerel, throats slashed from ear to ear."

Senior officials also believed the rumors about Japanese sabotage. Governor Poindexter told President Roosevelt on December 7 that local Japanese posed the main danger to the Islands. Minutes later, General Short informed Poindexter that Japanese landing parties were en route, and Poindexter responded by calling in FBI agent Shivers to discuss rounding up every Japanese in Honolulu.

On December 11, Lieutenant Smith, after spending several

days confiscating Japanese ham radios in Aiea Heights, concluded that, "One thing is shaping up; there was fifth column work attending this raid—probably a lot of it."

Navy Secretary Knox arrived on Oahu that same day and spent two hours with General Short who, having based his defense of the island on the presumption of sabotage, was determined to convince Washington it had occurred. Short's description of mythical Japanese fifth column activities led Knox to report to Roosevelt, "The activities of Japanese fifth columnists immediately following the attack took the form of spreading on the air by radio dozens of confusing and contradictory rumors concerning the direction in which the attacking planes had departed." When Knox's report was made public on December 15, General Short's desperate hand could be seen in its conclusion that "The most effective 'fifth column' work of the entire war was done in Hawaii, with the possible exception of Norway."

Within ten days of the attack the official position began changing. The *Star-Bulletin*, FBI, and military governor of Hawaii all declared there had not been a single proved case of espionage or sabotage by Japanese residents of the territory. The *Star-Bulletin* editorial of December 16 attacked the "weird, amazing, and damaging untruths" circulated by military dependents evacuated from Hawaii and printed in mainland newspapers. On December 17, General Delos Emmons, in his first broadcast as the new military governor, said no act of sabotage had been committed in Hawaii during or after the attack. In April, 1942, FBI Director J. Edgar Hoover confirmed it, and a month later Secretary of War Henry Stimson announced that, "The War Department has received no information of sabotage committed by Japanese during the attack on Pearl Harbor, and no evidence of sabotage in Hawaii." A year after that, Colonel Kendall Fielder, still in charge of military intelligence in Hawaii, stated he was "surprised to learn that some of the many Island rumors about the Hawaiian Islands during the first few days of the war are still prevalent on the mainland."

On Hawaii it became accepted that the sabotage stories were false, but they continued circulating anyway on the mainland. Representative Rankin of Mississippi argued in Congress that the internment of every Japanese was justified because "the Japs who had been there [in Hawaii] for generations were making signs, if you please, guiding the Japanese planes to their objects of iniquity." He added, "I say it is of vital importance to get rid of every Japanese whether in Hawaii or on the mainland. They violate every sacred promise, every canon of honor and decency. Do not forget that once a Japanese, always a Japanese."

Editorial writers and columnists like Westbrook Pegler and Walter Lippmann repeated the sabotage stories, and *Time* magazine claimed that Honolulu "teemed" with Japanese spies. Its January 5, 1942, issue alleged that, "In the 159,905 Japanese in the Hawaiian Islands (more than one-third of the population), Tokyo had plenty of talent . . . Fed on tolerance, watered by complacency, the Jap fifth column had done its job fiendishly well and had not been stamped out."

Two weeks later, *Time* reported that, "In the minds of many of Hawaii's 105,000 haoles (whites) invasion loomed as a very real threat. What would the Islands' Japanese do then? Islanders who remembered that Jap high-school boys from Hawaii had helped pilot the planes that attacked Pearl Harbor looked uneasily at Hawaii's thousands going freely, imperturbably about their business. What about the houseboy, the cop on the corner, the farmer down the road? What about the Japs [in the Hawaii Territorial Guard] set to guard the Islands?"

The sabotage rumors were used to justify the imposition of martial law. According to notes made on December 7 by the Secretary of Hawaii, Charles M. Hite, General Short had appeared at Governor Poindexter's offices in the Iolani Palace at about 1245 "obviously under great strain." He had requested and urged martial law, saying for all he knew landing parties were en route. He argued that martial law was necessary to prevent espionage and sabotage, and promised that if the attack was not a prelude to a landing it would be lifted "within a reasonably short time."

After signing the declaration, Poindexter told Hite he had never hated doing anything so much in all his life. A month later, he told the Roberts Commission he had only agreed because the Army had advanced the argument that Hawaii's large Japanese population could be better handled by military than civil authorities.

Martial law gave Hawaii's military governor a monopoly on legislative, judicial, and executive power, and freed him from observing the laws of the Territory of Hawaii or the U.S. Constitution. (The United States Supreme Court later ruled that the imposition of martial law had been illegal.) Hawaii's military government was a peculiarly American institution, the final fruit of an obsession with internal security and subversion. Press censorship was total, military trials usually resulted in a guilty verdict, and those disobeying curfew and blackout regulations had to buy war bonds or donate blood. Wages and employment were frozen and absenteeism became an imprisonable offense. Military regulations this harsh were never imposed in Britain, even during the worst months of the Blitz, when civilians were attacked nightly and Germany was preparing a cross-Channel invasion.

The Army offered the continuing danger of espionage and sabotage as justification for keeping martial law after the June 1942 victory at Midway made a Japanese invasion of the Islands impossible. Some military officers argued that the very absence of sabotage or espionage on December 7 was evidence of a sinister cunning, a view echoed by the 1944 Army Pearl Harbor Board, which concluded, "It is obvious that the reason why the Japanese aliens did not commit sabotage was that they did not want to stimulate American activity to stop their espionage and intern them."

The Pearl Harbor sabotage rumors also fed anti-Japanese hysteria on the mainland, and provided one of the principal rationales for the mass internment of West Coast Japanese-Americans. Responding to this injustice, dozens of prominent Hawaii residents signed affidavits denouncing the sabotage rumors and attesting to the loyalty of the local Japanese. Chief of Police William Gabrielson swore that "no authenticated case of sabotage of any kind whatsoever or evidence of fifth column activities on the part of alien Japanese or citizens of Japanese ancestry on the island of Oahu has been found." John Midkiff of the Waialua sugar plantation testified he had found no evidence of arrows cut in the cane fields and did not see any Japanese drivers "park vehicles across the roads or do any act which might lead to confusion or place others in danger."

The 1943 *Collier's* article about the treacherous Japanese milk truck prompted the *Advertiser* to comment that, "The 'Jap dairy truck story' has . . . been repeatedly exposed as just another of the countless Pearl Harbor yarns, rumors and canards that took to the air on and after December, 1941. But the story still keeps bobbing up like an uneasy ghost."

There were economic and political motivations behind these editorials and affidavits. Business interests feared labor shortages if Hawaii's Japanese residents were interned, and politicians worried the sabotage rumors might become a powerful argument against Hawaiian statehood.

On the mainland, the rumors continued to proliferate. A 1942 Hollywood film, *Air Force*, depicted local Japanese firing on an American plane after it made an emergency landing on Maui on December 7. A character in the film asserted that during the attack on Oahu, trucks driven by Japanese vegetable farmers had driven along a runway, smashing the tails off a line of fighter planes. Military authorities in Hawaii censored those inflammatory scenes before *Air Force* was shown in the Islands.

In her 1950 book *Hawaii's War Years*, author Gwenfread Allen reported that, "Many islanders discount official denials and still believe such stories as the one about the prominent Honolulu Japanese who, kimono-clad, waved a Japanese flag to the attacking planes, and the equally fantastic tale about the owner of a uniform of 'the Japanese military governor of the Islands,' who was prepared on December 7 to assume control under direction of Hirohito."

More than fifty years after the attack, I encountered stories about Japanese disloyalty and sabotage. A Navy survivor insisted that Japanese workers at KGMB had played music throughout the night of December 6 to provide a radio beacon for Japanese pilots. Another survivor said the owner of a tavern near Schofield Barracks had been a commander in the Japanese navy, and used a shortwave radio to beam Japanese pilots to Pearl Harbor. A Caucasian civilian who witnessed the attack as a boy and believed there had been sabotage on December 7, said, "The loyalty of the Japanese is bullshit. The Japanese who enlisted and fought in Europe during the war just thought it was a great opportunity to go and kill haoles." And even civilian and military witnesses who denounced the sabotage stories as lies sometimes mentioned shortwave radios in Japanese homes, and Japanese maids failing to appear for work on December 7. Even they could not entirely abandon the comforting fiction that the treachery of local Japanese had somehow contributed to the humiliation of Pearl Harbor.

CHAPTER 19

A DEEP SHOCK WAVE

"Surprise is an ineffectual word to describe our feelings," a civilian witness to the attack wrote twenty years later. "It was a kind of surprise so tremendous that it was like a deep shock wave going through us."

Navy wife Peggy Ryan remembered that within minutes, a small crowd of young Navy wives and small children, still in nightclothes, had gathered in her lane and were looking wonderingly at the sky, and at each other. "Probably we were in a state of shock," she concluded.

This word, "shock," is used frequently to describe the moment someone realized the attack was not an exercise but, "the Real McCoy," as Webley Edwards announced on KGMB. The shock was magnified by the unexpectedness of it all. Hawaiians no more expected a Japanese raid than Californians did. Seconds before, they had been listening to the radio, sleeping off hangovers, taking showers, praying in church, or dressing their children; one moment seeing an ocean and sky that had never before offered a surprise, the next swimming through burning oil or diving for cover.

The shock was particularly traumatic for military wives who had just seconds to embrace and exchange last words with husbands hurrying to join a battle in progress. Afterward, they watched the attack from their homes, knowing the explosions they were seeing might be claiming the lives of their husbands. There are some similarities in their situation to the first Battle of Bull Run, when civilians, including the wives of some of the troops, drove out in carriages from Washington to watch the battle. But those women had a chance to say more leisurely good-byes, and had chosen to witness the battle.

Wives and children living at Pearl Harbor's Mapalapa Junior Officers Housing took shelter in a deep railway cutting below their quarters. Most of the thirty-two women were in their bathrobes. Their children wore pajamas. When the last Japanese planes departed, they held a meeting and decided to return home to change diapers and feed their children. Their quarters were spread across the top of a hill overlooking the harbor. According to Charles Ide, who was nine years old at the time, when the wives saw the devastation below, "They just stood there and stared, some began to cry, some fell on their knees to pray, others began to get hysterical. Were their husbands alive or dead? They never felt so alone and helpless."

Journalist Joseph C. Harsch encountered a distraught military wife at the Royal Hawaiian Hotel. The sight of naval officers and their wives calmly eating breakfast while a ship, visible through the windows, was zigzagging and dodging bomb splashes confirmed his impression that the commotion was only a drill. Suddenly, an hysterical woman ran into the dining room shouting, "The battleships are burning! I saw red balls under their wings! They were shooting at our car! I was taking my husband down to his ship!"

Mary Ellen and Wells Lawrence woke when low-flying Japanese planes rattled the Venetian blinds in their quarters at Wheeler Field. They dashed next door to the home of his flight leader. At first, the two couples were "frozen with shock," Wells Lawrence told me, uncertain what to do next. As they stood in the living room, a bullet flew through the ceiling and nicked the floor between their feet, throwing sparks at their legs. The men ordered their wives to take cover behind the fireplace wall and turned for the door. Mary Ellen grabbed her husband for a last embrace, and told him, "Come back!"

She had reason to be concerned. The smoke of other burning planes had camouflaged many of the single-seater P-36s in his squadron. Lawrence readied one with ammunition, but as he was requesting orders from his squadron commander, another pilot jumped into the plane and took off. He was immediately killed in a dogfight, while Lawrence survived.

Navy Lieutenant Bernard Clarey was eating breakfast with his wife and fifteen-month-old son in their home on Moanalua Heights. He thought the exploding shells came from some terrible accident at the ammunition dump at Ewa. When a spectacular explosion at Hickam launched a bomber through the roof of a hangar he decided a shell from Ewa must have landed there.

As the explosions continued he became increasingly uneasy. He asked his wife to drive him to Pearl Harbor so he could report to his submarine. They put their son in the backseat of the roadster, something he would never have done had he imagined the truth. A block past his house, they passed civilian cars loaded with toys and clothes speeding in the other direction. Some had baby buggies strapped on top. They reminded Clarey of the newsreels of refugee caravans in Europe. As he turned onto the Kamehameha Highway he saw the *Arizona* in flames. He told his wife to leave him. Their tone of voice changed as their conversation turned serious, and the atmosphere was so charged that their infant son began crying hysterically.

Pearl Harbor flashbacks remain so powerful and disturbing because what happened that day was so shocking and unexpected. One moment a sailor was brushing his teeth, the next he was blasted into the water or chased by Japanese bullets. A man told me he recalled his father returning from Pearl Harbor stinking of gasoline, and still had 1941 flashbacks whenever he filled up his car. Several survivors admit to still jerking their heads skyward at the sound of a low-flying plane, and instinctively checking its markings.

A private from Hickam Field was evacuated from Hawaii crying and hallucinating. Twenty-five years later, he remained a patient at a Veterans Administration psychiatric hospital, under constant sedation, and responding to any mention of Pearl Harbor by saying, "Noises, noises, noises. Just another day. Leave me alone."

Bernard Clarey became a rear admiral and commander of the Pacific Fleet submarine force. In 1963, he had the job of welcoming a Japanese submarine to Pearl Harbor. He told me, "To have to greet them as friends and train them . . . well, let's just say I had mixed emotions about it." The Rising Sun flag on one of the submarines "suddenly brought back all the events of December 7."

Ensign Ike Sutton spent the morning racing across the harbor in Admiral Bloch's launch, pulling wounded and dying sailors from the water. His December 7 memory flashes include being strafed by Japanese planes, dead sailors wearing dress whites, because they had been at religious services, his life vest smeared with blood, and the skin of burned men coming off in his hands. When he woke screaming in the night, as he still did for over fifty years, it was because he had seen the faces of the men who had died because he had decided to wait until the launch was full of wounded before racing to Hospital Point.

The shock was so great for Carl Carlson that not until he was dying of cancer almost sixty years later did he offer to tell his story to Daniel Martinez, a National Park Service historian assigned to the *Arizona* Memorial. Carlson had been in the number three gun turret on the *Arizona* when it exploded. When he regained consciousness, he stretched out a hand and touched a flashlight. He used it to lead his shipmates to safety, then swam through burning water to a mooring quay, and then to shore, where he saw a man whose fire-blackened skin was flapping as he walked. Martinez asked Carlson if he wanted his ashes scattered over the *Arizona*, as other survivors of that battleship had. Carlson said no, after almost burning to death on December 7 he could never consider cremation.

The most frightening and enduring Pearl Harbor memories seem to afflict survivors who, like Ike Sutton, swam through Pearl Harbor or helped pull men from waters that had become a witches' brew of body parts, life rafts, burning fuel, corpses, and wounded.

No single sailor probably spent more time in the water than Sterling Cale, who swam for two to three hours while hoisting dead and wounded sailors onto a barge. He did not discover just how much Pearl Harbor haunted him until six years later, when he was serving as chief medical officer at the navy rifle range at Puuloa Point on Oahu. During a family picnic a sneaker wave suddenly washed his two-year-old son out to sea. The boy had been sitting on a flimsy picnic table and was able to cling to it. Cale jumped into the water for the first time since the attack and immediately froze, unable to move his arms or legs. Finally the family dog, a veteran of the canine corps, swam out and grabbed the boy by the seat of his pants. Cale has not attempted to swim since. He becomes nauseous if he approaches the water, and refuses to walk along a beach with his wife.

He appears less affected by his experiences aboard the *Arizona*, and believes this may be because the corpses he collected on it proved to be only a fraction of those he later encountered during a military career spanning three decades. During World War II, he saw hundreds of dead Americans and Japanese while serving as a medic with the 1st Marine Division at Guadalcanal and Saipan. Shortly before the Korean War, he transferred to the army and was involved in some of its most bitter and costly battles, including the retreat from the Choisin Reservoir. He then served four tours of duty in Vietnam as a translator, medical officer, province senior advisor, and intelligence agent seconded to the CIA. After retiring from the army he was hired by the State Department and sent back to Vietnam as the deputy director of a regional public health division. It was in this capacity that he became the first American civilian official on the scene of the My Lai massacre, arriving before the bodies had been buried.

I first met Richard Fiske, the former Marine bugler on the *West Virginia*, in 1990. We sat on a bench at the *Arizona* Memorial visitor center, facing Ford Island and the mooring quay that had anchored his battleship. Because he has been a volunteer guide at the memorial, I had assumed it would be easy for him to sit with me and recount his Pearl Harbor experiences. He had brought an album with faded black-and-white photographs of his former shipmates. As he turned its pages his voice cracked and his eyes watered. "When I moved back to Hawaii and came out here, I had no idea it would be such an emotional experience," he admitted. "My first day as a volunteer was awful because I kept reliving the attack and breaking down."

He showed me a picture of Ford Island, taken from this very shoreline and showing much the same view as we had today. "Except for the palm trees being taller it's the same," he agreed, flicking his eyes between his album and the island; between 1941 and the present. "Sometimes I look out there and, honest to Pete, I *see* those planes coming in."

After Pearl Harbor, Fiske fought at Iwo Jima, becoming one of six men from a thirty-four-man platoon to survive a month of combat unscathed. While working at the *Arizona* Memorial one day he met Mrs. Sugawara, who had lost three brothers on Iwo Jima. She threw her arms around him and uttered a long wail, then handed him an envelope containing a ten-dollar bill, a gift that still puzzles him.

One day a Chinese woman approached him, her face contorted with hate. "Mr. Fiske, how can you allow the dirty Japs to come aboard this ship?" she demanded.

He described his experiences at Pearl Harbor and Iwo Jima, saying that after spending so many years at the memorial, and seeing so many Japanese visitors, he had at last come to forgive them.

She shook her head. Japanese soldiers had murdered her parents and grandparents. "No!" she said, "After all that, you should hate them as I do."

"If you have so much hate in your heart, there's no room for love," Fiske replied. But it was obvious she disagreed. Unarmed civilians who have suffered atrocities are always slower to forgive a former enemy than soldiers who can fight back.

Fiske despised the Japanese until 1965, when he almost died from a bleeding ulcer. Before discharging him from the hospital, his military doctor said, "I can cure your stomach but not your head," and suggested he was carrying around so much hatred it made him ill. Fiske unburdened himself. By the time that doctor left his room he was bawling like a baby. "And that's the day I began to become human again," Fiske says.

Now on weekends he sometimes flies above Pearl Harbor with his Japanese-American son-in-law, who likes to practice touch-and-go landings on Ford Island. He sees the harbor as the Japanese pilots did on December 7. Could he—could anyone?—have imagined this in 1941? Or imagine his only granddaughter would be half-Japanese, "a little doll" he loves to pieces? Or that he would spend his retirement guiding Japanese tourists through a memorial to Pearl Harbor that is also Jones and Finley's grave?

The fiftieth anniversary of the attack was another watershed for Fiske. A delegation of Japanese Pearl Harbor pilots came to Honolulu and Fiske met Zenji Abe, the bomber pilot who had attacked the *West Virginia* and had organized the Japan Friends of Pearl Harbor, and Takeshi Maeada and Hirata Matsumura, who had torpedoed the *West Virginia*. Either pilot might, or might not, have been the one Fiske locked eyes with on December 7.

Fiske believes he and the Japanese pilots were drawn to one another. They spent December 7 signing autographs and posing for photographs. As they parted, Abe put his arm around Fiske, and said, "Richard-san, please do me this favor, taking this $300 and buy two roses and take them out to the *Arizona* every month and blow taps. This is my simple way of saying I am so very sorry."

Throughout the 1990s Abe sent Fiske money for flowers, and every month Fiske brought a red and a white rose out to the *Arizona* Memorial. He tossed them into the water and blew the American and Japanese versions of taps. During the 1990s, he traveled to Japan seven times at the invitation of his Japanese friends, blowing taps at the Hiroshima Memorial and other Japanese sites, and meeting the retired engineer who designed the torpedoes used at Pearl Harbor. The Japanese pilots returned several times to Honolulu. Mr. Maeada brought his grandchildren so they could become friends with Fiske's grandchildren, a relationship both men believe will continue after their deaths. In 1996, Fiske met the Japanese Emperor at the consulate. Several months later, the Emperor awarded him the Order of the Rising Sun, Silver Ray in recognition of his efforts at promoting Japanese-American friendship.

The shock of December 7 also explains the Pearl Harbor Survivors Association. I have met several members at the *Arizona* Memorial, where they work as volunteers, answering questions and introducing the documentary. The first time they invited me to attend a meeting of the Aloha Chapter, I imagined a version of the VFW, or one of the other fraternal World War II groups organized around warships, flight wings, and combat divisions. But the PHSA is different. The Aloha Chapter meeting I attended was a Sunday brunch at the Pearl Harbor officers' club held months before the fiftieth anniversary. The seventeen survivors attending it wore matching green aloha shirts and had brought wives, children, and grandchildren— several of them Japanese-Americans. They were an attractive and relaxed group of elderly men and included a former Army private, a pilot, a Marine Corps bugler (Richard Fiske), an artillery corporal, and a rear admiral. None had known one another on December 7. Some had almost been killed, others had been miles from the fighting.

I could understand why men sharing months of combat would travel thousands of miles to meet again and reminisce, or why those sharing a military triumph might want to remember it. But these Pearl Harbor Survivors had built one of the most active veterans' organizations in the nation on the foundation of a two-hour catastrophic defeat. They held five-year reunions in Hawaii, biennial national reunions, yearly district and state reunions, and monthly chapter meetings. They sponsored a golf tournament and a ham-radio network. They sold PHSA hats, decals, belt buckles, coffee mugs, official rings designed in a "fireburst pattern," and "My Grandfather Is a Member of the PHSA" T-shirts. Their quarterly magazine, the *Pearl Harbor-Gram*, had grown from twelve pages in 1960 to over forty in the 1990s. At the time of the fiftieth anniversary they had more than ten thousand members, 10 percent of the military personnel present on Oahu on December 7, and twice as many as in the early seventies.

At the Aloha Chapter brunch the members sang "Happy Birthday Dear Survivor" and decided to pay for the Aloha Chapter to be listed in the telephone book so visiting mainland survivors could contact them. They discussed the PHSA license-plate bill that was slowly moving through the Hawaii legislature (it has since passed), and the meeting closed with a survivor saying, "We must remember the reason we exist is to keep America alert—so if anyone has any ideas how we can do this better, well, just let me know."

Mainland survivors have seized on Hawaii as the common ground and wear aloha shirts to reunions featuring luaus. They have adopted a political agenda in keeping with their motto, "Remember Pearl Harbor—Keep America Alert," petitioning Congress to declare December 7 a "National Remembrance Day," and to provide a medal for any veteran present on Oahu during the attack. They lobby state legislatures to provide license plates identifying the driver as a Pearl Harbor Survivor, and greet each Secretary of the Navy with letters demanding a warship be named the U.S.S. *Pearl Harbor*, at first receiving polite replies to the effect that "while this name indeed signifies the selfless bravery and heroism of many Americans, it must be said that it does not represent a significant victory in the sense normally memorialized in the assignment of a ship name." The most extraordinary thing about campaigns like these is that they often begin years after the attack, so that California and Alaska, for example, did not start issuing survivor license plates until 1988, and it was not until 1996 that the Navy acceded to the survivors' demands and launched the U.S.S. *Pearl Harbor*.

The survivors have traditionally argued for a strong defense and have been staunchly anti-Communist. They have also been quick to take issue with anyone arguing against the use of atomic bombs to end the war. They keep a competitive eye on Hiroshima Day, and one *Gram* editorial complained that Americans seem to pay more attention to the anniversary of Hiroshima than Pearl Harbor. Another issue had a long article about a Japanese delegation that had visited the high school in Richland, Washington, to object to its symbol, a mushroom cloud celebrating the town's role in the production of nuclear arms, including the plutonium that destroyed Nagasaki. The high-school principal walked out of a meeting with the Japanese after reminding them that America had not started the war. The story was subtitled, "High School Principal Takes a Stand on His Own Principles."

The business of a meeting of the PHSA executive board revolves around questions like, "Should the PHSA handbook be put in the master ring binder?" "Should the 6th district be permitted to transfer the PHSA emblem onto hats to be worn at the district convention?" "Should the Olympic Peninsula Chapter of Bremerton, Washington, be allowed to put the PHSA emblem on a recreational vehicle flag?" But strip away the luaus and souvenirs and you are left with what brings the survivors together: the conviction that they have witnessed the most important event in twentieth-century American history, and that nothing in their lives since equals the shock of December 7.

CHAPTER 20

HOW COULD THEY
DO THIS TO ME?

The thing the Japanese of Hawaii feared most had happened, leaving them threatened by angry neighbors, panicky soldiers, and a possible enemy invasion. They were as shocked by the suddenness of the raid as anyone, dismayed by Caucasians who questioned their loyalty, and furious at Japan for putting them in this precarious position.

Japanese maids ran home to remove their kimonos and returned in haole clothes. Some were too embarrassed to face their employers again, and never returned. One maid told her employer, "I am so ashamed, I wish I could change my face."

Novelist Margaret MacKay, a longtime resident of Honolulu, described Sumi, the maid of a friend, as "a good, neat little person" who had been "content to dress in the disciplined way required by the old Honolulu families, in kimono, sash and sandals." Sumi stood at the window, staring at the burning harbor, refusing to speak. The next morning, she appeared in a crisp white-linen dress to serve breakfast, and said, "If you please, I not wear kimono anymore. I am American."

Some Japanese fell into the Oriental habit of concealing their embarrassment with smiles and laughter. William Diem drove his family up the Kamehameha Highway to escape the attack. They stopped at a crest with a spectacular view of the harbor, the same spot where Bob Kinzler had seen the burning battleships. Diem noticed that one of the other spectators was "an elderly Jap with a grin on his face from ear to ear."

Angry servicemen expelled Japanese-American defense workers from Pearl Harbor at bayonet point, and removed Japanese nurses from hospitals so they would not touch Americans wounded by Japanese bullets. Japanese pedestrians were cursed and punched, and it was said Filipino cane cutters were sharpening their machetes.

A handful of Japanese rejoiced. An inebriated man on Kauai praised the attack, and some rural grammar-school children shouted "Banzai!" A Japanese man on the isolated Hawaiian island of Niihau helped a downed Japanese flier terrorize the native Hawaiian populace. Ida Spear, who had been eight years old and living with her family in a mountainside home twelve miles from Pearl Harbor, insisted to me that she had seen Japanese neighbors waving Japanese flags and shouting "Banzai!"

Such incidents were rare, but often repeated and exaggerated. Far more common were Japanese like the boy who told his parents, "The Japanese are rats for attacking us when Japan and the United States were in the midst of peace negotiations," and the one who wondered, "Where were our planes?"—using the word "our" without imagining anyone would question which planes he meant.

Ted Tsukiyama, a junior at the University of Hawaii, woke to thunderous explosions and wondered, *Am I really hearing this? How could they be so stupid? They're crazy! They're attacking the USA! Who the hell do they think they are?* When he heard that Governor Poindexter had placed the University of Hawaii ROTC under the Territorial Guard he threw on his uniform and headed for the Manoa campus. "I had no second thoughts, not one, about putting on that uniform," he told me. "The enemy was attacking. Our outfit was about 80 percent Japanese, and on December 7 no one was thinking, 'Hey, we can't trust you because you're Japanese.' "

As he arrived, his instructors were fitting firing pins in the cadets' Springfield rifles. His company was deployed along Manoa Stream, and ordered to defend Honolulu from Japanese paratroopers who were supposedly approaching from St. Louis Heights. Tsukiyama told the *Star-Bulletin*, "There was no doubt or indecision as we advanced, it was going to be either 'them or us.' " He told me, "We were scared shitless, but we felt proud to be defending our country. I wanted to punch and kick the first damned Japanese I saw."

Another ROTC cadet, Ralph Yempuku, was the only one of five brothers who elected not to return to Japan with his parents when they left Hawaii in 1934 due to his father's poor health. He became intramural sports director at the University of Hawaii and on the morning of December 7 was at the Ala Moana Hotel, preparing to escort the Willamette football team on a sight-seeing tour. Two Navy pilots ran down the steps of the hotel, buttoning shirts and shouting they needed a ride to Pearl Harbor. Yempuku drove them in his car, stopping at a pharmacy to buy Bromo-Seltzer for their hangovers. At the Pearl Harbor gate he saw dead bodies piled in trucks like sardines.

Yempuku considered himself an American with the misfortune to resemble the enemy. "There's no way I can change it," he told his fellow cadets on December 7. "Until the day I die I'm going to look like a Jap!" He was *angry* at the Japanese, but not just because they had attacked his hometown, but because the raid was so embarrassing for him, and he admits having thought, *How can they do this to me?*

Future U.S. Senator Daniel Inouye was a senior at McKinley High School. As he biked to the first-aid station at Lunalilo School to help the wounded he passed groups of frightened Japanese civilians. He thought, *They worked so hard. They wanted so desperately to be accepted, to be good Americans. And now, in a few cataclysmic minutes, it was all undone.* He realized he was in trouble, too, and looked up, and shouted, "You dirty Japs!"

Spud Ishimoto was a mechanic at Pearl Harbor and had excellent relations with his haole coworkers. When the attack started, he dived behind a pile of lumber. He spent the rest of the day rescuing sailors and repairing engines. He returned home to find his father preparing to hand over the family's most prized possession, a Japanese ceremonial sword.

George Akita, the prize-winning student orator, wrote of hearing, "the rat-tat-tat of a machine gun from a swooping plane." He headed to church anyway and was almost killed by a shell exploding near the Schumann Carriage Company. At Sunday school he and the other students, most of them Japanese, sang, "Are we downhearted? No! No! No! Are we downhearted? No! No! No!" At the end of the day he wrote, "We have to be brave. This crisis will test out our guts and gumption."

Nancy Sato was terrified of being strafed by Japanese planes. As she ran home people were cursing the "damned Japs." But whom did they mean, she wondered? The Japanese pilots? Herself? Both? The worst part was no longer being accepted for what she was—an American—and knowing she would always be a "Jap." That afternoon, she threw her Japanese-language books into a bonfire.

Sue Isonaga was spending the weekend of December 7 with FBI agent Robert Shivers and his wife Corinne at their home near Diamond Head. She had started working as the Shiverses' housekeeper when she was a high-school student. The Shiverses had just arrived in Hawaii and had little previous contact with Orientals, but within months they had all become close friends. The Shiverses were unable to have children, Isonaga's father had died, and soon they were treating her like a daughter, and introducing her to everyone as "our child." She had started working as a teacher a few months before, but stayed with them on weekends. Shivers's last words to his wife on December 7 were, "Don't let Sue out of your sight."

When Isonaga heard a radio bulletin announcing the attack she burst into tears. She joined Corinne Shivers on the lawn, stunned to see Japanese markings on the planes. Diamond Head was a military installation, and a potential target. An FBI agent evacuated them to a house in Manoa Valley where the haole women were hysterical and a man passing out revolvers shouted, "At the sight of a Jap, don't ask questions, shoot to kill!"

"I have never forgotten that moment," Isonaga says.

She also remembers that later, when she worked at the Kahuku emergency feeding station, a woman accused her of trying to poison everyone, and when she was waiting to buy a movie ticket she overheard a Portuguese girl saying, "If it wasn't for these damn Japs, we wouldn't have to stand in line." One day, a Filipino man ran after her, cursing and shouting, "Because of you Japs Bataan fell." She shouted back, "I had nothing to do with the fall of Bataan, and if you keep going on, I'll report you to the FBI. I was raised here and I'm an American citizen."

When Japanese planes strafed Private Tom Tsubota at Waimanalo Beach he wondered if he knew the pilot. He had returned to Honolulu six months before, leaving Tokyo after his university instructor warned he would never pass his examinations unless he joined the military. At that moment he realized he would rather die for the USA than Japan.

Richard Ishimoto had a weekend pass and was staying with his parents in downtown Honolulu. He jumped on a bus heading for Schofield Barracks. Outside Hickam Field an hysterical MP boarded the bus and jabbed him with a rifle, screaming, "The Japs blew up my buddy!" Ishimoto showed the MP his military identification card, and this calmed him.

Edwin Kawahara was returning from the latrine to his Schofield Barracks tent when the Japanese hit Wheeler Field. He was one of thirteen hundred nisei draftees and volunteers under arms in Hawaii on December 7. Like all niseis born before 1926, he had been registered at birth at the Japanese consulate and had dual citizenship. But unlike many, he had renounced his Japanese citizenship when he turned eighteen.

He hurried to company headquarters, where he found his deputy company commander, Lieutenant Robert Louis Stevenson, who removed the cipher and division field codes from the office safe and handed them to Kawahara, saying, "Edwin, guard these with your life."

Kawahara still treasures this moment, saying, "It was magnificent to be the recipient of such total trust. I knew then that my love for the USA had been right all along."

Stevenson has no recollection of the incident because it had never occurred to him not to trust Kawahara. Stevenson is a third-generation kamaaina whose mother's family admired the Scottish author Robert Louis Stevenson. He had absorbed Hawaii's traditional racial attitudes, which were far more tolerant than those of mainland soldiers. His company, formerly in the Hawaii Territorial Guard, was 60 percent Japanese. There were no racial tensions and the only incident he recalls from before the war involved the refusal of Regular Army officers to admit non-Caucasian Territorial Guard officers to their club. This so angered the guard's commander, Colonel Wilhelm Andersen, that he boycotted the club and built a multiracial one.

Stevenson's most vivid December 7 memory is of a Private Nakamura, who had a broken arm encased in a cast stretching from his wrist to his shoulder. Nakamura nevertheless climbed onto a truck taking the company to windward Oahu to repel an expected invasion. Stevenson ordered him to stay behind. By the time he had returned from a short errand Nakamura had ripped off the cast and climbed onto the truck, and Stevenson believes he still has a twisted wrist because of that incident. A year later, Nakamura was guarding the waterfront from a machine-gun emplacement when Stevenson overheard a haole woman tell him, "You dirty Jap! You should be behind barbed wire."

Larry Nakatsuka, the author of the "Mr. Sato" columns in the *Star-Bulletin*, slept through the first bombs and woke to the ring of his telephone. It was his editor, Riley Allen, who wanted a report from the Japanese consulate for an extra edition. He was giving the job to Nakatsuka because he knew the consular staff and was the *Bulletin*'s only Japanese reporter.

Nakatsuka arrived to find Consul General Kita standing on the front steps of the residence in his pajamas. "Don't you know there's a war on?" he asked.

The impassive Kita dismissed the explosions and planes as an elaborate exercise and refused to make a statement.

Nakatsuka returned to the consulate at noon and thrust the front page of the *Bulletin*'s War Extra edition in Kita's face. Two police detectives ran up the consulate steps, shouting that they were putting the building under guard. They forced their way into a back room and found Takeo Yoshikawa burning codes and intelligence documents in a washtub.

Reflecting on this episode, Nakatsuka says, "There was never any doubt in my mind that I was anything but an American, and I thought then that it was my job to get what I could out of the senior representative of the enemy in Honolulu." He never feared being attacked by vigilantes because it never occurred to him anyone would perceive him as the enemy. Instead, he feared that if Japan occupied Hawaii, he would be among the first to be lined up and shot.

Seiyei Wakukawa remained a Japanese citizen because of America's restrictive immigration laws, but considered himself one hundred percent Americanized. He had written a thesis about the liberation movements in Japan's colonies of Taiwan, Korea, and Manchuria that was strongly critical of Japanese aggression. A week before, he had led a Japanese delegation to the post office to purchase defense bonds. He feared a Japanese invasion, and told me, "I thought I could prove my loyalty to the Americans, but if the Japanese army landed, I knew I would be shot."

The attack caught Tadeo Fuchikami in the RCA office. General Marshall's last-minute warning from Washington was still in his delivery pouch. Because it was not marked "Urgent" he had not rushed it to Fort Shafter. He thought, *Hey! It can't be Japan. Those Jap warlords are all cuckoo, like Hitler, but they're not strong enough to beat the old USA!* Despite the exploding shells, it never occurred to him not to deliver his messages ("Hey! It was my job."), or that a young Japanese man riding a motorcycle and dressed in a uniform, even the uniform of a delivery boy, might be in danger.

The streets were empty and on his way to Fort Shafter he passed spectators standing in front yards, pointing to the sky and laughing, certain this was a fabulous exercise. Then the roads filled with fire trucks, ambulances, and taxis with sailors returning to Pearl Harbor. Civilians drove into the high valleys to escape the attack, or in the opposite direction to witness it. A woman screamed, "Hey! You dirty Jap!" and Fuchikami wondered whom she meant. The military wives on his route were hysterical. Whenever he delivered a message, they gave him another for the mainland assuring relatives they were safe. His pockets were soon stuffed with telegrams and money.

The soldiers at one roadblock almost shot Fuchikami because his uniform was dark green and its RCA patch resembled a Rising Sun. They had heard that Japanese paratroopers in green overalls with a red shoulder patch had just landed in Kalihi Valley. (This paratroop rumor may have started when an American Army mechanic parachuted from a damaged aircraft over the north shore of Oahu, or when people saw Fuchikami racing down sidewalks to deliver his cables.)

Fuchikami delivered General Marshall's last war warning at 11:45 A.M., more than two hours after the last Japanese planes had departed. The clerks at Fort Shafter stamped his chit and pretended nothing unusual had happened; perhaps they did not want to lose face in front of a Japanese. The message was decoded and handed to General Short at 1458. He told a staff officer, "The damn thing won't do any good now." Several days later FBI agents accused Fuchikami of intentionally delaying General Marshall's warning, and only then did he realize how important it had been.

Wymo Takaki worked as a machinist on a civilian barge that was dredging near Ford Island on December 7. When his family returned to Japan in the 1930s his father had encouraged him to stay and become an American citizen. He attended high school in

Honolulu, boarded with haoles who became his foster parents, and became so worried Japan might invade Hawaii that in 1941 he stocked a cave on the north shore with emergency provisions so he could hide out until American forces recaptured Oahu.

When bullets ricocheted into his dredging barge he dived for cover. Several minutes later, the Norwegian captain ordered him to climb to the bridge to fetch some binoculars. He remained on the bridge for several minutes, mesmerized by the dive-bombers racing down the Halawa Valley, and the strings of torpedo bombers attacking Battleship Row. He was on the western side of Ford Island, so a thicket of trees obscured the battleships, but he saw the tops of their superstructures falling like trees.

He saw a destroyer firing on a midget submarine, and green and yellow shell bursts. A parachute opened and a Japanese pilot drifted into the water and sank from view. Fifty years later, Takaki still wondered if he had hoped to surrender, or shoot some Americans with his pistol, or had wanted to survive but changed his mind and drowned himself.

Takaki brought the binoculars to the captain and together they watched a Japanese plane crash into the harbor. The pilot wore a life jacket and was treading water. The captain, chief mate, and Takaki jumped into a work boat and headed toward him through blood-tinted water Takaki would remember whenever he cut himself shaving and saw the water in his bathroom sink turn red. He lay in the bow of the boat so he could pull the pilot aboard. As they neared the man he calmly removed his goggles, helmet, and life preserver and drowned himself.

Takaki fished the pilot's possessions from the water. Back on the dredger, his crewmates insisted he translate the writing on the life preserver. Takaki explained he could not read Japanese and the other men, Hawaiians, mainland haoles, and Chinese who had been his friends twenty minutes before turned on him. One man grabbed his shirt, and shouted, "You dirty Jap spy, read it to us! C'mon, read it!" Another choked him. The captain drew his pistol and they backed away. He put Takaki ashore, an action Takaki would later characterize as reckless, saying, "After I attended Army counter-intelligence school I realized that captain had made a gross mistake by releasing me on the back side of the harbor. After all, what if I really had been a Jap spy?"

A Japanese plane strafed him as he ran home along the Kamehameha Highway. Bullets came rushing toward him and he dived into a drainage ditch. After that, whenever he heard people trying to excuse the Japanese by saying they never strafed civilians he told them it was a damned lie.

In the space of thirty minutes he had almost been killed twice: once by a Japanese plane, and once for being a Japanese spy. He shook with fear that evening and told his Caucasian foster mother he was too scared to return to work.

"If you don't, they'll be sure you're a Jap spy," she said.

He went back on December 9 and saw lines of corpses covered with sheets. A Marine guard pointed a gun at his chest and shouted he was a "fucking Jap" and forbidden to enter Pearl Harbor. Several days later he was permitted to return to collect his machinist's tools. This reassured him. *Only in America can good things like this happen,* he thought. *With these tools I can serve my country.*

CHAPTER 21

THE UNITED STATES NAVY SHELLS HONOLULU

There were many instances of self-sacrifice and heroism on December 7. Men pulled shipmates from the harbor, and went belowdecks on burning ships to rescue buddies. Pilots stood on runways next to burning planes, firing pistols at Zeros. A black mess attendant on the *West Virginia*, Doris Miller, grabbed an abandoned machine gun, fired at dive-bombers, and earned the Navy Cross. On the *California*, Machinist's Mate Robert Scott drowned because he had insisted on remaining at his belowdecks station after a torpedo holed his compartment. On the *Nevada*, Machinist Donald Ross made two perilous trips to the forward dynamo room to rescue trapped shipmates, while in the port antiaircraft battery Ensign T. H. Taylor continued directing fire despite being wounded, burned, and deafened by shattered eardrums that sent blood coursing down his cheeks.

While Joseph C. Harsch was applying for war correspondent credentials at Army Intelligence offices at Fort Shafter a calm Army sergeant's voice announced over the intercom, "Paratroopers landing on Diamond Head. Troop transports and cruisers approaching Kailua Beach. Two battleships off Barbers Point." On hearing that, the colonel making out Harsch's card strapped on his holster and strode out the door to meet the enemy.

There was also fear and panic.

Kathy Cooper was staying with her parents in a large house on Admirals' Row directly under the flight path of the Japanese bombers. Her brother lay on his back on the roof, taking photographs as they flew past. She watched from the patio, and felt reverberations in her chest from the deafening noise. One Japanese pilot flew so close she thought, *My God! If I had a ball, I could hit him with it.* She became furious at the thought that if she was killed, her husband might remarry. Then a jittery young sailor appeared, carrying a huge rifle and explaining he had come to guard the women from the Japanese. He was so scared Cooper sat him down in the kitchen and gave him a cup of coffee.

A former colonel I met remembered "confusion plus," and men being "simply petrified and frightened stiff." Another recalled a senior officer who "went all to pieces and had to be sent back to the States on a stretcher." General Frederick Martin, the commander of the Hawaiian air force, visibly aged while witnessing the destruction of his bombers at Hickam. His ulcer acted up and he told his chief of staff, "What am I to do? I believe I am losing the power of decision." Later that afternoon, he was admitted to the Hickam Field Hospital.

While the attack was in progress, George Bicknell bumped into General Short at Fort Shafter. Short, whom Bicknell later characterized as being "in a state of animated confusion," asked what was happening at Pearl Harbor. When Bicknell replied he had just seen two battleships sunk, Short replied, "That's ridiculous!"

After the Japanese had left, American gunners shot down American warplanes, and American fighters strafed Japanese-American fishermen returning to Kewalo Basin in sampans. The U.S.S. *Gamble* opened fire on an American submarine, and machine-gunners protecting Kaaawa Beach shot at stars, mistaking them for signaling lights. Reservists manning antiaircraft batteries at Kaneohe fired on one another, then turned their guns on civilians coming to watch what they imagined was a Japanese landing. Shore-based gun batteries and ships fired on American fighter planes returning from the carrier *Enterprise*, hitting three and killing their pilots. A Japanese-American block warden was shot by another warden who failed to recognize him. A sentry killed a civilian who had stuck his head and arm through a fence while trying to retrieve a hat blown off by the wind.

During the attack, panicked naval gunnery crews forgot to use fuses or set them improperly, or mistakenly fired shells that only exploded on contact. Their shells fell on buildings, gardens, and houses across Honolulu, crashing into the yard of Thomas Fujimoto's home, barreling through the roof of Lewers & Cooke, destroying the Schumann Carriage Company, and cratering Kuhio Avenue. One shell burst on the grounds of the Iolani Palace, another exploded in the driveway of the governor's residence, its splinters flying across the street and killing an elderly Chinese. American ordnance killed a woman in Nuuanu Valley, two amateur boxers at the corner of Nuuanu and Kukui, four defense workers driving to Pearl Harbor in a green Packard, and eleven-year-old Matilda Faufata, who died in her mother's arms. Not a single American shell exploded near the high-level Japanese bombers flying at ten thousand feet.

Navy shells were falling on the Waipahu plantation as Elwood Craddock and his cousin returned from hunting birds near Wheeler Field. They exploded in fields behind Craddock's house, throwing up clouds of dirt and sending pineapples flying into the air. Craddock assumed they were enemy bombs. Later he learned they were shells fired broadside at the Japanese planes by sailors who had forgotten to set the fuses.

U.S. naval shells kept hitting Honolulu long after the last Japanese planes departed, yet civilians persisted in holding the Japanese responsible. A month later, Honolulu Mayor Lester Petrie wrote, "And it must not be thought that the victims of the tragedy were slain in a military attack. The ruthless Japanese deliberately slew helpless civilians in areas where the death toll would be greatest.

The city proper escaped only because it did not offer so easy a target for mass slaughter."

The Navy shells hit fifty-seven sites and killed forty-eight civilians. Most of the casualties were U.S. citizens, but police and newspapers broke them down by race, giving separate numbers for Americans, Portuguese, Japanese, Chinese, Koreans, Puerto Ricans, and Hawaiians, thereby denying these other races, even in death, the honor of full citizenship. A haole writing about the attack explained that, "Most of the casualties were Japanese, because there are few white people on the streets so early on a Sunday morning."

It was considered an exquisite irony for the Japanese to have killed members of their own race. Three years later, English teacher Herbert Coryell wrote an account of his experiences, describing a shell that exploded in the Lunalilo School, killing four people, and insinuating it was "ironic" for Hawaii's Japanese to be killed by Japanese bombs because they had expected special treatment from the attackers. He said, "Fortunately there were no children in the school at the time. If there had been they would have been chiefly of Japanese ancestry. One of the things that makes our island Japanese so bitter toward the Tokyo Japs is that the Tokyo Japs rained down their bombs on them and strafed them with machine gun bullets, quite disregarding their common racial extraction."

Throughout the war, the Navy never admitted the real source of the "mass slaughter" in Honolulu. But in 1943, during closed-door hearings of the Army Pearl Harbor Board, an Army ordnance officer who had investigated forty bomb sites testified that the shells were "antiaircraft ammunition of another service, sir, whose time fuses had failed to function in the air." The commander of Hawaii's coastal artillery added that a great deal of the ammunition had been defective and unfortunately those "duds" had detonated on contact with the ground. Only one Japanese bomb had hit Honolulu and he believed that had been an accident. "All the rest of them were Navy five-inch shells," he insisted. "I went out and dug up the fragments and looked at the markings on them. I know they were Navy shells; so does the Navy."

For decades, the relatives of civilians killed on December 7 remained bitter about their treatment. The government refused them compensation and funeral expenses, and until the fiftieth anniversary even excluded them from events commemorating Pearl Harbor. They have recently found a champion in Nanette Purnell, a cemetery historian who, after noticing a number of civilian graves dated December 7, 1941, has researched civilian casualties for the last decade. She has consulted hospital and plantation records, police reports, obituaries, and news accounts, and traveled to Washington, D.C., where she discovered that the civilian casualty report mentioned in the congressional investigation was missing from the National Archives. She has compiled a map showing all fifty-seven impact sites, and collected personal information about many of the victims. When we met I asked her why a Hawaiian woman who was not even alive in 1941 had become the champion of the civilian casualties. She said, "I felt sorry for them because they really are the forgotten victims of Pearl Harbor."

She described some of the most poignant victims. There was seven-month-old Eunice Wilson who had been sitting on a front-porch rocking chair in her mother's lap as her father walked up the path. At that moment, a shell exploded, killing both her and her father in front of her mother's eyes. There were the four members of the Hisacki family, killed when a shell fell on the street outside their Saimin stand and blew shrapnel through the front door. There was Joseph Adams, a Hawaiian man killed with his son in their sedan as they drove to work. "He left nine children—imagine, nine!" Purnell said. "The surviving kids had to drop out of school to work, and it changed their lives forever." That was what made the civilian deaths so compelling. Because they involved people of all ages, and people watching children and spouses blown to pieces, they had the potential to be more shattering than the military casualties.

The shelling increased the panic among civilians. People pulled furniture from their houses, and scattered it across their lawns to protect it from fire. They loaded cars and fled to the heights to escape the shelling, while residents of the same heights headed in the opposite direction to escape enemy paratroopers. Those inside rushed outside to escape fire; those outside, fearing shrapnel, ran indoors. Broken water mains sent geysers flying fifty feet into the air, and fire engines and ambulances mounted sidewalks to pass jammed intersections. Nothing moved at normal speed, and Honolulu became a silent movie in which everything was blurred, fast, and jerky.

One of the calmest residents of Honolulu was Pat Morgan's next-door neighbor, the manager of the Yokohama Specie Bank. They had never met, but she often watched him playing tennis on his backyard court. On December 7, he played a doubles match with some Japanese friends that continued without interruption throughout the attack. The men wore tennis whites and green eyeshades. Their wives watched from the sidelines. Morgan was so upset she wanted to yell and shake her fist. She still wonders if they expected to be arrested so they passed the time playing tennis.

Civilians living on the heights had a long-distance view of the attack, as if observing it through the wrong end of a telescope. Don Woodrum remembers seeing Pearl Harbor "without the close-ups we expect from television." It struck Pat Morgan as strangely beautiful, the orange flames blazing inside clouds of smoke, and little boats cutting across the harbor, disappearing in and out of black walls of smoke.

The rumors of paratroopers, saboteurs, and poisoned water spread fast. A radio announcer urged listeners to remain calm, but because his voice quivered his message had the opposite effect. Governor Poindexter came on the air at noon and is remembered for being so nervous he could hardly speak. Teenage boys drove through plantation towns honking horns, and shouting, "Poisoned water! Don't drink it!"

Civilians with ham radios picked up the police band and overheard the rumors of invasions and poisonings. The rumors ricocheted between the military and the civilians, who reported them to the police, who broadcast them over the radio, where they reached more soldiers and civilians. Twice on the evening of December 7, police bulletins declared another attack was in progress. One said, "All cars turn off your lights! Pearl Harbor is being bombed again." A civil-defense bulletin announced, "Get your car off the street! Drive it on the lawn if necessary!"

At various times it was believed that Japanese paratroopers had landed on the North Shore, in Nuuanu Valley, in Manoa Valley, and on St. Louis Heights; that Japanese transports had landed troops off Barbers Point, off Lualualei, and off Nanakuli; that saboteurs had poisoned the reservoir at Aiea and the water tower on St. Louis Heights; and that an enemy agent had taught a dog to bark in code, although it was not specified whether it was barking in English or Japanese.

Reports of slowly oscillating signal flares were traced back to a man who had dropped a lighted flashlight that rolled down a steep hill. A "radio transmitter" turned out to be an electric pump making a loud hum. Soldiers at Barbers Point mistook a school of fish for an enemy submarine, and fired on clumps of seaweed they took for survivors swimming ashore.

According to Honolulu Police Department logs, a "suspected looter" turned out to be a man removing belongings from his own bomb-shattered home, "a headquarters for Japanese paratroopers" was a backyard luau tent, "a fifth columnist transmitting intelligence via shortwave radio" was a man listening to news from the mainland, "a man up a telegraph pole signaling Japs at sea" was a telephone lineman, and "spies signaling with blinker lights" were two men lighting cigarettes.

On December 8, an *Advertiser* article headlined "SABOTEURS LAND HERE" claimed, "the saboteurs were distinguished by red disks on their shoulders." The saboteurs and enemy paratroopers turned out to be football players from San Jose College dressed in warm-up suits, kites snagged in a tree, six children on a Sunday school outing, and the branches of a eucalyptus tree. A civilian crowd beat a Chinese-Japanese man after mistaking him for a saboteur, and two air-raid wardens beat an elderly Chinese-Hawaiian warden to death after mistaking him for a Japanese parachutist.

For a surprise raid on a civilian city to cause fear and panic is not unusual. But Hawaii's multiracial population, and its lonely situation, magnified those emotions. For months, the military had been scaring itself and Oahu's civilians with warnings that local Japanese might support the enemy. Hawaii's isolation, once a source of comfort, now fed the panic as people realized that not only were they too distant from the mainland for quick reinforcements, but they had nowhere to flee to from a Japanese invasion. When Pat Morgan and her brothers heard that enemy paratroopers were approaching her house they armed themselves. "We did not know which bullet went into what," she said, "but our plan, such as it was, was to shoot from the veranda, then drive up the Tantalus Road and disappear into the mountains. There was nowhere else to run to. After all, we couldn't just drive to Arizona."

On the night of December 7, the first night of a blackout and curfew that would last almost three years, civilians saw shells flashing like sheet lightning, and the dull red glow of burning battleships, projected onto the night sky. At midnight, they saw a rare lunar rainbow, which native Hawaiians believe symbolizes an imminent victory. All night, they felt the ground shaking from trucks trailing artillery pieces, and heard the rifle shots of nervous guards, the antiaircraft fire of panicky gunners, and the grinding gears of mortuary wagons transporting the dead to cemeteries in Nuuanu Valley.

PART FOUR

AFTER THE ATTACK

CHAPTER 22

THE A LIST JAPANESE
PACK THEIR BAGS

Yukiko and Fumiko Fukuda remember little of the attack, but their father's arrest remains vivid, and no wonder since it resulted in their being repatriated to Japan, nearly starving to death in Hiroshima, and receiving only half pensions from the Hawaii State Department of Education. One Fukuda sister told me, "Our father was wearing a short-sleeved shirt and work pants." The other said, "He was weeding and hoeing our small garden and although he had a cold, the FBI agent and policemen did not allow him to pack a bag."

Mr. Fukuda was one of 370 Hawaiians of Japanese ancestry picked up on December 7 who were on the "A List" compiled by Lieutenant Colonel Bicknell, FBI Agent-in-Charge Robert Shivers, and Detective John Burns of the Honolulu Police Department. The detainees included Shinto and Buddhist priests, the teachers and headmasters of Japanese-language schools, and the 242 unpaid Japanese consular agents who assisted Japanese aliens in filing birth, death, and marriage certificates. Many on the A List expected to be detained and stood patiently on street corners, dressed in suits and ties, their suitcases packed, waiting.

In the following days more Japanese were rounded up, 1,441 in all. Aside from consular agents and language teachers, the largest contingent were "kibei," people who had been born in Hawaii, educated in Japan, and held dual citizenship. A third of the Hawaiian detainees were released within several months, leaving fewer than a thousand interned in camps. There was a similar roundup of suspected Japanese sympathizers in California, but it was not until March of 1942 that 110,000 West Coast Japanese were rounded up and interned.

It is easier, and now very much in fashion, to believe that in 1941 every Japanese in Hawaii was a Wymo Takaki or Ted Tsukiyama, cursing the "Damned Japs," and praying for an American victory. Few issei remain alive, and fewer still will admit to having divided loyalties or supporting Japan. The myth of total Japanese loyalty, of their "100 percent Americanism," is a moving and compelling one. It flatters Caucasian Americans by depicting the Japanese as eager to emulate them, and it is one of the cornerstones of the considerable economic and political power Japanese-Americans enjoy in the Islands. But it is also at odds with logic and the facts. On December 7, 40,000 of Hawaii's Japanese—almost 10 percent of the total population of the territory—held only Japanese citizenship. Most would undoubtedly have become American citizens had U.S. immigration laws permitted it, but some suffered divided loyalties, and a few took pride in the attack and might well have assisted Japanese troops during an invasion. Had they refused, Japanese military authorities could have executed them for treason. At a time when French, Dutch, Norwegians, Belgians, Danish, Poles, and Russians were helping the Nazi occupiers of their nations, it stretches credulity to argue that at least some Japanese aliens would not have collaborated with a Japanese occupation force in Hawaii.

Some Japanese-Americans will admit, or at least hint at the presence of pro-Japan sentiments in Hawaii. Larry Nakatsuka stressed to me that the Japanese community in 1941 was hardly monolithic, saying, "There were many splits, so summary conclusions will always be wrong."

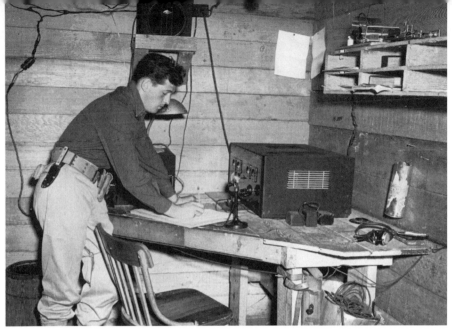

Pvt. Joseph Lockhard, who picked up the attacking Japanese planes on a mobile radar unit. (USS *Arizona* Memorial, National Park Service)

A Japanese plane roars off the deck of a carrier the morning of December 7, 1941. (USS *Arizona* Memorial, National Park Service)

Sailors at Ford Island Naval Air Station watch the burning U.S. battle-ships. (USS *Arizona* Memorial, National Park Service)

A tattered U.S. flag flies over Hickam Airfield after the attack on Pearl Harbor. (USS *Arizona* Memorial, National Park Service)

The USS *Arizona*'s band at Bloch Arena. There were no survivors of the band on December 7. (USS *Arizona* Memorial, National Park Service)

The USS *Arizona* burns amidships with its forecastle collapsed. (USS *Arizona* Memorial, National Park Service)

The day after the attack, servicemen killed at Kaneohe Naval Air Station are buried. (USS *Arizona* Memorial, National Park Service)

A dead sailor on the shoreline of Kaneohe Naval Air Station. (USS *Arizona* Memorial, National Park Service)

A Japanese Zero fighter plane during the attack. (USS *Arizona* Memorial, National Park Service)

Mr. John Adams, his father, and another passenger were killed while driving to their jobs in Pearl Harbor. (National Archives)

A Japanese midget submarine beached on the windward coast of Oahu after the attack. This captured piece of enemy equipment became a patriotic icon and was hauled across America to encourage the sale of war bonds. (USS *Arizona* Memorial, National Park Service)

An oil painting on silk by an unknown Japanese artist of nine of the ten Japanese sailors who participated in the midget submarine attack against Pearl Harbor. Missing is Ensign Kazuo Sakamaki, who was presumably excluded because he permitted himself to be taken prisoner. (USS *Arizona* Memorial, National Park Service)

In March 1943, the Japanese-American volunteers who became the core of the much-decorated 442d Infantry Battalion assembled on the grounds of Iolani Palace in Honolulu prior to their departure for training on the mainland. (Hawaii State Archives)

Left: Sterling Cale at the Pearl Harbor Reconciliation Ceremony on December 6, 2000. *Right:* Richard Fiske with Zenji Abe, who once bombed Fiske's ship, at Pearl Harbor Reconciliation Ceremony on December 6, 2000.

The USS *Arizona* Memorial. (USS *Arizona* Memorial, National Park Service)

Nancy Sato told me that of course some of the older Japanese-Hawaiians were pro-Japanese, "although they weren't much of a threat to anyone." Her neighbor's son had always been pro-Japanese, even after joining the U.S. Army. His family listened to Japanese shortwave broadcasts throughout the war, and considered the war in Europe to be completely different from the one against Japan. Sato's mother, an alien, often declared, "I hope we win the war in Europe," where her son was fighting. But Sato believes half of her mother was hoping Japan would win. When President Roosevelt died, her mother viewed it as retribution for the invasion of Okinawa. "See! That's what happens when he invades our country," she gloated. "That's why he died." When Sato was in school, she also had a Japanese-language teacher who had served in the Japanese army and tried to persuade his students to worship the Emperor. "But we kids knew we were Americans, so he didn't get very far. When I heard he was interned in California I thought, 'Yeah, well, he *should* have been interned.' "

More evidence that a small minority of Japanese aliens might have applauded a Japanese victory came in 1953, during the first postwar goodwill visit of a Japanese naval vessel to Pearl Harbor. Several of its crewmen wandered into the Likelike drive-in, and quickly attracted a crowd of elderly first-generation Japanese-Americans (issei) who bowed and called the astonished sailors "Admiral" and "Fleet Marshal." For several years after the war, a small minority of issei had insisted the American victory was a hoax, organized so-called "victory clubs" and contributed to a fund to provide entertainment for the Emperor when he came to claim Hawaii. On October 27, 1945 (prewar Japan's Navy Day), hundreds climbed Aiea Heights, expecting to witness the triumphant entry of the Japanese fleet into Pearl Harbor. Two years later, the president of one such club was insisting reports of a Japanese surrender were propaganda, and that General MacArthur was a prisoner of war. By 1950, membership had dropped, some said to five thousand, others to five hundred, but the last club, Hisso Kai, did not disband until 1977.

Seiyei Wakukawa told me, "If there had been an invasion, many

Japanese would have stood on the sidelines, waiting to see how the wind blew. But once the Japanese army had established its primacy I think almost all would have collaborated. But I think many haoles would have done the same. So to say you couldn't trust the Japs is like saying that the French people couldn't trust themselves during the occupation of their country, which turned out to be true!" Few of Wakukawa's friends applauded the Japanese attack, and most worried about their safety. But one man did burst into his house on December 7, crying, "They have finally done it!"

Military intelligence officers visited Wakukawa after December 7 and questioned him closely about a portrait of Karl Marx hanging over his desk. He was also watched by the Oahu Citizens Committee for Home Defense, a group of prominent Japanese-Americans recruited by FBI agent Shivers to promote loyalty within their community. One prominent Japanese college professor sat for hours in his car in front of Wakukawa's house. Shivers later confirmed that niseis had supplied the FBI with the names of Japanese aliens they believed should be interned.

Wakukawa was detained on December 17 and placed in solitary confinement at the U.S. immigration station in downtown Honolulu. He was later transferred to Sand Island and questioned by intelligence officers who believed he knew the significance of the Mori telephone call, then moved to a rudimentary camp in the New Mexico desert. He wrote to President Roosevelt protesting his treatment and was paroled in 1943, but forbidden to travel to Hawaii or the West Coast. He settled in Chicago and taught Japanese, later moving to Columbia University, where he translated Japanese material for the Navy. Japanese academics were in demand and Harvard recruited him to write a paper about Japanese land systems that would become the basis for a land-reform program imposed on Japan during the postwar occupation.

Alfred Preis, the future architect of the *Arizona* Memorial, was also brought to the immigration station with his wife on December 8. He had fled Vienna to escape the Nazis but because he and his wife had Austrian passports, they were considered potential enemy aliens, even though Germany had not yet declared war on the United States. A guard separated Preis from his wife and ordered him to empty his pockets, another urged him up a flight of stairs at the point of a bayonet. He stumbled into a room lit by burning cigarette ends and reeking of fish because most of the other detainees were Japanese fishermen. The next morning, he broke down when guards confiscated his wedding ring and ordered him to scrub the toilets with his bare hands. The Sand Island detention camp was more tolerable, and everyone ate excellent meals prepared by detained German chefs. The European internees bickered, the Japanese lived in harmony, the native Hawaiian guards napped in detainees' tents, and the only shot ever fired came when a guard fell asleep under a coconut tree and accidentally discharged his gun, bringing down a coconut. The camp commander ordered Preis to befriend Otto Kuehn, the Nazi spy. For weeks, he listened to Kuehn's unconvincing pleas of innocence, watched for suicide attempts, and marveled at the irony of a man who had fled the Nazis being ordered to guard the life of the only Nazi spy in Hawaii.

I asked Preis if he was still bitter about his internment. He looked shocked. "But I *hoped* to be interned!" he insisted. "I wanted America to win the war, and if I hadn't been picked up, I would have lost confidence in the authorities."

Preis was one of 112 Germans and Italians—both aliens and naturalized citizens—who were interned on December 8, three days before the United States and their homelands went to war. Former intelligence officer Don Woodrum believes that one hundred percent of the German and Italian communities in Hawaii were interned while less than one percent of the Japanese community suffered the same fate because there were so few Europeans that the government could easily grab them all. "So we took all the German chefs from the hotels, Little Joe Pacific the Italian shoe repairman, a man claiming to be a Finnish count, and all the other European alcoholics and eccentrics."

The more closely you examine the detention of aliens on Hawaii, the more curious it becomes. Consider that Robert Shivers,

John Burns, and Kendall Fielder—the same men responsible for choosing which Japanese should be detained—were among twenty-two non-Japanese a committee of prominent Japanese-Americans would honor in 1985 for "contributing to the success and well-being of the Japanese immigrants to Hawaii and their descendants." And consider that in a foreword to a booklet published on the hundredth anniversary of Japanese immigration to Hawaii, Governor George Ariyoshi praised these same three Caucasian men as "outstanding individuals whose dedication to humanitarian interests had significant impact on the economic and social well-being of Hawaii's Asian immigrants . . . [and] who promoted fair treatment of persons regardless of their race, color or creed."

One reason for the testimonials is that the December 1941 detentions on Hawaii were also its last detentions, and in March 1942, when a Japanese invasion of Hawaii was still widely feared, and when Japanese were being interned on the West Coast, 99 percent of Hawaii's 160,000 Japanese residents, who posed a much greater theoretical threat, remained free largely through the efforts of Robert Shivers, John Burns, Colonel Kendall Fielder, and General Delos Emmons, who had replaced General Short as commander of the Army's Hawaiian Department.

There were economic and practical considerations involved, and it was argued by these men and others that Hawaii's Japanese were too numerous and too necessary to its economy and war effort to be interned. President Roosevelt's cabinet had sent a directive to Emmons on December 19 instructing him to intern Hawaii's forty thousand Japanese aliens on the island of Molokai, and the Joint Chiefs of Staff had recommended that he evacuate Hawaii's Japanese to mainland internment camps. Emmons ignored both directives at considerable risk to his career. He was a recent arrival to the Islands who had initially mistrusted the Japanese, but now defended them because Shivers, Fielder, and Bicknell had persuaded him that most of Hawaii's Japanese were, in Fielder's words, "as American as you are, or I." Fielder credited Shivers with convincing him that the Japanese were loyal, and Sue Isonaga can recall Fielder telling her,

"I came not knowing anything about the Japanese, but Bob Shivers pushed me in the right direction." In a 1943 letter to Charles Hemenway, president of the Hawaiian Trust Company, Shivers explained that according to an order signed by General Short on December 7 not a single person could be interned or released from internment in Hawaii without his approval. That order, he continued, "pretty well placed control in my hands, which enabled me to carry out the ideas and plans which I knew were yours as well as mine. . . . Fortified with this fact [the absence of Japanese sabotage], we were able to stand up for what we thought was right against the opposition of, as you know, some high-placed officials."

Sue Isonaga remembers Shivers telling people, "I just can't see mass internment. Why, look at Sue, she's just as American as you and I are. I'm not putting them in camps and ruining their lives."

Shortly after arriving in Hawaii Shivers had approached a prominent young Japanese-American attorney, Masaji Marumoto, who was the first Oriental admitted to the Harvard Law School and the first to argue a case before the United States Supreme Court. He complained to Marumoto that he was being "bombarded with all kinds of anti-Japanese information" and wanted to know the Japanese side of the story. Marumoto introduced him to Japanese community leaders, who began meeting Shivers for breakfast every Sunday. Shivers and Marumoto also met weekly to discuss how to encourage loyalty within the Japanese community. Their wives became friendly and the couples became so close that after leaving Honolulu Shivers wrote Marumoto, "We miss you . . . more than I thought we would at the time we left. You know, Masaji, how much I value your friendship and the association our families had together." After 1945, Marumoto became the first Japanese president of the Hawaii Bar Association and the first Japanese judge of Hawaii's supreme court. When I met him his memory was failing, but he spoke at length about what had been one of his greatest honors, being Robert Shivers's first Japanese friend.

Sue Isonaga lived with Robert and Corinne Shivers throughout the war. He gave her away at her 1949 wedding and after he died she exchanged frequent visits with Corinne. She named her oldest son Robert, and her brother has a daughter named Corinne. Her daughter is named May, after Mrs. Shivers's sister. She showed me photographs of her children and was proud that her son had married a Caucasian-Japanese woman, one daughter had married a Chinese man, and the other, a Caucasian. Because after all, Bob Shivers had often told her, "The sooner we're all intermarried the better it will be."

Mementos of the Shiverses were scattered throughout Isonaga's home. She filled Mrs. Shivers's vases with flowers, and displayed their silver tea service in a glass case. A large photograph of them bore the inscription TO OUR OWN SUE, WITH LOVE and showed a plain-looking woman with a sweet expression and a dark-haired man with an earnest, hound-dog face. As Isonaga spoke about visiting the Shiverses' graves on Father's Day, his birthday, the anniversary of his death, Memorial Day, Christmas, and Valentine's Day I realized that long after whatever distant blood relations Shivers may still have in Mississippi have forgotten him, Sue Isonaga and her children and their children will be honoring his grave.

Hawaii's culture also contributed to the relatively gentle treatment of its Japanese residents. What discrimination and prejudice existed lacked the brutal edge of mainland racism. Newcomers among the military and defense workers distrusted the Japanese, but kamaainas understood the difference between the nisei and the more passive, or pro-Japanese, issei. This is why Lester Hicks, president of the Hawaiian Electric Company, gave a speech in February of 1942 condemning a proposal to intern Hawaii's Japanese as "fantastic," and declaring that they had "woven themselves into our community fabric . . . in such intimate fashion as to be an integral part of us."

General Briant Wells (Ret.) denounced Navy Secretary Knox's charge of Japanese fifth column activity in Hawaii as "slanderous" and told the Roberts Committee, "Our whole country is made up of people from all races and one race is just as good as another citizen as far as rights are concerned."

Bob Shivers, replying to accusations made by Kimmel, said, "In spite of what Admiral Kimmel or anyone else may have said about the fifth column activity in Hawaii, I want to emphasize that there was no such activity in Hawaii before, during, or after the attack on Pearl Harbor. Consequently there was no confusion in Hawaii as a result of fifth column activities. . . . I speak with authority when I say that the confusion in Hawaii was in the minds of the confused."

In the panicky days following the attack, the internment of small numbers of Japanese in Hawaii was an understandable and sometimes, as Nancy Sato and others believed, merited reaction. If in some cases it was an injustice, it was at least a forgivable one. On the West Coast, where virtually all the Japanese were interned, they could at least have no doubts or questions about why they were singled out. But the Hawaiian detainees felt stigmatized by their selective internment, and the question, "Why me?" still haunts them.

When I met Seiyei Wakukawa in 1990, he was a brittle old man living comforted by a cocoon of books covering every table and filling floor-to-ceiling shelves in a ground-floor apartment in a Nuuanu Valley neighborhood that had changed little since 1941. His internment was "the great mystery of my life," he said, particularly because he had toured Japanese schools and churches during the summer of 1941, encouraging loyalty to America, and his University of Hawaii Ph.D. thesis had been profoundly antifascist, containing strong criticism of Japanese territorial aggression on the Asian mainland. "Until this day I cannot imagine the basis for their conclusion I was dangerous to the nation," he said, sadly shaking his head.

Had he been interned because of his portrait of Karl Marx? Because he was rude to his interrogators? Because the agent who searched his office reported, "This guy is a very smart fellow—he didn't leave a single thing to implicate himself"? Because the haole professors who rejected his thesis ("it was rather too radical for the time, too Marxist-oriented") had spread rumors that he was a parlor pink? Or because his older brother had been a special attaché at the Japanese embassy in Washington and appeared in a *Newsweek* photograph as one of the diplomats burning official papers on December 7?

This brother had sent him a telegram on December 5, saying, "This is a good-bye. Take care of yourself." It was kept from him, he says, by pro-Japanese relatives in Honolulu who worried he might warn the Americans. Perhaps the authorities had intercepted it, and that explained his detention. Or perhaps prominent Japanese on Robert Shivers's Moral Committee had betrayed him? "But if they were such one hundred percent Americans, why would they persecute someone as anti-Japanese as myself?" he wondered. "Perhaps they were suspicious of me because I was a radical. I still don't have much love for them. They have been highly praised here, but I believe they would have been just as loyal to the invading Japanese. Many cooperated with our government because it was convenient. Some were friends of mine from college days, and after the war, they did not suspect that I harbored grudges against them."

Our conversation caused Wakukawa to become so distraught that to cheer him up I mentioned the Civil Liberties Act of 1988 that granted every surviving American of Japanese ancestry interned during the war twenty thousand dollars in reparations. Wakukawa planned to spend his twenty thousand moving to a larger apartment and publishing his book about Japanese immigration, and considered it an official acknowledgment that he had been unjustly imprisoned.

Like some of the attempted Pearl Harbor reconciliations between Japanese and Americans, the internment compensation program, an attempt to reconcile Japanese-Americans and other Americans, has stirred up ghosts. Ike Sutton, the ensign who was strafed while pulling sailors from Pearl Harbor, later settled in Hawaii. He won a seat in the state legislature and ran for lieutenant governor on the Republican ticket in 1990. Even though the votes of Japanese-Americans are crucial in any Hawaiian election, he could not restrain himself from attacking the reparations program during a televised interview, saying, "Well, why not give forty thousand dollars then to the Japanese boys who strafed me?"

Survivors of Pearl Harbor and the Bataan Death March protested that the legislation was unjust because Japan had never paid reparations to American POWs for their years in horrifying Japanese prison camps. In August 1990, the Pearl Harbor Survivors mounted a campaign against a bill passed by the California legislature requiring schoolchildren to be taught that there was no military basis for the internment, and that it resulted from "race prejudice." The survivors persuaded a legislator to introduce a resolution stating that the camps had not been "concentration camps" but relocation centers, and that the program was prompted by military necessity.

Attacks on the reparations program infuriate Japanese-Americans. Attorney Earl Nishimura had been prominent in the Hawaiian campaign for reparations. When I mentioned the objections of some Pearl Harbor Survivors he pounded his desk, and said, "We fought two wars—against the enemy, and against skeptics. We were as good Americans as anyone!"

Ted Tsukiyama thought the argument linking Japanese reparations to American POWs with compensation to the internees was outrageous. "We had no compunction about fighting the Japanese," he said. "But now they want to lump us together with those damned Japs. How can they *still* do this to us?"

The Fukuda sisters are as obsessed as Wakukawa with solving the mystery of their internment—in their case why they were among only forty Japanese families chosen to accompany male detainees to the mainland. Their father had been one of the 242 Japanese consular agents. Even though his was an honorary post carrying no diplomatic immunity, U.S. authorities offered him a choice between internment in America or repatriation to Japan. He was one of a handful of Japanese aliens from Hawaii to choose repatriation, mainly because he feared he would be unable to earn a living in Hawaii because the government had closed his language school and forbidden the teaching of Japanese.

The Fukuda sisters and their mother were among several hundred Japanese families asking to be repatriated with the men. One sister said, "We were brought up to obey our parents. We had no preparation for working outside the home, and we thought our decision would help him in being released to Japan." The other added, "We were living miserable financial lives, yet were sad to leave our friends and school life."

They were among forty Japanese families from Hawaii that the U.S. State Department chose for repatriation. They traveled by ship to San Francisco, then to New York to join their father on the *Gripsholm*. Its sailing was canceled and they were incarcerated in a resort in North Carolina with Japanese and German diplomatic families. They were later reunited with their father at a repatriation camp in Crystal City, Louisiana, where they remained for the duration of the war, attending a special high school in the camp and enjoying rations and clothing equivalent to those of American enlisted personnel. (The Fukudas proudly showed me their high-school yearbook, pointing out photographs of football teams and cheerleaders, and the smudged signatures of their German, Japanese, and Italian classmates. They were about to fly to San Diego for a reunion. Camp Crystal T-shirts and a souvenir book were in the works and, like the Pearl Harbor Survivors Association, sons and daughters of the internees were being urged to attend.)

When the war ended, their father still believed he could no longer make a living in Hawaii and insisted on repatriation to Japan. The sisters would have preferred to return to Hawaii, but they wanted to remain a family. They shivered through a Japanese winter because they had bartered their warm clothes for food. Their father took them to Hiroshima, hoping to show them his birthplace, but the bomb had obliterated all traces of it. He died three weeks after arriving. When the sisters and their mother tried returning to Hawaii they discovered that they had forfeited their citizenship by choosing repatriation. They regained it in 1952 and went home to become public-school teachers, but found they were a decade behind other teachers their age, and unable to qualify for a thirty-year pension. Fumiko Fukuda complained that, "Now teachers our age are really enjoying these years because they have better pensions, while we're living on a one-third pension."

Their smiles were pained, and they spoke softly, even apologetically, while voicing their complaints. They blamed Pearl Harbor, the war, and their internment, but not their father, for putting them in this flimsy tract house and leaving them wondering, as Yukiko said, "What would have happened to us had we not been interned."

They had turned their internment into their retirement hobby. "We're just kind of curious to see how things were decided," Fumiko said.

"And to find out how we and the other forty families were selected for repatriation," her sister added.

They became experts in this narrow field, and books and yellowing documents cluttered their sitting room. They had made three trips to the National Archives in Washington, D.C., where they discovered a list containing their father's name, their own files, and the official record of their transcontinental journey, complete with details such as, "After the expatriate party boarded the *Army Queen* [a ferry to Oakland], the Red Cross, under the supervision of Mrs. T. Bacigalupi, served the expatriates all the fresh milk and several kinds of sandwiches they required."

On their last visit to Washington they found an exchange of letters between Secretary of War Stimson and Secretary of State Hull that solved the mystery of their selection for repatriation. Stimson wrote Hull that General Emmons opposed repatriating the Japanese being held in camps in Hawaii because he feared they might divulge information about the Islands' defenses upon returning to Japan. Hull overruled this objection, saying it was essential that forty Japanese families from Hawaii be chosen for repatriation. Japan held Americans captured on Guam, Wake Island, and the Philippines, and the State Department believed that their repatriation and humane treatment depended on Japanese aliens from Hawaii receiving equivalent treatment.

The letter explaining the fate of the Fukuda sisters was sent by an assistant secretary of state to Navy Secretary Frank Knox. It said, "Realizing the difficult situation in Hawaii, the Department has left to the discretion of the War Department the selection of thirty or forty Japanese [families] who are considered less dangerous or who, for special reasons, it is considered desirable to remove from the Hawaiian area."

The Fukudas like to believe that their family was in the "less dangerous" category, and that this document proved their loyalty. Even so, they consider their smaller pensions an injustice, and they, too, see themselves as victims of Pearl Harbor.

CHAPTER 23

A DEEP, POWERFUL
THIRST FOR REVENGE

An odd exhilaration followed the fear and panic during the at-tack. Mary Ellen Lawrence remembers everyone singing on the evacuation buses, and the excitement and pride of being given the opportunity to measure up to the heroism of British civilians. Kathy Cooper compared the attack to newsreels of the London Blitz. A Punahou schoolteacher wrote in her diary, "More men lay dead and wounded on Oahu than had fallen in any of the heaviest attacks on London, and soon many Anglophile haoles were grandiloquently calling the single two-hour raid 'the Blitz.' "

After the exhilaration, however, came an anger that sometimes lasted a lifetime. A chief petty officer who remembered pulling bodies from the harbor "like fish," said, "If I could have gotten my hands on any one of those Japanese, I would have crushed him like an insect." A crewman on a minelayer was furious, "Because the Japanese envoys had been down on the dock only a week or so before and there was the ambassador in Washington talking peace." A gunner's mate on the *Oklahoma* described "a deep, powerful thirst for revenge on the part of every enlisted man." Pat Morgan told me, "We were all consumed with an urge to do something violent."

Kathy Cooper had "an utter feeling of horror, helplessness, and anger, consuming anger. If a Japanese pilot had walked into the house, I would have tried to kill him." Matilda Faufata, whose daughter was killed in the raid, heard her husband shout, "Some Jap is going to pay for this," and had to restrain him from carrying out his threat. The grave-diggers at the Oahu cemetery were so furious they refused to bury the dead until enemy corpses were segregated from the American ones. Admiral Halsey vowed the Japanese language would be spoken only in hell, and told his men, "Kill Japs, kill Japs, kill more Japs."

The fact that people had seen the faces of the Japanese pilots, and even "the slant of their eyes," magnified the anger. It was said the Japanese had waved, smiled, and laughed, taunting the sailors before killing them. Marines at Ewa Field reported a tail gunner who stopped firing long enough to thumb his nose. Another released the handles of his gun and clasped his hands above his head, shaking them like a victorious prizefighter. Then he grabbed his gun and shot more Americans. Because the planes flew slow and low, particularly during the early torpedo runs, no doubt some men did see the pilots. But some of the reports of gloating Japanese were exaggerations, a way of personalizing the attack and increasing the anger.

The treachery of having attacked on a Sunday morning, without a declaration of war, and while Japanese envoys were holding talks in Washington, was considered unforgivable. Within a week of December 7, respondents to a mainland poll had chosen "treacherous," "sly," and "cruel" as words best describing the Japanese people. Authorities in Virginia jailed every Japanese resident. The Tennessee Department of Conservation requisitioned six million licenses for "hunting Japanese," only to be told by the state purchasing department it was "open season on Japs," so no license was necessary.

Like Hiroshima, Pearl Harbor has become an unacknowledged backdrop to Japan–U.S. political and economic transactions. The years preceding the fiftieth anniversary of the attack were a particularly emotional time. A U.S. senator described the export of Japanese cars to America as "an economic Pearl Harbor," a television advertisement for American automobiles featured references to Emperor Hirohito and exaggerated Japanese accents, and it was reported that an Alabama country club rejected the membership application of a Mr. Hiroshi Isogai, manager of the Honda All-Lock Manufacturing Company, "amid lingering ill feelings about World War II." When this decision was reversed, members admitted their first vote was motivated by "resentment dating back to Japan's 1941 attack on Pearl Harbor."

When Rhode Island began celebrating a holiday known as "V-J Day"—Victory over Japan Day—the Japan Society of Rhode Island mounted a campaign, supported by Japanese business interests, to change it to "Rhode Island Veterans Day." Cliff Wilson, the commander of the Rhode Island American Legion, said, "If they were offended when we called it V-J Day, wc were pretty offended when they bombed Pearl Harbor. Why should we have to pacify them?"

American investor T. Boone Pickens ran full-page newspaper advertisements headlined "AMERICA YOU LOST THE ECONOMIC WAR," and beginning, "That taunt was hurled recently at Boone Pickens and fifty American shareholders in Japan, along with 'Yankee Go Home!' and 'Remember Pearl Harbor!' " Pickens argued that his investment company had been unable to gain a single seat on the board of a Japanese company controlled by Toyota, despite owning 26 percent of its stock. America seemed to be losing the economic war with Japan, Pickens said, "not because Japanese workers are smarter or more industrious than Americans . . . [but] because corporate Japan takes advantage of our open markets, but plays by an entirely different set of rules—rules that mock American principles of free and fair trade." There it was again, the idea that a Japanese victory had to be the fruit of Japanese treachery.

One of the most forgiving Pearl Harbor survivors I met was Robert Hudson, who told me the qualities he saw in the Japanese, such as devotion to the elderly, love of family, and respect for education, were also the values of 1941 America, the same ones he had fought to defend. He had retired to Honolulu so he could pursue his great passion, researching Pearl Harbor. He began exchanging Christmas cards with Kazuo Sakamaki, the Japanese midget-submarine captain captured after the attack, and enjoyed what he termed "a delightful correspondence" with former Zero pilot Aeiichi Hayashi, and with a Mr. Fujita, who had strafed the Naval Air Station at Kaneohe. They in turn sent him figurines, swords, and expensive dolls with handstitched kimonos, a symbolic atonement for Pearl Harbor and the torpedoes that had sank his ship, sending him swimming through burning oil. His favorite peace offering is a carved rosewood box that had come with a note asking, "Will you kindly accept this appreciation of our friendship?"

Hudson invited two of his new Japanese friends, Fujita and Sakamaki, to attend the fiftieth anniversary ceremonies at Pearl Harbor. A Navy public affairs officer and officials at the National Park Service, which administers the U.S.S. *Arizona* Memorial, had encouraged him to make this gesture, and Navy and State Department officials in Honolulu and Washington, who had been searching for ways to include the Japanese in the ceremonies, also approved of a Pearl Harbor survivor inviting his former enemies to Honolulu. But when news of the invitations reached members of the Pearl Harbor Survivors Association, there was an uproar.

One of Hudson's fellow crewmen on the U.S.S. *Oglala* wrote, "I was beside myself as [to] how to answer that letter stating that you want to have Sakamaki and Fujita, the pilot who bombed Kaneohe, as your *guests* at the 50th reunion in 1991. As of today I presented the idea of yours to 140 members of the Pearl Harbor Survivors Association [at a meeting of a California chapter]. So now I can answer and feel that it's not just me: 139 out of 140 think this is not advisable, nor very healthy for you to do this. I suggest you forget it completely."

Hudson dismissed the letter as an isolated protest, and was prepared to continue. Then he received a letter from the national president of the Pearl Harbor Survivors Association saying, "You have caused the Aloha [Hawaii] Chapter to get up in arms with your proposal. . . . There are not many in the Association that feel the same way as you do toward the Japanese. In fact, that is one of the concerns of the local fathers, that some of our members might cause an incident while over there for the anniversary . . . Your slogan, 'YESTERDAY'S ENEMY TODAY'S FRIENDS,' I simply do not agree with."

The survivors' objections persuaded the Navy to withdraw its support, and Hudson rescinded his invitations to Sakamaki and Fujita, writing lengthy apologies.

Before arriving in Honolulu for the first time, I read about a Pearl Harbor survivor who was protesting the use of a Japanese-made Komatsu backhoe to excavate an addition to the national cemetery that would one day hold his remains. "Is it too much to ask that this practice be stopped on the hallowed grounds of our national cemeteries?" he asked. "Do other Pearl Harbor survivors feel as I do? Does 'Remember Pearl Harbor' mean anything today?"

I considered this a good example of the hypersensitivity of the wartime generation, but a few days later I was in the shrine room of the U.S.S. *Arizona* Memorial, angry beyond all reason at a Japanese woman born at least a quarter century after a Japanese bomb had ignited the *Arizona*'s forward magazine, killing 1,177 of its crewmen. I was reading the names of the dead carved on a marble wall, searching for the seventeen sets of brothers, when I heard an urgent whisper, "Please, sir . . . please, sir . . . please!" and turned to face a young Japanese woman wearing a pained smile. She waved the back of her hand, motioning me to move aside so she could pose her sister in front of this list of dead American sailors. I shook my head and turned my back. Her shutter went clickety-clack anyway.

Let me be clear about this: had she been American, British, Russian, Chinese, or even German, I would have smiled and moved. I put my reaction down to my age. I was born in 1946, into the earliest postwar generation, one that grew up listening to our fathers' war stories and surrounded by their wartime souvenirs, and for whom *bravery* was defined by Omaha Beach, *evil* by the Holocaust, and *treachery* by Pearl Harbor. We were too close to the war for historical perspective, but too removed from it to understand its ironies and moral ambiguities. After watching all those black-and-white documentaries and reading those fat histories, and after comparing our restless and unfulfilled generation with the one before it, perhaps it was not surprising that we felt a secondhand nostalgia for a time we had never lived, and a war we had never fought, nor surprising that our secondhand memories could sometimes become secondhand grudges.

The descendants of Pearl Harbor survivors have formed the Sons and Daughters of Pearl Harbor Survivors (SDPHS), which has a yearly national convention that was held in Covington, Kentucky, in December 2000, a growing membership that has reached 2,500, a national chaplain, and a newsletter called the *The Offspring*, in which a member declared, "I am the proud son of a Pearl Harbor survivor. Although I can't smell the smoke, hear the rattles and bangs of weaponry used December 7, 1941, I feel the intensity of an emotion."

As Hawaii prepared for the fiftieth anniversary of Pearl Harbor, opinion polls reflected an increased dislike and distrust of the Japanese in the state. The increased resentment was new; its existence is not. "There is anger left," a kamaaina who lived through Pearl Harbor told me, "and it comes to the fore when the Japanese are overwhelming."

Japanese investors had been buying Hawaiian enterprises and real estate since the 1950s and by 1991 they owned fast food chains, construction companies, dry cleaners, car dealerships, golf courses, and office buildings. They owned the state's largest bakery, a controlling interest in its largest shopping mall (the Ala Moana Center), three-quarters of its luxury hotel rooms, and half the rooms in Waikiki. Like most islands, Hawaii has always been starved for capital, so at first Japanese investment was welcomed, particularly because it coincided with the decline of Hawaii's sugar and pineapple industries. But as it increased, attitudes changed. By 1987, Japanese spending and investments accounted for 45 percent of Hawaii's economic activity. "Hardly a hotel is built, or a major commercial development begun," the First Bank of Hawaii reported, "without some participation by Japanese investors."

Jokes about Hawaii becoming the next Japanese prefecture suddenly became less amusing. If Japan accounted for 45 percent of the Islands' economic activity in 1987, it was easy to imagine them reaching 51 percent. Japanese speculation in residential real estate upsets Hawaiians the most. The Japanese favored Waikiki and beachfront communities like Kahala, Black Point, and Portlock, where Genshiro Kawamoto, a Tokyo property speculator, bought the Henry Kaiser estate for $42 million.

The Japanese bought Hawaiian houses as speculations, reselling them in Tokyo weeks later to a second tier of buyers who have never seen them. They bought them as retirement homes and long-term investments, sometimes leasing them back to the original seller. They bought them as vacation homes, occupying them for a few weeks every year. After acquiring Oahu's best waterfront properties they moved inland into middle-class neighborhoods, buying ranch houses in Hawaii Kai and windward Kailua.

They bought everything they could during the early 1990s because the yen was strong and the dollar weak, and even Hawaii real estate sold for a tenth of its Japanese equivalent; because they already owned Hawaii's best resorts and beachfront hotels and these houses were the only quality left; and because the houses were the spoils of a trade war that, at the time, they were winning.

If I mentioned Pearl Harbor to an Hawaiian in 1991, I heard, "They couldn't invade us, so now they're buying us." "What they couldn't do with their bombs they're doing with their yen." Or, if the speaker had a certain perspective, "We have turned their yen into bombs." (Cy Gillette told me, "It's our damn fault. . . . This is the difference now, we're doing Pearl Harbor to ourselves.") It was always "they" or "them"—words signifying the enemy in a society under assault.

I heard public testimonials to the Japanese contribution to Hawaii's prosperity; in private, I heard something different. A real-estate agent who had fattened herself on Japanese commissions described them as "arrogant sons of bitches." The widow of a Pearl Harbor–era Army officer said, "I sometimes have trouble getting to my husband's grave at Punchbowl because Japanese tourists are in the way." A woman who had converted her family's ranch into a private amusement park where Japanese tourists paid to ride horses and go-carts complained, "We used to ranch cattle, now we ranch Japanese."

Wallace Fujiyama, now a successful Honolulu lawyer, told me, "Some of these Japanese speculators are raping this state. They're very snobbish and cliquish. People here bend over backward for the Japanese, but no one has ever really looked at whether this is good for our community."

As Hawaii became an economic colony of Japan, the Hawaiians were feeling the customary resentment of the colonized toward the colonizer. What made their resentment unique, and gave it a nasty edge, was that the victors of a war were being colonized by the losers, and the place being colonized was one the losers once attacked.

It was sometimes argued that opposition to Japanese investment was motivated by racism, and pointed out that Britons and Canadians had been investing in Hawaii for years without being vilified. But if racism alone explained the resentment, then why had investments by other Asian nations escaped similar censure? And why were many Japanese-Americans living in Hawaii such bitter critics of the foreign Japanese? In truth, the resentment was directed less against race than nationality.

Hawaiians of all races often prefaced their complaints, "I am not 'Japan-bashing,' but . . ." and claimed to be concerned about "foreign speculators" of all nationalities, although there was little doubt which nationality they feared most. Some people were honest, or foolhardy, enough to acknowledge it. A headline described then Mayor Frank Fasi saying, "Act Now or We'll Be a Tokyo Suburb." Honolulu's finance director warned that, "Japan could buy all of Oahu," since Japan had accumulated $52 billion because of trade imbalances with the United States, while all of Oahu's real property was worth only $51 billion. It was preposterous to imagine the Japanese doing so, but the point was that it was possible, and in 1991 that appeared to be a Japanese victory more enduring than Pearl Harbor.

The Japanese recession of the 1990s has forced the sale of some Japanese trophies and resulted in a sharp reduction in Japanese investment and tourism in Hawaii. The fact that the Hawaiian economic bubble burst in concert with the Japanese one provided more evidence of the extent to which the Islands had become an economic colony of Japan, and how closely their economy and destiny was linked to Japan. While mainland America was enjoying the great economic boom of the 1990s, Hawaii's economy remained, like Japan's, stagnant, with the lowest level of economic growth of any U.S. state and a huge increase in personal bankruptcies, unemployment, and the number of residents on welfare. At the beginning of the twenty-first century, Americans from the West Coast began investing in Hawaiian real estate. There is now some grumbling about rich dot-com millionaires buying up Hawaii, but it lacks the nasty edge of comments previously directed at Japanese investors.

Some of the shadows Pearl Harbor casts over the Japanese presence in Hawaii are more faint. A haole man informed me that every Japanese-owned golf course on Oahu, even those proposed or under construction, faced military property, and Japanese developers were even planning a resort opposite the gates of the naval weapons arsenal at Lualualei.

Other shadows are dark and unmistakable. A haole woman gave me a written summary of the issues facing Hawaii that included the observation, "The Japanese people need *Lebensraum* now, even more than ever—not just to move but to play golf etc. Couldn't do by military conquest, so do by purchase."

The mayor of Maui threatened to withdraw his island's "aloha" for Japanese tourists if the Japanese Navy joined the U.S. naval forces in exercises on the uninhabited island of Kahoolawe. Neither the mayor nor the environmental or native Hawaiian groups opposing these exercises spelled it out, but it was clear that for the Japanese to shell a Hawaiian island was an outrage of a greater magnitude than for the Australians or British, who had been persuaded to skip this phase of joint maneuvers without threats of withheld aloha.

Mr. Del Oleson wrote to the *Advertiser*: "We were called upon, both men and women, to defend these islands and hundreds of others, from an aggressor who had three goals in mind. To conquer, to control and to own. . . . Yet it was only a delay, not a victory. There are people among us who, because of greed, have placed 'For Sale' signs on land we saved for future generations."

A real-estate agent working with Genshiro Kawamoto discussed him in the shamed voice of a traitor. "Yesterday I had seven closings with Kawamoto," she said. "All day I've been clicking my heels and saying '*Sieg Heil.*'" (There was a pattern here: the Japanese needing *Lebensraum*, the sudden increase in Japanese investment in Hawaii characterized as a "blitzkrieg," and saying "*Sieg Heil*" to Japanese investors.)

A leaflet published by Na'opio Aloha'aina, an organization of Waianae coast residents opposed to the Japanese-financed West Beach resort development, contained numerous veiled references to 1941. The Waianae coast is Oahu's last relatively inexpensive neighborhood and has large communities of native Hawaiians, Filipinos, and other "locals," as the Honolulu newspapers call them in crime reports, in order to distinguish them from haoles, who, no matter how long they live in Hawaii, are never, in this context, "locals."

The Aloha'aina protest leaflets warned that the Japanese resort would result in congestion, pollution, water shortages, and the destruction of the family farms supplying most of Oahu's local produce. A headline described the Japanese as bringing "WINDS OF DANGER!" to Waianae, an echo of the World War II miniseries *Winds of War*. The leaflet contained crude racial stereotyping: "We called West Beach Estates to ask about future condo prices. The guy said, 'Soddy. We only sell $20 million parcels now. *Sayonara.*' " It charged that West Beach would cause more traffic fatalities: "Japan's big bucks tourism will increase injuries and death among our local people . . . Should we just sit back and wait for this new bloodshed?" One page showed a cartoon with an enormous Rising Sun as its background. It had a single, slanted Oriental eye staring at two versions of Oahu. The present-day one was straddled by a huge Japanese yen Y, and crisscrossed with tour buses flying Japanese flags. Two Japanese jumbo jets flew overhead, dropping skyscraper hotels that fell like bombs. The leaflet's second version of Oahu was labeled "1941," and here planes with Japanese markings dropped bombs on warships moored in Pearl Harbor.

On an April Fool's Day before the fiftieth anniversary, the hosts of a popular morning radio program pretended that Japanese investors had bought their station overnight. In the space of several minutes I heard many of the same racial clichés common among Americans in 1941. Then, the Japanese had been nearsighted, bucktoothed, rice-eating midgets who spoke poor English and could not shoot straight. Now there were jokes about "little men," and the new owners of the station being so small the microphones had to be lowered several feet. Someone banged a gong and spoke fractured English, pronouncing all his *r*'s as *l*'s. A new game, "Banzai Bumper Stickers," offered a sack of rice as first prize. An announcer promising to explain Japanese investment in Hawaii began, "It all started on December 7 . . ."

Some listeners believed the hoax. Japanese-American callers were the most upset. "How sorry I am for you guys at the station," said one Japanese-American woman, "and I pray every day that they don't buy in my neighborhood."

Imagine the uproar if a radio host in Chicago pretended his station had been purchased by Africans, then made jokes about the staff being told to carry spears and the cafeteria offering boiled missionary. Yet the Japanese-Americans of Hawaii considered themselves so American that instead of protesting the racial stereotypes, they presented themselves as more outraged than anyone that another

Hawaiian property had fallen to Japanese investors, just as their parents and grandparents had insisted they were furious at the "damned Japs" after Pearl Harbor.

Behind the nervous jokes about Japan's buying Hawaii was the belief that for the Japanese to own so much of the state had somehow rewritten history, and challenged the assumption that World War II had been a morality play in which treachery was rewarded with suffering and defeat. And if you considered that war as simply a lengthy episode in a century-long competition between America and Japan for control of the Pacific and Asia, as many Japanese do, then Japan's economic victory in the eighties became as significant as the American military victory of the forties, and promised more lasting consequences.

The Zeros now were the stretch limousines of the Japanese speculators, made more sinister by their smoked windows and black-uniformed chauffeurs. They cruised Kahala, Kailua, and Hawaii Kai, stopping for passengers to photograph a house or approach its occupants with an unsolicited offer. Other Japanese flew over desirable neighborhoods in helicopters, selecting targets from the air. Everyone had stories of a friend or neighbor opening the front door to face a Japanese with a checkbook. The offers often came unexpectedly and at unlikely times, such as early in the morning.

A Japanese gentleman showed the neighbor of Dorothy Bicknell's piano tuner a suitcase containing $250,000 in the expectation that the sight of so much cash would persuade him to sell his house. Dorothy Anthony told me Japanese nationals had bought six apartments in her condominium in the last months, in one instance offering $700,000 to a neighbor who had paid $300,000 for his apartment the year before. Who could resist such a profit?

The Admiral Yamamoto of the speculators was Genshiro Kawamoto, ranked as among the six richest men in Japan, and credited with unlimited resources of cash and cunning. He purchased seventy-eight Oahu homes in four months, closing on twenty-five windward houses in a single day, afterward telling a reporter for the *Boston Globe* that Hawaiian houses were poorly constructed and "lousy, candy houses." He refused to inspect homes unless owners provided a new pair of slippers at the door, and recommended Honolulu change its zoning laws so they more closely resembled those of Japan.

It was rumored that he was behind proposed legislation prohibiting foreigners from buying more real estate, so that his houses would become more valuable. It was feared he would buy radio and television stations "to tell us how to think." Talk-show hosts invited listeners to guess where the "Kawamotomobile," a stretch limousine of legendary proportions, would appear next, and callers were divided between those fearing it would pull up next door, and those hoping it would roll to a stop in their driveways.

The obsession with Japanese investment led newspapers, television stations, and magazines to run frequent polls. Two-thirds of Hawaii residents agreed that, "The sale of land in Hawaii to Japanese investors is the biggest contributor to the high cost of living here," while only 31 percent "trusted the political motives of the Japanese nationals." Almost half believed Hawaii was on the verge of becoming a colony of Japan.

One of Mr. Kawamoto's neighbors was Bob Bekeart, a Navy veteran who had been based at Pearl Harbor aboard the destroyer tender *Dobbin* in 1941. He had married a native Hawaiian woman and returned to Oahu after the war, living ever since in Portlock, a waterfront neighborhood near Koko Head popular with Japanese nationals. As I arrived, a burglar alarm sounded in a neighboring house belonging to Kawamoto, and for the next fifteen minutes we shouted over its clanging.

Bekeart complained that ever since the Japanese had begun buying houses and leaving them empty their alarms had become a nuisance. They shorted and there was no one to turn them off, or they were tripped by the cat burglars who preyed on the Japanese. "I'm surrounded by absentee Japanese," he shouted. "But I won't move. They'll have to take me out of here feetfirst." When the alarm fell silent he said, "You know, I look after Kawamoto's house, and report when his burglar alarm goes off, but I can't even get an aloha from him or his yardman."

The morning of December 7 had found Bekeart with his wife at their home in Manoa, out of sight of Pearl Harbor. After hearing the news bulletin on the radio he went to his room to get ready for war. He told himself, *We're going to get these guys and within two months we'll all be marching through Tokyo. It's winter now in Japan, so I should take my heavy raincoat, my warm Hart Schaffner & Marx double-breasted suit, and my brown Stetson.* He wore the suit, carried his alligator raincoat over his arm, and put everything else into a ditty bag. He was dressing for Tokyo.

He never again underestimated the Japanese and believed they would soon own his neighborhood. "They have great allegiance to brand names," he explained, "and Portlock has a reputation as a place for rich haoles, although it's really a place that's making the haoles who leave it rich."

For Sale signs sat outside many houses lining the ocean side of Portlock Road. The houses faced Maunalua Bay and had lawns running down to a seawall and views west across the water to Diamond Head. Once Mr. Kawamoto's burglar alarm fell silent, we walked through a gate and across an absentee Japanese owner's lawn to the seawall. "There's a three-million-dollar house over there, and a fourteen-million one down there," Bekeart said, swinging his arms like a weather vane. "That one went for nine hundred and ninety-five thousand, and that one belonged to Dolly Parton, but even she sold out."

In 1941, sailboats and sampans had filled this bay and its waters were clear, its beaches white and inviting. But during the fifties and sixties, dredging for the nearby Hawaii Kai development had turned the sand gray and left the bottom lined with sludge. Every day, a concession towed out a floating platform, and a flotilla of Jet Skis filled the bay with their insect buzzing. The customers were mostly tourists from Japan, and several years before, one of Bekeart's daughter's school friends had gone swimming and been run over and killed there by a Jet Ski.

Until recently, these Portlock lawns had run together seamlessly, and neighborhood children played across them. Some of their new owners had built walls and fences. There had been a community association and frequent block parties, but participation had dropped off. Bekeart said they still held a newcomers' party, but every year fewer people bothered to attend it. Instead of a place to live, Portlock had become a place to make an investment.

As we walked along the shore toward Koko Head, Bekeart said, "That one should sell for three million soon. Look, they've turned that one into a Moroccan bordello, don't you agree? And that one was owned by a friend who gave great Fourth of July parties. He was tending bar at his party last year when a Japanese man drove up and offered him a million. He said no and a few days later the offer became $1.2 million. He couldn't resist, and forty-eight hours later, the buyer had flipped it for $1.3 million."

Native Hawaiian families had lived in Portlock before the war. They were fishermen and squatters lacking legal title. The outlines of their fish ponds remained visible, and Bekeart said Hawaiians sometimes set up temporary encampments near them. Hawaii is one of the last places where haoles should complain about foreigners taking their land, and it is easy to discern some rough justice in haoles being displaced in turn by the Japanese, and with considerably more compensation than they offered the Hawaiians they once chased off this same shoreline. Still, I could not help feeling sorry for Bekeart and his neighbors. They had lived here most of their adult lives, raising children and investing themselves in an easygoing and friendly community that had, like many such places in Hawaii and on the mainland, vanished.

CHAPTER 24

NO CAN EAT GOLF BALLS!

For six weeks following the attack Japanese-American soldiers of the Territorial Guard watched over Honolulu's telephone lines, utilities, and reservoirs. Some mainland soldiers made derogatory comments, and one regular Army officer asked Hawaii Guard commander Wilhelm Andersen, within hearing of his men, how he dared sleep in a place "where these Japs can slit your throat." Yet the nisei soldiers were proud they were trusted to bear arms and defend Oahu against a possible Japanese invasion. Then, on January 19, Ted Tsukiyama and other niseis in a unit camped at the Koko Head rifle range were suddenly brought to Schofield Barracks and discharged.

Ted Tsukiyama told me, "Our officers gave us a farewell speech and cried. We had Chinese, Hawaiian, and black American officers [the black officer was Nolle Smith, who had been born and raised in Hawaii and never considered black], and none ever imagined this would happen. For me, being discharged because of my race was more traumatic than learning that the Japanese had bombed Pearl Harbor. We could accept the fact by then that Japan was our treacherous enemy. But to have our own country, in its most extreme time of need and danger, repudiate us, was more than we could take. The very bottom had dropped out of our existence."

The regular U.S. Army also dismissed Ralph Yempuku in January. He blamed the new troops from the mainland, who looked at the niseis and saw the enemy in American uniforms. He overheard one soldier saying, "Jesus, we're too late. The Japs are here already."

Three days after the raid, military policemen rounded up Japanese workers at the Pearl Harbor Navy Yard and marched them to the gate. Spud Ishimoto remembers, "They made us march double time, even the ladies from the laundry. At the main gate they took away our badges, threw them in a wastebasket, and said, 'We don't want to see you Japs around here anymore.' But you figure you can't get mad at them. They're not in their right mind. They're just hot, hot, hot. They look at my face and see the people who killed their buddies, and think, 'Goddamn him to hell.' "

A Marine guard at the Pearl Harbor gate pushed Wymo Takaki back into the road with his rifle, and shouted, "Fucking Jap! You're not going to work here." Takaki later worked at Wheeler Field. The soldiers there were kind, he says, "But I hated the mail calls when they would read out names and their buddies would shout back, 'Killed, killed, he's in the hospital.' I felt guilty because they had been killed by people looking like me."

Instead of feeling bitter, niseis like Takaki, Yempuku, and Ishimoto became even more determined to prove their loyalty. They made public displays of burning anything "Japanesy," destroying so many Japanese documents, photographs, and phonograph records that the Office of War Information later had trouble finding enough for research purposes. They blacked out the Japanese flags in graduation and wedding photographs, pulled Japanese signs off shrines and stores, and ceased speaking Japanese in public. More than 250 Japanese adopted Chinese, Hawaiian, Portuguese, and haole names, so that the Haraguchis became the Kanekoas, the Jujitas the Ah Hees, and the Nakamuras the McFarlanes.

Young niseis became the authority figures in their families, setting down rules for their parents such as "Don't talk in Japanese,"

"Don't talk on the telephone, because you don't speak English," and "Don't bow like a Japanese." They took out newspaper advertisements reaffirming their loyalty. One in the *Star-Bulletin* said, "We're ganging up on you, Tojo, in a way you and your Nazi friends don't understand. . . . Get it Tojo? It isn't the Jap way, the Nazi way, nor the Fascist way. It's the FREE AMERICAN WAY." Every patriotic activity became a test of loyalty the Japanese were determined to win. They wrapped more bandages, dug more public bomb shelters, and bought so many war bonds that in 1942 Hawaii had a per capita purchase rate four times the national average.

Japanese students formed a "kiawe corps" to clear kiawe trees from beaches and prevent invading Japanese soldiers from using them as shelter. Japanese community leaders formed the Emergency Service Committee that exhorted Japanese residents with slogans like, "We must take our bumps, keep our chin up. Don't brood or gripe." It arranged for anti-Japanese sayings to be baked into rice cakes, and soon, at tea parties across Honolulu, elderly Japanese were reading, "The chrysanthemum does not prosper in Hawaii" and "The sun rises but always sets."

It was stirring, touching, and sometimes too much. Japanese in Hawaii launched a drive to buy a bomber to attack Tokyo. In 1943, they contributed $10,340 to purchase bombs to "drop on Tokyo." One of the organizers of this drive declared, "We're real Americans and we're going to act and fight like Americans. We hope that this money will be used for bombs which will give Tojo and his cutthroats bloody hell."

When Masao Akiyama, a nisei who had studied in Japan, refused induction into the Army in 1944, admitting he could not be "100 percent American" because his mind was with Japan, the Japanese community disowned him. Dr. Ernest Murai, chairman of the Emergency Service Committee, called his action contemptible, saying, "We doubt that there are many others like Akiyama waiting to be discovered. But if there are . . . it will be the job of all of us to smoke them out."

Seiko Ogai submitted an essay titled "Am I Haole?" to a competition sponsored by the regional director of the Office of War Information in Honolulu. It described his brother, then serving in the Army in Europe, as "about as American as a bottle of soda water" and told how he was proud of "his wallet with pictures of Caucasian and Hawaiian girls, not an Oriental face in the group." Ogai had written a covering letter with his essay declaring, "I do not especially want any of the prizes, but I did want . . . to let others know that a Jap is not necessarily a Jap." His essay won first prize.

Despite their humiliating dismissal from the Territorial Guard, the niseis campaigned to be allowed to serve in the armed forces. Yempuku, Tsukiyama, and other former ROTC and Territorial Guard soldiers formed an all-nisei labor battalion called the Varsity Victory Volunteers that quarried rock and constructed roads and military installations. Nisei personnel in the 298th and 299th Infantry Regiments, which had been federalized before the attack, remained in the Army, as did nisei serving in an engineering construction battalion. In June 1942, Japanese personnel from these units were sent to the mainland for training and consolidated into the 100th Infantry Battalion, which took so many casualties in the early days of the Italian campaign it was known as the "Purple Heart Battalion."

The exemplary record of the 100th and the fierce lobbying of Hawaiian niseis persuaded the War Department to raise an all-nisei unit to fight in Europe. In January 1943, almost 10,000 Hawaiian niseis answered a call for 1,500 volunteers. About 2,500 were combined with a smaller number of mainland Japanese to form the all-Japanese 442d Regimental Combat Team, which absorbed survivors of the 100th Battalion on its arrival in Italy. It fought until the end of the war in the Italian, French, and German campaigns, coining the slogan "Go for Broke!" and becoming the most decorated unit in United States military history, and one of the most written-about and praised military units of the war.

In just three years, the "Go for Broke" myth of the nisei soldier as superhuman fighter and super-patriot had replaced the myth of the treacherous Japanese-American fifth columnist. Compare the expulsion of the Japanese from the Territorial Guard in 1942 with the official 1944 Army *Pocket Guide to Hawaii*, which advised new arrivals, "In 1941 there were 157,990 people of Japanese descent here. That means that 34 out of every 100 civilians were Japanese. Now get this straight. Most of them went to American schools. They learned to pledge allegiance to the same flag you salute. They like American soft drinks. And one of their favorite radio comedians is Bob Hope. They're Americans."

The sacrifices of the nisei soldiers made anti-Japanese racism unseemly in Hawaii, and gave the Japanese community a claim on the Territory's future prosperity at a time when martial law and immigration from the mainland were weakening the haole oligarchy. A direct line can be drawn from the war record of the 442d to the postwar defeat of the Republican Party, statehood, and the economic and political successes of the niseis and their children.

Some niseis served in the Pacific War, mostly as intelligence agents charged with interviewing prisoners, infiltrating enemy lines, and translating radio communications. They were scattered among battalions, and had American bodyguards to prevent them being mistaken for the enemy. They worried about being tortured and executed as traitors if captured, and about having to interrogate or shoot relatives serving in the Japanese Army.

Ralph Yempuku's four brothers all fought for Japan. He parachuted behind enemy lines in Burma for the OSS (Office of Strategic Services) and organized hill tribes into partisan bands that ambushed Japanese convoys. He often thought, *What will I do if my brother is in that convoy? If he is one of the prisoners I have to interrogate?* He supported dropping the atomic bomb, even though his parents lived near Hiroshima, and went there searching for them while serving with the occupation Counterintelligence Corps.

Ted Tsukiyama became an interpreter for the 10th Air Force in Burma. He remained so angry over Pearl Harbor he wanted to kick in the balls of the first Japanese he met, and persuaded another nisei interpreter to let him into a prison stockade. "I wanted revenge," he said, "but they were not the arrogant supermen I had imagined, just beaten dogs, and my desire to kick them disappeared."

Wymo Takaki believes Pearl Harbor was a "lucky accident" for the niseis since it gave them an opportunity to prove their patriotism. After failing the physical for the 442d and flunking the test for nisei interpreters, he told the recruiting officer who finally accepted him, "I was strafed in Pearl Harbor and I'm still angry. It's my battle." He was sent to military language school at Fort Savage, Minnesota, where he learned enough Japanese to translate the writing he had seen on the life jacket of the airman who had ditched in Pearl Harbor and committed suicide. It turned out to be the man's name, Asahi. "When someone shoves the kanji [Japanese script] letters in your face and is choking you and calling you a dirty Jap spy, you don't forget those letters," he told me.

He arrived in Japan after the surrender, but in time to fight one of the first intelligence battles of the Cold War by interviewing Japanese POWs returning from Soviet prison camps, searching for "sleeper" NKVD intelligence agents. He made a career of Army Intelligence, serving seven years in Japan and marrying a Japanese woman. He volunteered to fight in Korea, first as a frogman, then as a parachutist—anything to see combat and demonstrate his patriotism.

He volunteered again for Vietnam after being shocked by stories of draft evaders fleeing to Canada. He worked undercover for the military, posing as an agricultural specialist, and sometimes a Chinese-American or Japanese businessman. The Vietcong held the Japanese in high regard because after World War II three hundred Japanese soldiers had stayed in North Vietnam to avoid the humiliation of returning home. They fought for the Vietminh against the French and a residue of pro-Japanese feeling among the Vietcong made it easy for Japanese nationals to travel through Vietcong territory. Many had flag stands on their cars, Takaki remembers, "and whenever there was any danger you could see all these Japanese businessmen and technical advisers racing around with their jeeps flying Japanese flags. Here were American GIs dying, and these guys were being protected by that flag. Oh, I was displeased with that."

Takaki cultivated a former Japanese soldier who had become a prosperous South Vietnamese businessman and had close ties to the Vietcong. At the start of the Tet offensive, Takaki hitched a ride back to Saigon with this man. When heavy gunfire stopped them outside Saigon the businessman ordered his chauffeur to slip a Japanese flag onto a pipe attached to the bumper. Takaki heard guns and mortars, then saw the Japanese flag, framed by explosions. "I was under fire again, like at Pearl Harbor, and seeing the Japanese flag," he says. "I started screaming, 'Hey! I don't want to be protected by this flag! I was at Pearl Harbor, I can't forgive the Japanese. Let me out!' The businessman restrained him from jumping from the car, but Takaki still feels guilty about being saved by this "enemy flag."

In 1987, Takaki lay in Tripler Army Hospital after surgery for cancer, reviewing the unfinished business of his life. He remembered Asahi, the Japanese airman who had drowned himself in Pearl Harbor, and promised himself that if he lived, he would find this man's relatives in Japan and relate to them the circumstances of his death. After leaving the hospital, Takaki and his wife flew to Japan, where they found Asahi's name on a list of the Japanese enlisted men killed at Pearl Harbor. They called an association of former World War II pilots only to be told no record was kept of the enlisted men because, as the association's secretary put it, "those youngsters were supposed to die."

After two months, Takaki and his wife tracked Asahi's relatives to a village on the southernmost island of Kagushima. His parents had died without fulfilling their lifelong dream of visiting Pearl Harbor, but his other family members welcomed them. There were tears, gifts, reminiscences of Pearl Harbor, and a visit to the local school, where a romantic oil portrait of Asahi hung in the principal's office.

———

When I arrived in Hawaii I had assumed Takaki's generation of niseis would have forgiven Japan for Pearl Harbor, and pictured them as a bridge between Hawaii and Japan, and like other hyphenated Americans, sympathetic to their country of ancestry.

I was first disabused of this notion at a meeting of the executive committee of the MISLS (Military Intelligence Service Language School) veterans' association, an organization of Hawaiian niseis who had attended language school on the mainland because none of them knew Japanese well enough to become interpreters immediately. The MISLS veterans reminisced about the "good old days up on the CBI [China-Burma-India] border," traded playful punches to each other's stomachs, and joked about their golf scores. They popped open beers and apologized to me for a "light agenda" that consisted mostly of opening their junk mail. The main event was a brief speech by a member of a Japanese-American group hoping to build a Japanese cultural center in Honolulu. He wanted the veterans to make individual donations and consider pledging a substantial gift from their endowment. This sounded to me like a sensible final destination for their money, yet most were hostile to it. After some rough questioning, the cultural-center advocate conceded that many of its visitors would be Japanese tourists, and his organization had decided not to charge admission. That was received coolly by the veterans, who were seeing their decision in terms of, "Should we help finance the construction of what will be a free tourist attraction for citizens of the former enemy nation?"

No ethnic group in Hawaii is more touchy about Japanese tourists, real-estate speculators, and the growing influence of Japan on island affairs than niseis of the Pearl Harbor generation.

Seiyei Wakukawa thought Japanese "land rollers" should be controlled. Sue Isonaga told me, "We feel it's an invasion, and that they're ruining things for the local people. It's just gone too far." Ted Tsukiyama felt "foreign" and "uncomfortable" among Japanese from Japan. The wife of an AJA war veteran who taught Japanese exchange students at the university complained they were "loud, rude, and come from rich families that throw their money around."

Edwin Kawahara wanted me to know that his wartime Japanese language courses had not made him pro-Japanese. "I enjoy my Japanese," he said "but as any other American would enjoy speaking another language and understanding another country's culture." When he visited Japan he discovered that Japanese from Hawaii were considered foreigners and treated rudely. He was an insurance agent, a low-status profession in Japan, so that even when he had dealings with people from Japan in Hawaii, they made him feel inferior.

Attorney Wallace Fujiyama, who had been accompanying his father's baseball team over the Pali Highway on December 7, accused the recent wave of speculators of flaunting their money, breaking their word, and being rude to the Hawaiian Japanese. "We get guys who've owned some noodle shops or used-car dealerships. They're not accepted in Japan so they come to make a big name for themselves here. They don't understand the sacrifices we made during the war. We worked hard to have our place in the sun and nobody says to me now, 'Hey, boy, cut my grass,' 'Park my car.' But now they're rocking the boat for all of us. We are still just a bunch of farmers to them, and they look down on us as uncouth. As far as I'm concerned we should get a big bulldozer and bulldoze them into the ocean!"

I found Tadeo Fuchikami, the RCA messenger entrusted with the last warning from Washington, living in a weathered bungalow in the same Kalihi neighborhood he had ridden through on December 7. No one had asked him about Pearl Harbor since 1966, when he had been a technical consultant for *Tora! Tora! Tora!* and taught the nisei actor playing him how to handle an antique motorcycle. He was retired and told me, "Golf is the thing that gives my life meaning."

When not playing golf, he made sculptures out of coat hangers and golf balls he found in the weeds bordering Honolulu's public courses. His sitting room was filled with wire stick men with golf-ball bellies that doubled as coaster racks, and wire cats with golf-ball bodies and pink plastic hair whose wire arms held notepads and digital clocks. They were middle-class American in concept, but their delicate legs, tiny clocks, and clothespin noses were unmistakably Japanese.

Fuchikami explained he had been a skilled plumber in 1941, but an appendix operation had prevented him practicing his trade for several months so he was temporarily delivering telegrams. Had General Marshall's last warning been marked Urgent, he would have rushed it to Fort Shafter on a special run. Had it even been marked Priority, he would have gone there first. Instead, there was nothing distinguishing it from a happy-birthday or anniversary cable, so he followed his usual route. It was not until several days later, when FBI agents accused him of having intentionally delayed its delivery, that he suspected it was important, and not until the early 1950s did he learn its contents.

"Hey, when I first heard about that, I felt really bad," he said, putting his hands behind his head and rocking backward in a leather recliner built for American men three times his size. "I wished I could have had the message sooner. Then I would have warned people and I might have been a national hero. For a while, I thought that Day of Infamy might have been my fault."

I had no doubt the national hero Mr. Fuchikami wanted to have been was an American one, celebrated for delivering a message that might have sent hundreds of Japanese to their deaths. Nor did I doubt that when he saw Japanese tourists, he saw foreigners, and when he saw families of blond Californians, he saw fellow Americans. When he shot out of that leather lounger like a missile, and said, with a cruel smile on his face, "I'm all for the USA whipping their asses," I was sure he wanted the USA to whip some Japanese asses.

These asses belonged to the Japanese businessmen who were at this moment buying local golf courses where golfers like Mr. Fuchikami saw Japanese tourists being placed ahead of them. Many of those protesting the golf-course purchases were Japanese-Americans, and in one celebrated case, a Japanese-American doctor had recently been removed from the board of governors of the Honolulu Country Club following a public confrontation with the club's new Japanese owner.

Japanese tenant farmers were also protesting their eviction from agricultural land bought by Japanese golf-course speculators. A celebrated case involved farmers Ryoie and Nancy Higa, whose supporters coined the slogan "You can eat vegetables but you no can eat golf balls." The Higas had received an eviction notice from their new Tokyo-based Japanese landlord, Sanjiro Nakade, that was dated on December 7, a circumstance the Waianae Farmers Ag-Water and Land Use Concerns Committee described as an "anniversary present from Japan." Their reply to Nakade said, "Sanjiro Nakade–In Hawaii, we eat vegetables, not golf balls. . . . You are trying to do with money what Imperial Japan failed [to do] with bombs in 1941."

Tadeo Fuchikami could not afford a country-club membership, but the Japanese golf invasion had still affected him. He used to treat himself to the private courses, and enjoyed playing at Makaha, he said. "But now that the Japs have raised the greens fee for outsiders to almost a hundred dollars we poor retirees have no hope to play there—maybe once a year if I'm lucky and someone treats me."

The Japanese occupation of Oahu's golf courses was particularly galling for Fuchikami, who had served with the American occupation forces in Japan and learned golf from his commanding officer. The Japanese civilians there had been a pitiful lot. "Boy! Now the shoe sure is on the other foot." He shook his head and, close to tears, whispered, "I just can't understand how this has happened."

To answer Fuchikami's question you had only to look at the wall of electronics in his living room. He had an elaborate stereo system whose miniature speakers pumped out the slushy French love songs he liked, two videocassette recorders, and two large-screen televisions with earphones so he and his wife could sit together while watching different programs. As my eyes hopped from Sony to Hitachi he gave a sheepish grin and, proving he really was "one hundred percent American," offered a typical American excuse, "You know, I would really *like* to buy American," he said, "but the quality . . ."

At first I considered Fuchikami an eccentric, touched by his love of golf. Then I met Ralph Yempuku, who had become a successful impresario since leaving the wartime OSS. He promoted foreign circus acts and sumo wrestling in Japan, also booking these shows into Honolulu's Blaisdell Arena, where I met him in a windowless office papered with posters of his sumo stars.

On the twenty-fifth anniversary of Pearl Harbor, he had told the *Star-Bulletin* that the sacrifices made by niseis had been worthwhile, including the risk he took of killing his own brothers, because, "Today, our children don't face any of that business of not feeling one hundred percent trusted . . . That is why I felt the nisei boys who died didn't die in vain. They made a helluva lot possible for coming generations."

Now he was not so sure. "I think the majority of all the people like me who served in the war felt that we have been, well, not 'cheated'—that is too harsh a word—but as far as this thing with the Japanese has been concerned that we have been sold down the river by our government," he said. "The 'thing' with the Japanese he referred to was their purchase of Hawaiian real estate. "I jump over all those years from Pearl Harbor to today, and I find myself getting the same feelings about the Japanese who are coming over here to Hawaii, taking over the hotels, and putting their money into everything."

He leaned across his desk and lowered his voice. "Most of my friends are local Hawaiians. I go out with them every day, and they are beginning to talk about the Japanese. They say, 'Hey, what the hell are these Japanese up to? They're buying here and there, taking over golf clubs, this and that. You know? Taking our land away.' And one of them, maybe it was a slip of the tongue, said, 'Hey! What the hell are you Japanese doing?' I don't think he really meant it, but it gave me a shiver, you know?"

Just remembering the comment made him angry. "Between you and me," he said, "you cannot trust a Japanese farther than you can spit. They proved this between 1931 and 1941, they proved it during the war, and they're proving it now. They will talk nice and bring gifts, then before you know it you've got this knife in the back. This is what happened at Pearl Harbor and it's happening again."

He saw the skepticism on my face and slammed his hand on his desk, saying, "Don't ever lose sight of the fact the Japanese of today are the same kind of Japs that were in Japan in 1941. Just because they bow and bring gifts, you think, 'Well, the Japs have changed from the arrogant militarists who ran Japan and started these wars and bombed Pearl Harbor.' No! This is the same mistake our government is making. I say this: *They are the same Japanese.* Give them time and they will do the same thing they did in 1941."

I was amazed at these 1941 echoes. Again Hawaiians believed themselves menaced by Japan, and again the Japanese of Hawaii were making strident speeches and extravagant gestures, and determined to be second to no one in their contempt for the enemy. His denunciation of Japanese duplicity reminded me of the essay by the Army wife in the Hawaii War Records Depository that described polite Japanese smiles as "masks of deceit."

CHAPTER 25

NOW WE'RE AN AMERICAN CITY

"The day I arrived in Hawaii was the day I vowed never to leave," Dorothy Bicknell told me. She came aboard the *Lurline* in 1936 and the moment she saw people climbing aboard from the pilot boat, carrying armfuls of flower leis with their overpowering fragrance she knew she wanted to stay forever.

Eva Marie Judd said, "As soon as I stepped off the boat I told myself, 'This is it!' I loved the racial mixture and physical beauty."

Dorothy Anthony and her husband arrived days after their wedding and his graduation from Harvard Law School. Moving to Hawaii struck them as madcap and exotic. She was immediately seduced by the open trolley cars and the little Chinese ladies in black pearls, dripping jade, and driving big cars at a time when on the mainland you rarely saw a woman behind the wheel.

"It was the most glamorous place," Mary Ellen Lawrence remembered. "I think it was the colonial atmosphere, and the way it smelled, with flowers everywhere, Chinatown being so exotic, and the drive to Wheeler through miles of pineapple fields. I was struck dumb by Hawaii."

I had not asked these women about their earliest memories of

Hawaii. Instead, they had offered these remarks during conversations about the attack, perhaps because it seemed natural to connect prewar Honolulu with Pearl Harbor; to connect the innocent, romantic city that had bewitched them with the day changing it forever. The attack would have a similar effect on mainland cities, but Honolulu would undergo the most wrenching transformation. Prewar Hawaii has been called "a polite tyranny," a place of "benevolent paternalism," and a "tough little oligarchy." It was ruled by the descendants of the nineteenth-century New England missionaries who controlled its political, economic, and social life through positions in the Big Five, former sugar-trading houses occupying five granite palaces a shadow's reach apart in downtown Honolulu. The Big Five monopolized Hawaii's agriculture, transportation, trade, and communications, and Honolulu's haole oligarchy maintained a firm grip on the Territory through a series of interlocking directorates. For example, in 1941 Castle & Cooke's Matson Lines controlled 98 percent of the shipping between Hawaii and the mainland, a Castle was president of the Honolulu Gas Company, a Cooke was president of the Hawaiian Electric Company, and another Castle headed the Honolulu Rapid Transit Company.

The declaration of martial law on December 7 released the Big Five's chokehold on Hawaii, accomplishing in a day what might otherwise have taken years, and ending the colonial system as surely as the Japanese occupation ended those of the British, Dutch, and Americans in Southeast Asia. The shift in power first became apparent on December 8, when the U.S. Army Corps of Engineers requisitioned Punahou School for its headquarters, making office space for itself by throwing chairs and textbooks out the windows of an institution that had educated generations of the haole elite.

The military government of Hawaii immediately assumed all legislative, judicial, and executive power in the Territory. It seized control of all land and maritime transportation, fixed prices, set wages, awarded defense contracts (often to mainland firms), censored the press, abolished civilian courts, and regulated everything from bowling alleys, rent, and garbage collection to prostitution, gasoline sales, firearms, and water chlorination. By facilitating the entry of war workers and mainland capital, it also introduced labor organizers and business competitors to the Islands. Army rule may have been profoundly undemocratic, but it shattered the monopoly power of the prewar oligarchy. The Hawaii it returned to civilian rule in late 1944 was more populous, wealthy, and cosmopolitan than the one it took over on December 7, 1941.

The niseis, native Hawaiians, and Filipinos who returned from the armed forces after the war resisted attempts to reimpose Big Five paternalism. They and the new mainland immigrants joined forces, joined the Democratic Party, and organized labor unions. Racial barriers in employment ended, mainland firms entered Hawaiian economic life, and the Asian population, led by the Japanese, gained considerable economic and political power.

Although Hawaii was undergoing such changes throughout the 1950s, Honolulu still bore a physical resemblance to the 1941 city. There were no skyscrapers or freeways, and the construction and tourist booms that would transform Oahu began at the end of the decade, encouraged by statehood and passenger jet service to the mainland. Even without Pearl Harbor and martial law, the Big Five's monopoly would have slowly been weakened, jets would have turned Waikiki into a skyscraper resort, and agricultural production would have declined, but all the changes would have been more gradual, and less shocking to Hawaii's culture and environment, and to Pearl Harbor-era kamaainas like Dorothy Bicknell, Eva Marie Judd, Dorothy Anthony, and Mary Ellen Lawrence.

At the time of the fiftieth anniversary, Dorothy Bicknell was confined to a wheelchair and had not traveled from her windward home into Honolulu in several years. This was fine with her, she said. "The last time I went to Waikiki, well, I might as well have been in Florida."

Eva Marie Judd lived three miles inland, in the same Maunalani Heights home where she witnessed the attack. From her windows, Waikiki was a concrete dam, blocking her views of the ocean. On December 7, she saw shells splashing in the Pacific, now she watched smog gathering whenever the city was locked in a Kona weather pattern.

Mary Ellen and Wells Lawrence lived in a condominium high-rise within sight of the church where they had been married and the school where he had taught mathematics for twenty-five years. Their Makiki Heights neighborhood was a densely populated and unplanned jumble of cottages and condominiums that had, in turn, stolen each other's mountain and ocean views. The Lawrences said they would not have settled in Honolulu if they arrived today. It had become like any other city, plagued by traffic jams and chicanery. Its sweltering summers were also a new feature, the fault of tall buildings blocking the trade winds. "There is less shade, less green, and more asphalt," he said. "And so many trees have disappeared that the weather is definitely changing and becoming hotter."

Dorothy Anthony was a block from the Lawrences in a condominium whose lobby had the marble walls, concrete waterfalls, security systems, and other now-common "amenities." The building's distinguishing feature was that the Manoa Stream, once celebrated by travel writers for its beauty and wild tropical flowers, ran through a concrete sluice bordering the lobby. From her seventh-floor apartment Anthony pointed to roofs climbing the bulldozer-flattened slopes of the Koolaus, and to nearby Punahou School, its once-spacious grounds crowded with new buildings. "I don't like what this city has become," she admitted. "If I was arriving today, I don't think I'd be as taken with Honolulu. Now we're an American city, and hardly different from those on the mainland."

More than a vague nostalgia for Hawaii's prewar colonial system motivated the complaints. Instead, the Pearl Harbor generation feared the loss of exactly what had once bewitched them, and continued drawing visitors and immigrants, Oahu's extraordinary natural beauty.

Cy Gillette called Honolulu "pretty horrendous." Elwood Craddock said "I stay away as much as I can. Last time we went, we sweated, it stank, and I came home with a sore throat." Don Woodrum referred to Waikiki as "an isolation ward for tourists." Sue

Isonaga said she never went downtown or to Waikiki for pleasure, and complained that every year there seemed to be fewer neighborhoods where she felt safe, a situation common to many postwar American cities, whose safe and pleasant neighborhoods shrink in size and number as the cities grow larger and more populous.

I tried keeping their complaints in perspective by reminding myself that before Pearl Harbor, Hawaii had been a stratified colonial society, while now it was a prosperous multiracial one that is as tolerant as any on earth. Before, Asians had been unable to rise to positions of power in the Big Five companies and could not be bus drivers and telephone workers, but since 1975, Hawaiian Asian-Americans have achieved a higher social and economic status than Caucasians. Before, Honolulu had been a pleasant but stagnant backwater, now it had fine libraries, an opera, theaters, and a respectable university.

Despite all the development, much of Oahu remained gorgeous. Its North Shore beaches were thrilling and wild, and curtains of soaring green cliffs overshadowed windward farms and ranches. The Koolaus' upper slopes remained a dragon's back of spiky peaks cut by narrow valleys and treacherous cliffs, and downtown Honolulu was as distinctive and interesting a small American city as you can find, a place of palm shadows, flowering hedges, and the sharp Pacific light you find in San Francisco on a good day, blessed with an exotic hodgepodge of architecture—a rococo Victorian palace, the heavy granite temples of the Big Five, and the tile-roof-and-stucco Territorial buildings popular during the 1920s.

I reminded myself of all that, and yet I could not escape the suspicion that almost everything added to Oahu since Pearl Harbor had detracted from its beauty, while everything pleasing to the eye predated it, nor escape the suspicion that you could say the same thing about plenty of such places on the mainland.

Before Pearl Harbor, Honolulu had been a smaller and less just city, now it was three times the size and more equitable, but had acquired a monotony of fast-food restaurants, package-tour hotels, and shopping strips. Before, there had been more than met the eye, now there was less. The Royal Hawaiian Hotel remained lovely and gracious, but most of its famous gardens had become a multilevel shopping center. The Waikiki Theater had preserved its fine Art Deco facade, but its remarkable auditorium had been chopped into a triplex. The military bases had kept their sprawling homes and gardens, but just outside their gates were developments lacking the backyards that made living in the Islands worthwhile. Honolulu had not just changed slightly since Pearl Harbor, it had become almost the opposite of its prewar self, and an exemplar of the post–Pearl Harbor, postwar changes visited on mainland cities.

Before Pearl Harbor, Honolulu had been a languid city where you worked half a day and took the morning off to welcome an ocean liner. Now its cost of living was so high it had the highest percentage of any state in the nation of two-income families, and the highest percentage of people holding two jobs. It was not unusual to find a husband and wife with three or four jobs between them, and cursed by a hectic schedule leaving little time for cooking, which was responsible for the state having the greatest per capita number of fast-food franchises in the nation.

Before 1941, Waikiki resembled a coconut plantation. There were still palm trees, but they were not as numerous or as large, and those shading beaches and streets were repeatedly neutered, so their nuts could not fall on pedestrians or cars, occasioning lawsuits. In fact, so few productive trees remained on Oahu that the owner of a bakery complained of having to make traditional Hawaiian coconut cakes with coconut imported from Thailand. Waikiki had lost many of its trees during the construction booms of the sixties and seventies. Elsewhere, residents were selling their mature backyard trees to Ko Olina, a 640-acre Japanese-owned resort on the formerly barren southwest coast. I sometimes saw trucks loaded with the palms, their fronds dragging on the highway. Residents of Nanakuli protested this loss. One man complained over the radio of seeing fewer palm trees every time he returned from work. He shouted, "Wake up, Nanakuli! Stop selling your heritage to the Japanese!"

Before Pearl Harbor, Hawaiians had been so unconcerned with

crime many had permanently lost their house keys, and in 1939, Maui's chief of police boasted that his entire county (which included the islands of Maui, Molokai, and Lanai) was crime-free. Now the only "House Without a Key" on Oahu was the bar of that name in the Halekulani Hotel. Honolulu's crime rates, particularly for violent offenses, were low compared to mainland cities, but most Hawaiians compared them to the city they remembered, and on that basis there was a crime wave. Guidebooks warned female tourists against jogging alone on cane roads, louvered windows were seldom used in new construction because they were difficult to secure against thieves, and new homes came with security systems and signs warning of dogs and alarms.

Sue Isonaga told me, "Before, I had no fear living here alone when my husband was fighting in the Korean War. Now I never leave my door unlocked, even if I'm only in the yard." Wymo Takaki had wanted to take his son on a hike to show him the remote cave he had stocked with provisions against a Japanese invasion, but his friends warned him that it was located in an area controlled by violent marijuana cultivators.

Public manners were excellent. Rarely did I hear a voice raised in anger or a horn honked in impatience, and I was the recipient of numerous acts of kindness difficult to imagine on the mainland. Yet, many residents believed the true "aloha spirit" had suffered since Pearl Harbor.

Eva Marie Judd described it as being "kindliness, thoughtfulness, and everyone being very polite," and said it had been genuine when she arrived but had become a veneer. Jack London once wrestled with defining aloha and came up with "the positive affirmation of one's own heart giving." The Hawaii State Commission on Environmental Planning held hearings on aloha and concluded that although difficult to define, it was "identified with empathy, tolerance, graciousness, friendliness, understanding, and giving." Whatever its precise definition, it was agreed to have roots in the Polynesian culture of native Hawaiians, which placed a high value on friendliness, cooperation, and sharing. In 1941, thirty-five thousand tourists a year visited Hawaii; now there were more than seven million and I sometimes encountered what is known in the Islands as "aloha fatigue," or people "forcing their aloha."

Before Pearl Harbor, the tourist industry promoted the harmless myth of the grass-skirted hula girl standing in front of a grass hut playing a ukulele. In fact, grass skirts were a late nineteenth-century import from Micronesia and were never worn by native Hawaiians. The ukulele, although adopted by Hawaiian musicians as their own, was brought by Portuguese plantation laborers. The last Hawaiian to live in a grass hut was an eccentric curiosity even in the 1930s, and probably the most photographed hula girl of all time was a woman in the Kodak Hula Show named Tootsie Notley.

The new Hawaii myth was that the islands were a vast adventure playground, in which every "adventure" required some form of exotic, and expensive, motorized transport. This myth convinced visitors that Hawaii must be seen from a helicopter, all-terrain vehicle, motorized rubber raft, or a parachute attached to a speedboat, but rarely on foot, perhaps because it is difficult to charge for walking. There were reports of a smog of motorboat exhausts hovering in the spectacular sea arches of Kauai's Na Pali coast, of jeeps altering the terrain of remote valleys and beaches, and of environmental problems caused by the washing and fueling of the sight-seeing craft that board nine hundred passengers a day at the mouth of the Hanalei River.

The tourist industry has portrayed the Islands as enjoying universally abundant sunshine and dry weather, as well as lush, tropical foliage. In fact, most Hawaiian islands have both sunshine and a rain forest, but not in the same place. They have a dry south-and-west-facing leeward coast with plenty of sunshine, which is accompanied by the barren Greek-island terrain that comes with under twenty-five inches of rain a year. The forests and waterfalls are found on the east-and-north-facing windward coasts, and are accompanied by frequent rainfall and clouds.

Before Pearl Harbor, the most common tools employed to make the real Hawaii conform to the visitor industry's mythical one were the pencils, etching knives, India-ink cakes, and split razor blades of the photographic retouching studio. In the 1920s, pioneers like Norman D. Hill, "Hawaii's Doctor of Photography," added fleecy clouds to drab skies, set lights blazing from black hotel windows, erased electric lines and telephone poles, filled every night sky with a harvest moon, highlighted palm fronds, enhanced rainbows, and created the image, in the language of one 1925 tourist brochure, of "an Eden of peace and pleasure, love and laziness, and plumbing that is American."

After Pearl Harbor, the most common tool for making Hawaii conform to the fantasy was the bulldozer. Developers reshaped, watered, and planted miles of leeward coastlines, transforming them into Brobdingnagian resorts that squatted like toads on lily pads of bogus tropical landscaping, and changing a wild and distinctive Hawaiian landscape into the manicured one of a California country club.

Former intelligence officer Don Woodrum, who became an advertising and public-relations executive, scoffed at the "Disneyland-type" hotels, saying, "This is a radical change for us. Before the war, visitors came to enjoy our unique culture and atmosphere, and they wanted hotels that would let them mingle with Hawaiians. But as Hawaii has lost what made it unique, people just come for the weather, and hardly ever venture outside the walls of these compounds. They have what I call 'concentration camp holidays.' "

Despite the complaints about crowded sidewalks and mainland defense workers, Oahu was uncrowded in 1941, with much of its population of three hundred thousand concentrated in the city. You could drive for miles through cane and pineapple fields without seeing a house, and walk along rural beaches empty except for a few fishermen. People hiked and gathered wild orchids on lower slopes of the Koolaus that have become dense carpets of houses. The windward coast was reached over a twisty mountain road instead of tunnels and an interstate highway, and was known for its agricultural villages and weekend beach shacks.

Today, Oahu feels crowded. Its population has more than tripled since 1941 and the windward villages of Kailua and Kaneohe have become sprawling commuter suburbs. Police patrol scenic lookouts to break up large gatherings of teenagers seeking open space, and lifeguards set out traffic cones to clear a corridor to the water through carpets of sunbathers. Waikiki has become more densely populated than New York or Tokyo. Every day, 120,000 people pack themselves into its square mile, so many that if they visited the beach at once, there would be trampling deaths. Cane and pineapple fields shrink each year, and it is not impossible that by 2041 Oahu will have lost most of its agriculture and accessible open spaces, becoming an urban island like Singapore or Hong Kong. Only military bases like Wheeler Field, Hickam, and Ford Island are likely to remain much as they are now, spacious and uncrowded, and still haunted by Pearl Harbor.

POSTSCRIPT

DECEMBER 5–7, 2000

EXORCISING THE GHOSTS

So many events had been scheduled for the fifty-ninth anniversary of Pearl Harbor that they had to be spread over several days. In addition to the traditional December 7 ceremonies, the National Park Service was holding a reception on December 5 to introduce new exhibits at the U.S.S. *Arizona* Memorial Visitor Center. On December 6, an ad hoc group calling itself "The World War II American and Japanese Friendship Committee" had arranged a reconciliation ceremony aboard the battleship *Missouri*, during which more than a hundred Japanese veterans, including three Pearl Harbor pilots, would shake hands with American veterans and survivors.

Sterling Cale planned to attend. But his wife, who came from a local Filipino-American family, remained bitter. She had told him, "I don't want to see any photographs of you shaking hands with them." When I mentioned the *Missouri* event to Ray Emory, the survivor who had identified the Pearl Harbor Unknowns, he said, "In 1991, some reporter asked me about reconciliation and I told him, 'Look, if my next door neighbor raped and murdered my mother fifty years ago, do you think I'd be inviting him over for lunch?' "

At the U.S.S. *Arizona* Memorial Visitor Center reception that evening I met Zenji Abe, one of the pilots who would shake Sterling Cale's hand the next day. He was a small, formal man with huge spectacles, an elderly version of the stereotypical Japanese aviator of 1941—short, near-sighted, and timid. But when he spoke, I sensed a fierce determination undiminished by age. I asked what had inspired him to buy the flowers that Richard Fiske scattered over the *Arizona* every month. His eyes blazed behind his owlish eyeglasses and he chopped the air with a hand to emphasize each word. "I do flowers because we attacked before war was declared, and that was wrong— very *wrong*!" He had begun feeling remorseful in 1983, he said, after the sudden deaths of his wife and son made him think how the sudden deaths of the servicemen he killed at Pearl Harbor must have devastated their families.

The December 7 ceremonies held on the lawn of the *Arizona* Memorial Visitor Center started at 0755, the same time the attack had commenced. There were echo taps, a missing man flyover, a sail-by, a rifle salute, a moment of silence, speeches, and prayers from a Navy chaplain and Japanese priest.

"Is this the way it was fifty-nine years ago?" I asked Sterling Cale. Had he seen the same fluffy pink clouds, the reflected sun sparkling off windows at Ford Island, the water smooth as a mirror, the trade winds stilled, the palm fronds frozen? Had he sensed the world holding its breath?

Yes, he said, it was just like this.

Pearl Harbor anniversary speeches often mentioned the "lessons" of that day. During the early years of the Cold War, the lesson was vigilance against Communism; during the Vietnam War, the danger of appeasing an Asian foe; during the Reagan years, the importance of a strong military. But other lessons, ones with an uncomfortable relevance to the present, went unexamined. Among these are how an obsession with internal subversion can leave you vulnerable to your real enemies; how technological superiority—the ability to decipher Japanese codes—is no guarantee of victory; and how a mix of racism and national pride can be a recipe for disaster, or as Colonel William Flood, the commander of Wheeler Field, put it on December 7, "To think that this bunch of little yellow bastards could do this to us when we all knew that the United States was superior to Japan!"

This year, however, there was no mention of lessons, and no attempt to use Pearl Harbor to further a particular political agenda. Instead, Kathy Billings, the superintendent of the memorial, gave a short speech reminding us that most of the dead had been no older than the painfully young servicemen sitting among us. Then Clark Simmons, a distinguished African-American attorney who had been a mess attendant on the *Utah*, delivered a moving keynote address that summarized the attack and closed with the motto of the Pearl Harbor Survivors Association, "Remember Pearl Harbor and Keep America Alert."

By the time of the seventieth anniversary, perhaps only a handful of survivors will attend this ceremony, and ten years after that, none. But Pearl Harbor will continue to be remembered, and marked, perhaps by speakers who are the sons and daughters, or grandsons and granddaughters, of Pearl Harbor survivors, and who will claim to be overcome by "intense emotions" every December 7. For the rest of us, the most lingering legacies of the attack may be a vague sense of insecurity, a suspicion that sometimes the disaster our leaders and experts dismiss as impossible can happen, and can happen because beneath the sleek and reassuring skin of prosperous suburbs, glittering cities, and technological wonders lie some of the same flaws in the national character—overconfidence, racism, and pride—that turned Pearl Harbor into such a catastrophe. I suspect it is these flaws that will prove to be the most stubborn Pearl Harbor ghosts of all.

NOTES

8   Radar on Oahu from Tetley interview.
9   Description of last peacetime crossing: interview with Dillingham.
9   Davidson story: *HA*, December 4, 1941.

2: VICE-CONSUL MORIMURA SEES THE SIGHTS

12   Background on Yoshikawa's spying activities: Yoshikawa article in *Naval Institute Proceedings*; Shearer article in *Parade*, articles in *HA*, December 7, 1969, and December 3, 1981; article in *HSB*, December 7, 1960; *Farago*, particularly chapters 18 and 19; interview with Woodrum; postattack Investigative Reports of the 14th Naval District found in the appendix of the 194S investigation conducted by Major Henry C. Clausen, reproduced in PHA, part 35.
14   The best explanation of the importance of the Bomb Plot message is in *Layton*, pp. 162–68. See also *Farago*, chapter 18.
14   Voyage of the *Taiyo Maru*: *Farago*, pp. 24S–47, *HSB* and *HA*, November 1–6, 1941; *Layton*, pp. 174–75.
16   Yoshikawa's cables: *Farago*, pp. 291–312.
16   RCA office gives cables to counterintelligence: described in *Layton*, pp. 277–80.
17   Layton's conclusion about Yoshikawa's cables: *Layton*, p. 278.
17   The "Lights" cable: *Layton*, pp. 277–84; *Farago*, pp. 300–2; Prange, *Dawn*, pp. 450–51. Layton has the most reliable, detailed explanation of how information that could have averted Pearl Harbor had already been received in Washington the day before, and of why this information was not properly evaluated. He stresses the misuse of radio intelligence as the root cause of the disaster, while Prange believes it was the "gap between knowledge of possible danger and belief in its existence." The argument is over which was a more important cause of the debacle. I think it is virtually impossible now to "prove" that one or the other was more responsible; both were culpable, and both "root causes."

19 Prange points out the serious consequences of the failure to close the Honolulu consulate in *Dawn*, pp. 149–52.

19 Hughes's comments about Yoshikawa: *HA*, December 7, 1981.

20 Woodrum comment from interview.

20 Mayfield comment made to Roberts Commission, PHA, part 23, p. 650.

20 Shivers comment made to Roberts Commission, PHA, part 23, p. 857.

21 Kimball comment made to Roberts Commission, PHA, part 23, p. 923.

22 Army Intelligence report from a January 5, 1942, memorandum written by Second Lieutenant Clifford M. Andrew, available in HWRD.

22 Bicknell report from his unpublished manuscript.

3: GEORGE AKITA DELIVERS A SPEECH

23 Speech contest: *HSB*, December 5 and 6, 1941.

24 Excerpt from Akita's diary furnished by Akita to the author.

25 Discussion of intergenerational strains among Japanese community in Hawaii: Lind; Fuchs; Hazama and Komeiji; Saiki; Stephan; Ogawa; interview with Larry and Minnie Nakatsuka; series of articles by Nakatsuka under the pseudonym "Mr. Sato" published throughout summer 1940 in HSB.

26 Difficulties placed in way of "Americanization" found in Bicknell manuscript.

27 "Not very pretty to look at" comment made to the Army Pearl Harbor Board by General Wells, PHA, part 28, p. 1422.

28 Sources for efforts by AJAs to prove loyalty are same as for pp. 58–60.

4: THE VIEW FROM WALTER DILLINGHAM'S WINDOW

30   Interview with Dillingham.

31   Background material on Honolulu in 1941: *Hoehling*; *Sheehan*; *Porteus*; *Allen*; *Paradise of the Pacific*; *HSB*; *HA*; author interviews.

34   *Fortune* article: "Sugar-Coated Fort," August 1940.

36   Morgan article in *HSB*, July 11, 1941.

38   Kurusu's stop in Honolulu: *HSB* and *HA*, November 13, 1941.

38   Litvinov's stop: *HSB* and *HA*, December 5, 1941.

39   Visit from Thai royal family and dispute over the hula: unpublished autobiography of author Catherine Mellen, shown to the author by Richard Van Dyke.

5: OMENS ARE SEEN

44   Football game reported in copies of the December 7, 1941, *Advertiser* printed before its presses broke.

44   Omens in the Honolulu sky: *Mellen*, p. 168.

45   Good's comment is in Prange, *Dec. 7*, p. 27; Chapman's is on p.38; Layton's reaction to the national anthem on p. 47.

46   Short's "What a target": *Lord*, p. 6.

46   Mellen "considered it sinister": *Mellen*, pp. 168–69.

46   Poindexter's suspicions about Japanese rice purchases are from his testimony to the Roberts Commission, PHA, part 23, p. 821.

47   Testimony of Honolulu police chief to Roberts Commission is in PHA, part 23, pp. 795–96.

47   Story about the luau at Wahiawa is in *Ollila*, p. 104.

48   Search of Hawaii Importing reported in *Hazema* and *Komeiji*, pp. 129–30.

48   *Murder by the Yard* quotation: *Yates*, p. vii.

6: THE SUBMARINERS' WIVES THROW A PARTY

51   Kathy Cooper material from interview.

51   Moseley comment: Prange, *Dec. 7*, p. 104.

52   Same sources as pages S8–60; also author's interviews in Honolulu, and *Porteus*.

7: ALERTED FOR SABOTAGE

55   Dillingham statement: PHA, part 28, p. 1443.
55   Bicknell statement from his unpublished manuscript in HWRD.
56   Fielder statement made to Roberts Commission, PHA, part 22, p. 179.
56   Message from War Department: PHA, part 14, p. 1407. Prange, *Dawn*, p. 403.
56   Marshall misses his opportunity to intervene: PHA, part 3, p. 1421.
56   Stimson's statement in Prange, *Verdict*, p. 210.
57   Short's comment to Roberts commission: PHA, Part 22, p. 102.
57   Martin believes there will be no Japanese strike: PHA, part 28, p. 962; Prange, *Verdict*, p. 253.
57   Martin's report: Prange, *Dawn*, p. 94.
58   The "war warning": PHA, part 14, p. 1406.
59   Shoemaker's alert: Prange, *Dec. 7*, p. 15.
59   Martin's alert: Prange, *Dec. 7*, p. 23.
60   Dybdal account from interview.
60   Camp Malakole antiaircraft preparations: interviews with Myron Haynes.
60   Farthing calls a meeting: Prange, *Dec. 7*, p. 24.
61   Ahola's account from interview.

8: THE SUPREME OVERCONFIDENCE OF A GREAT ATHLETE

63   Belief in sabotage of *Advertiser* presses: Catherine Mellen autobiography.
65   Mass comment from *HA*, September 4, 1941.
65   May comment from *HA*, December 2, 1941.

65   Knox speech reported in *HSB* and *HA*, and in *Ketchum*, pp. 724–26.

65   *New York Times Magazine* article: Hanson W. Baldwin, "Our Gibraltar in the Pacific," February 16, 1941.

65   Collier's article by Walter Davenport, June 14, 1941, p. 11.

67   Wakukawa comment from interview.

67   The kamaaina woman whose father joked about a Japanese raid was Patricia Morgan (now Swenson), from interview.

67   The Marine bugler was Richard Fiske, from interview.

68   *Paradise of the Pacific* article appeared in January 1936.

68   Sutton comment about "great athlete" from interview.

68   Kinzler comment from interview.

68   Woodrum comment from interview.

68   Clarey comment from interview.

68   Cooper comment from interview.

69   McMorris comment from Prange, *Dawn*, p. 401.

69   Kimmel comment to Harsch from *Stillwell*, p. 264.

69   Layton quotation from Layton, p. 244.

69   Pye comment from Layton, p. 274.

69   Layton says an attack "far from our minds": *Layton*, p. 275.

69   Bicknell's summary from his manuscript in HWRD.

9: MRS. MORI TALKS TO TOKYO

71   Flynn records Mori call: from interview.

72   Text of Mori call reproduced in report of Roberts Commission in PHA, part 24, p. 2023.

72   Bicknell learns of Japanese consulate burning its papers: Prange, *Dec. 7*, p. 22; Bicknell manuscript in HWRD.

72   Bicknell worries about Mori call and meets with Short and Fielder: Bicknell manuscript in HWRD; Congressional investigation of 1945, PHA, part 10, p. 5089–122; *Lord*, pp. S–6; Prange, *Dec. 7*, pp. 40–41.

73   Bicknell mumbles about flowers on December 7: interview with Dorothy Bicknell.

74 Woodrum's reaction to Mori call: from interview.

74 Article about Mrs. Mori: *HSB*, December 5, 1957.

75 Bicknell's interpretation of call: see reference for pages 135–37.

76 Interview with Mr. and Mrs. Breitinstein.

10: ENSIGN YOSHIKAWA'S LAST CABLE

79 Yoshikawa's last evening and further life: Yoshikawa article in *Naval Institute Proceedings*; Shearer article in *Parade*; articles in *HA*, December 7, 1969, and December 3, 1981; article in *HSB*, December 7, 1960; *Farago*, particularly chapters 18 and 19; interview with Woodrum; postattack Investigative Reports of the Fourteenth Naval District, which can be found in the appendix of the 1945 investigation conducted by Major Henry C. Clausen, reproduced in PHA, part 35.

11: A WHITE RIVER FLOWS DOWN HOTEL STREET

83 Background for Honolulu on the eve of war: author's interviews; *Porteus*; *Hoehling*; *Allen*; *Sheehan*; *Lord*; *Paradise of the Pacific*; *HA*, December 7, 1941.

83 "Battle of the Music" reported in *HSB*, April 2, 1942.

84 Bicknell remembers Kita's parties: Prange, *Dec.* 7, p. 45.

85 Dorothy Anthony comment from interview.

85 Description of party at Royal Hawaiian cottage: interview with Ruth Flynn.

87 Kinzler comment from interview.

88 Mason p. 15

89 Temperance League investigates Hotel Street: testimony to Roberts Commission, PHA, part 23, pp. 835–52.

90 Prohibitionist tract quotation: Gilbert, pp. 11–12.

90 Honolulu Chief of Police Gabrielson testified to the Roberts Committee that December 6 had been an ordinary Saturday night: PHA, part 23, pp. 794–96.

90   Material on defense workers: *Sheehan; HSB; HA.*

91   Labor Day parade: *HA,* September 2, 1941.

91   Cale material from interview.

92   "Lights twinkling in their periscopes from *Sakamaki.*

92   Photograph of Japanese pilots doing hula: *Hudson,* p. 3.

12: HAWAII TAKES A DEEP BREATH

95   Midget submarines head for Pearl Harbor: *Sakamaki; Stewart; Jackson; HSB* series written by Burl Burlinghame and beginning December 6, 1988.

95   Description of Pearl Harbor on night of December 6: *Farago,* p. 361.

96   *Ward* fires on a midget submarine: same references as p. 169; also Prange, *Dec. 7,* pp. 91–92, 100–3, *Dawn,* pp. 495–98, *Verdict,* pp. 461–62; *Lord,* pp. 38–42.

97   First Shot Naval Vets: *HA,* December 7, 1978.

97   Opana radar station story: *Lord,* pp. 44–49; Prange, *Dec. 7,* pp. 95–99.

100   Missed chances in Washington: *Layton,* pp. 302–6; Prange, *Dawn,* pp. 493–95.

101   Fuchikami collects telegram: interview with Fuchikami.

103   "Prep" flag is raised: *Lord,* pp. 66–67.

104   Amateur army pilots shot down: interview with Myron Haynes.

104   Cornelia Fort story: *Clark,* pp. 113–16.

104   Vitousek story: interview with Roy Vitousek; Swenson manuscript; *Lord,* pp. 86–87; *HA,* December 7, 1966.

13: THE MANEUVERS ARE REALISTIC

106   Craddock story from interview with Craddock.

108   Short thought the Navy was having practice: PHA, part 22, p. 57.

108   Bicknell describes incredulity of other officers: Bicknell manuscript.

108   Yee Kam York: testimony to Roberts Commission, PHA, part 23, p. 926.

108   Ethelyn Meyhre: *HA*, December 7, 1966.

108   A woman near the university: Grace Tower Warren, who described her experiences in an essay, "War in Paradise," submitted to the HWRD.

109   Dorothy Anthony's reaction from interview.

109   Joseph C. Harsch from his article "A War Correspondent's Odyssey," found in *Stillwell*, p. 264.

109   Pye from testimony to Roberts Commission, PHA, vol. 22, p. 533.

109   Shivers persuades Hoover: *HSB*, December 8, 1981.

109   Ruth Flynn from interview.

109   Dillingham from interview.

110   Izuma and Johnson's experiences: article by Dr. Harold Johnson, "Reminiscences of December Seventh 1l," published in *Hawaii Medical Journal*, December 1966, pp. 143–44.

110   Smythe and Oyama stories: *HA*, December 7, 1976.

110   Judd story from interview.

110   Kimmel sees the attack: Prange, *Dec.* 7, p. 119.

111   Hudson's reaction from interview.

111   Dickinson reaction from "I Fly for Vengeance," *Saturday Evening Post*, October 19, 1943.

111   Fiske story from interview.

112   Cale story from interview.

113   Dybdal story and Pearl Harbor cruise from interview.

14. THE WARM AIR OF AN UNENDING SUMMER LAND

117   Japanese pilots' memories of the attack: Prange, *Dec.* 7, pp. 113–16; Fuchida, "I Led the Attack . . ."

117   The number of Japanese pilots is a matter of some controversy.

This figure from *HSB* article published on the twenty-fifth anniversary. David Aiken (see Chapter 1, p. 15) is making an extensive study of this subject, and his figures, when they are published, will probably be the most reliable.

118 Comment by Yoshio Shiga from *HSB*, December 8, 1981.

118 Genda visit described in *HA*, March 4, 1969.

118 Return of Bando to Pearl Harbor from *HSB*, December 8, 1981.

118 Hudson described the return of the six pilots in an interview.

120 Fuchida's conversion and frequent visits to Hawaii: Fuchida's book; *HSB*, December 8, 1966.

121 Fuchida attends the dinner party: interviews with Smyser and Dorothy Bicknell; *HSB*, December 8, 1966.

120 Fuchida's 1966 visit to the *Arizona* Memorial: *HSB*, December 8, 1966.

121 Don Stratton refuses to pose: *HSB*, December 7, 1981.

122 Fuchida's comment "joy in my heart" reported in *HSB* during his 1952 visit to Honolulu.

122 Fuchida's comment about Vietnam War reported in his 1978 obituary published in *HA*.

15. A VOICE FROM THE BOTTOM OF THE SEA

123 Midgets on December 7 from Stewart, "Those Mysterious Subs"; *Jackson*.

123 Sakamaki's experiences: *Sakamaki*; *Saiki*, chapter 12; interview with Sakamaki by Buck Buchwach, *HA*, December 7, 1969.

125 Sakamaki's 1981 visit reported by De Yarmin in interview.

125 Story of the raising of Midget D: *Jackson*; *Stewart*; *HSB*, July 6 and 16, 1960; *HA*, July 21, 1960 ("Clues Indicate Crew Escaped Midget Sub"), February 3, 1975, and December 7, 1985

126 Article in *Naval Institute Proceedings* is Stewart.

126 Okino Sasaki story: *Our Navy*, December 1967.

16. THE *ARIZONA* OPENS LIKE A FLOWER

131 Description of deaths on *Arizona*: Fleet Reserve Association booklet, p. 45; *HSB*, May 7, 1984; Prange, *Dec. 7*, pp. 144–45.
131 Interview with Cale.
131 *Mason*, p. 221.
132 Interview with Fiske.
133 Casualties are described in Cloward article and *HSB*, December 7, 1982.
133 Description of explosion and casualties on *Arizona*: *Lord*, pp. 98–99; Prange, *Dec. 7*, p. 146.
135 Interview with Emory.

17. THE "LITTLE YELLOW BASTARDS" DESTROY THE ARMY AIR FORCE

140 Ahola memories from interview and from article in *HA*, December 7, 1986.
142 Description of Hickam Field in early days from articles in Hickam Field historical archives.
145 Kinzler remembers attack on Schofield: from interview.
146 The book of Pearl Harbor photographs: *Cohen*, p. 98.
147 James Jones's account of the attack on Schofield: *From Here to Eternity*, pp. 822–47.
147 *From Here to Eternity* photograph: *Cohen*, p. 99.
147 Garcia material from interview.
149 Jones returns in 1973: Jones, *Viet Journal*, p. 249.
149 Picture caption: *Cohen*, p. 101.
150 Gillette's experiences at Kaneohe: from interview.
151 Attack on Kaneohe: Gillette interview; *HSB*, December 7, 1979; *Lord*, pp. 116–17, 153–54; Prange, *Dec. 7*, pp. 282–86.
154 Fortieth anniversary ceremonies at Kaneohe, return of Finn, Kikuyo Iida, and Nemish protest: material in files of Kaneohe MCAS public affairs office files; *HA*, December 6, 1981; *HSB*, December 7, 1981.

18. ONCE A JAPANESE, ALWAYS A JAPANESE

158   Thompson material from her article in HWRD.

158   Kay material from "Summary of Verbal Report Submitted to Colonel Bicknell and Lieutenant Dyson, U. S. Army," found in HWRD.

159   Kita thinks the planes are "French,": *HA*, January 4, 1948.

159   Description of *Women's Voice* article in Prange, *Dawn*, p. 843.

160   Layton quotation from *Layton*, p. 298.

161   Kimmel hit by bullet: Prange, *Dawn*, p. 516.

162   Kimmel says he was a scapegoat: AP interview published in *HA*, December 8, 1966.

164   Rumors about Japanese residents of Hawaii: *Porteus*, pp. 160–63; *Allen*, pp. 47–56; *Lind*, pp. 38–61; *HSB*, December 8–12, 1941; *HA*, December 8–12,1941.

165   Two heroic Japanese teenagers: *Clark*, p. 184.

166   Story of dead Japanese in truck: ". . . A Hell of a Christmas," in *Stillwell*, p. 224.

167   Knox makes his report: Prange, *Dawn*, pp. 586, 589.

167   Stimson announcement: *HSB*, May 14, 1942.

168   Notes made by Hite of Poindexter's conversation in his diary in HWRD; see also *Anthony*, pp. 5–10.

169   See *Anthony*, pp. 34–59, for discussion of military government in Hawaii; *Allen*, pp. 166–83.

170   Affidavits swearing to loyalty of Hawaii's Japanese residents: a file in HWRD.

170   Story about kimono-clad Japanese: *Allen*, p. 56.

19: A DEEP SHOCK WAVE

172   "Shock wave" comment by civilian witness: Patricia Swenson, in her unpublished manuscript.

172   Peggy Ryan memories: "A Navy Bride Learns to Cope," in *Stillwell*, p. 232.

173 Harsch memories: " 'A War Correspondent's Odyssey,' " in *Stillwell*, p. 264.

173 Experiences of Mary Ellen and Wells Lawrence: from interview.

175 Hickam Field private: *Newsweek*, December 12, 1966.

175 Clarey experiences and flashback: from interview.

175 Sutton experiences: from interview.

176 Cale interview.

177 Fiske experiences: from interview.

179 Details about the Pearl Harbor Survivors Association from issues of its quarterly, *Pearl Harbor-Gram*, 1987–1989.

20: HOW COULD THEY DO THIS TO ME?

182 Maid who wished she could change her face: Reported by Grace Tower Warren in "War In Paradise," in HWRD.

182 Mackay describes Sumi: from Mackay article.

183 William Diem account in HWRD.

183 Tsukiyama from interview.

184 Yempuku from interview and Knaefler article.

184 Inouye from *Hazama and Komeiji*, p. 125.

184 "Spud" Ishimoto from interview.

185 Akita from his diary.

185 Sato from interview.

185 Isonaga from interview.

186 Tsubota from interview.

186 Richard Ishimoto from interview.

186 Kawahara from interview.

186 Stevenson from interview.

187 Nakatsuka material: interview with Nakatsuka; *Lord*, pp. 170–71; *HSB*, December 7, 1941 (third extra edition); Prange, *Dec. 7*, pp. 344–45.

188 Wakukawa from interview.

188 Fuchikami from interview.

189 Takaki from interview.

21: THE UNITED STATES NAVY SHELLS HONOLULU

192   Pearl Harbor heroics: Editors of the Army Times, *Pearl Harbor and Hawaii: A Military History*, pp. 39–77.

192   Harsch: Harsch article in *Stillwell*, p. 264.

193   Cooper from interview.

193   Panic and shelling of Honolulu: *Allen*, pp. 5–8; *Lord*, p. 158; *Revolt in Paradise*, pp. 56–60; Prange, *Dec.* 7, pp. 331–36, *Dawn*, pp. 561–72; *HSB*, December 7, 1976; *HA*, and *HSB*, December 7–10,1941.

194   The death of Matilda Faufata is described in a poignant letter sent to the HWRD by her mother.

194   Craddock from interview.

194   Petrie comments published in *Western City* magazine, January 1942.

195   Herbert Coryell in HWRD.

195   The shells belonged to the U.S. Navy: PHA, part 28, p. 1059; *Lord*, p. 220.

197   Morgan from interview and Morgan manuscript.

197   Woodrum from interview.

197   Poindexter is nervous: Warren paper in HWRD.

199   Warden is beaten to death

199   Morgan arms herself: from Morgan manuscript.

22: THE A LIST JAPANESE PACK THEIR BAGS

203   Fukuda material from interview.

204   Internment of Japanese on Hawaii: *Hazama and Komeiji*, pp. 123–32; *Fuchs*, p. 303; *Allen*, pp. 134–38.

204   See *Stephan*, pp. 23–40, for an excellent discussion of the conflicting loyalties of the Japanese.

204   Nakatsuka from interview with Larry and Minni Nakatsuka.

205   Sato from interview with Nancy Sato (now Haynes).

205   Wakukawa from interview.

206   Preis from interview.

207   Woodrum from interview.

208   Most Japanese on Hawaii not interned, and praise for Shivers *et al*: booklet published by Honolulu Japanese Junior Chamber of Commerce *(Kanasha)*; also article by Smyser in *HSB*, December 7, 1979.

208   Isonaga from interview.

209   Marumoto's friendship with Shivers: Marumoto interview and article in *East-West Photo Journal*.

209   Isonaga from interview.

210   Wells: PHA, part 23, p. 804.

211   Wakukawa from interview.

212   Sutton from interview.

213   Nishimura from interview.

213   Tsukiyama from interview.

213   Fukuda sisters from interview.

23: A DEEP, POWERFUL THIRST FOR REVENGE

217   Lawrence from interview.

217   Cooper from interview.

217   Mary Hall's diary in HWRD.

217   Anger of military men: Prange, *Dec.* 7, p. 337.

217   Morgan from interview.

218   Cooper from interview.

218   Faufata from letter in HWRD.

218   Halsey vows revenge: *Dower*, p. 36. See *Dower*, pp. 36–41, for a discussion of the anger resulting from Pearl Harbor.

218   Japanese tail gunner thumbs his nose: Dickinson article.

218   Mainland poll: *Cantril*, p. 501.

218   Tennessee hunting licenses: *Melosi*, p. 5.

218   "Hunting Japanese": *Time*, December 22, 1941.

219   Economic disputes haunted by Pearl Harbor: *New York Times*, July 11, 1990.

219   Pickens advertisement: *New York Times*, September 6, 1990.

220   Hudson from interview.

221 Backhoe story: *Pearl Harbor–Gram*, January 1988.

222 "I am the proud son . . .": *Pearl Harbor–Gram*, January, 1988.

222 Opinion polls: *Fortune*, February 26, 1990.

222 Statistics about Japanese investment in Hawaii: *Hawaii Business*, January and April 1990; *Forbes*, February 22, 1988; *HA*, April 17, 1990; *HA*, April 27, 1988; *HSB*, April 9, 1989; numerous articles in *HSB*, and *HA*, February-May 1988 and April 1990.

228 Bicknell and Anthony from interviews.

229 Polls of attitudes toward Japanese investment were made in March 1990 and published in a series of articles in *HSB*, April 23–28, 1990.

229 Bekeart from interview.

24: NO CAN EAT GOLF BALLS!

232 Tsukiyama from interview and *HSB*, December 7, 1978.

233 Yempuku from interview.

233 Ishimoto from interview.

233 Takaki from interview.

233 Japanese prove their loyalty: *Allen*, pp. 81–84, pp. 350–51; *Ogawa*, pp. 313–27; *Hazama and Komeiji*, pp. 130–50.

234 Murai comment reported in *HA*, July 9, 1944.

235 Ogai essay in HWRD.

235 Japanese units in World War II: *Allen*, pp. 266–73; Ogawa, pp. 313–27, 349–63; *Hazama and Komeiji*, pp. 150–76.

236 Yempuku from interview.

236 Tsukiyama from interviews.

237 Takaki from interview.

239 Wakukawa, Isonaga, Tsukiyama, and Kawahara interviews.

240 Fujiyama from interview.

240 Fuchikami from interview.

240 Golf: *Hawaii Business*, January 1990; *HSB*, March 20, 1988; *HA*, March 21, 1988; *New York Times*, April 16, 1990.

243 Yempuku: from interview and *HSB*, "Divided Families" series

by Tomi Knaefler, appearing the week of the twenty-fifth anniversary of the attack.

25: NOW WE'RE AN AMERICAN CITY

245 Bicknell, Judd, Anthony, and Lawrence from interviews.
246 Martial law: *Anthony*, pp. 34–59.
247 Bicknell and Judd from interviews.
248 Lawrence from interview.
248 Anthony from interview.
248 Gillette, Craddock, Woodrum, and Isonaga from interviews.
251 Isonaga, Takaki, and Judd from interviews.

SELECTED BIBLIOGRAPHY

This is a listing of the works consulted in the writing of this book, not an all-inclusive Pearl Harbor bibliography. The best one-volume histories of World War II in the Pacific have been published in the last ten years—John Costello's *The Pacific War* and Ronald H. Spector's *Eagle Against the Sun*. Anyone wishing to learn more about the role racial hatred played in the war should read John W. Dower's excellent *War Without Mercy*. If there can be such a thing as a "last word" on Pearl Harbor it is probably shared by Rear Admiral Edwin T. Layton's memoir, *And I Was There*, which lays out the failures to make use of radio intelligence before Pearl Harbor, and Gordon Prange's *At Dawn We Slept*, which is without question the most inclusive book written on the subject. The best revisionist history is John Toland's controversial *Infamy*, but no one should read it without also reading Prange or Layton. The best reconstructions of December 7 are Walter Lord's *Day of Infamy* and Prange's *Dec. 7, 1941*.

The best single work on twentieth-century Hawaii is Lawrence Fuch's *Hawaii Pono*. Ed Sheehan's *Days of '41* is a fine poetic description of Honolulu in the year before the attack. *Hawaii Under* the Rising Sun by John J. Stephan contains a thoughtful and realistic assessment of Japanese loyalty in Hawaii.

The files in the Hawaii War Records Depository at the University of Hawaii contain letters, excerpts from diaries, and essays that make up a fascinating record of civilian attitudes and reactions to the attack.

BOOKS

Allen, Gwenfread. *Hawaii's War Years*. Honolulu: University of Hawaii Press, 1950.

Anthony, J. Garner. *Hawaii Under Army Rule*. Stanford, Calif.: Stanford University Press, 1955.

Barnes, Harry Elmer. *Perpetual War for Perpetual Peace*. Caldwell, Idaho: Caxton Printers, 1953.

Beekman, Allan. *The Niihau Incident*. Honolulu: Heritage Press of Pacific, 1982.

Biggers, Earl Derr. *The House Without a Key*. New York: Grosset & Dunlap, 1925.

Brown, DeSoto. *Hawaii Goes to War: Life in Hawaii from Pearl Harbor to Peace*. Honolulu: Editions Limited, 1989.

———, ed. *Hawaii Recalls: Selling Romance to America. Nostalgic Images of the Hawaiian Islands: 1910–1950*. Honolulu: Editions Limited, 1982.

Cantril, Hadley, ed. *Public Opinion 1935–1946*. Princeton, N.J.: Princeton University Press, 1951.

Clark, Blake. *Remember Pearl Harbor!* Rev. ed. Honolulu: Mutual Publishing, 1987.

Cohen, Stan. *East Wind Rain: A Pictorial History of the Pearl Harbor Attack*. Missoula, Mont.: Pictorial Histories Publishing Company, 1981.

Cooper, George, and Gavan Daws. *Land and Power in Hawaii: The Democratic Years*. Honolulu: Benchmark Books, 1985.

Correspondents of *Time*, *Life*, and *Fortune*. *December 7: The First Thirty Hours*. New York: Knopf, 1942.

Costello, John. *The Pacific War 1941–1945*. New York: Rawson, Wade, 1981.

Culliney, John L. *Islands in a Far Sea: Nature and Man in Hawaii*. San Francisco: Sierra Club Books, 1988.

Daws, Gavan. *Shoal of Time: A History of the Hawaiian Islands*. Honolulu: University of Hawaii Press, 1968.

Dower, John W. *War Without Mercy: Race and Power in the Pacific War*. New York: Pantheon, 1986.

Editors of the Army Times Publishing Company. *Pearl Harbor and Hawaii: A Military History*. New York: Walker, 1971.

Farago, Ladislas. *The Broken Seal*. New York: Random House, 1967.

Farrell, Bryan. *Hawaii: The Legend That Sells*. Honolulu: University of Hawaii Press, 1982.

Fleet Reserve Association, *U.S.S. Arizona: Ship's Data*. Booklet. Honolulu: Fleet Reserve Association, 1978.

Fuchida, Mitsuo. *From "Pearl Harbor to Golgotha."* San Jose, Calif.: Sky Pilots of America International, undated [probably mid-1950s].

Fuchs, Lawrence H. *Hawaii Pono: A Social History*. New York: Harcourt Brace, 1961.

Fussell, Paul. *Wartime: Understanding and Behavior in the Second World War*. New York: Oxford University Press, 1989.

Gessler, Clifford. *Tropic Landfall: The Port of Honolulu*. Garden City, N.Y.: Doubleday, 1942.

Gilbert, Dan. *What Really Happened at Pearl Harbor?* Grand Rapids, Mich.: Zondervan, 1942.

Harrington, Joseph D. *Yankee Samurai: The Secret Role of Nisei in America's Pacific Victory*. Detroit, Mich.: Pettigrew Enterprises, 1979.

Hazama, Dorothy Ochiai, and Jane Okamoto Komeiji. *Okage Sama De: The Japanese in Hawai'i*. Honolulu: Bess Press, 1986.

Hibbard, Don, and David Franzen. *The View from Diamond Head: Royal Residence to Urban Resort*. Honolulu: Editions Limited, 1986.

Hickam Air Force Base, Public Affairs Division. *Hickam: The First Fifty Years*. Honolulu: Public Affairs Division, Hickam AFB, 1985.

Hoehling, A. A. *The Week Before Pearl Harbor.* New York: Norton, 1963.

Honolulu Japanese Junior Chamber of Commerce, Kanasha Program Committee. *Kanasha: In Appreciation.* Honolulu: Honolulu Junior Chamber of Commerce, 1985.

Hudson, Robert Stephen. *Sunrise Sunset: December 7, 1941, Pearl Harbor.* Honolulu: Hudson Historical Enterprise, 1986.

Jackson, Charles L. *On to Pearl Harbor and Beyond.* Dixon, Calif.: Pacific Ship & Shore, 1982.

Jardine, John, with Edward Rohrbough, and Bob Krauss, ed. *Detective Jardine: Crimes in Honolulu.* Honolulu: University of Hawaii Press, 1984.

Jones, James. *From Here to Eternity.* New York: Scribners, 1951.

———. *Viet Journal.* New York: Delacorte, 1974.

Kahn, David. *The Code Breakers.* New York: Macmillan, 1967.

Ketchum, Richard M. *The Borrowed Years 1938–1941: America on the Way to War.* New York: Random House, 1989.

Kimmel, Husband E. *Admiral Kimmel's Story.* Chicago: Regnery, 1955.

Layton, Rear Admiral Edwin T., USN (Ret.). *"And I Was There": Pearl Harbor and Midway—Breaking the Secrets.* New York: Morrow, 1985.

Lenihan, Daniel J., ed. *Submerged Cultural Resources Study: USS "Arizona" Memorial and Pearl Harbor National Historic Landmark.* Santa Fe, N.Mex.: Submerged Cultural Resources Unit, Southwest Cultural Resources Center, Southwest Region, National Park Service, U.S. Department of the Interior, 1989.

Lind, Andrew. *Hawaii's Japanese.* Princeton, N.J.: Princeton University Press, 1946.

Lord, Walter. *Day of Infamy.* New York: Henry Holt, 1957.

MacDonald, Alexander. *Revolt in Paradise.* New York: S. Daye, 1944.

Mason, Theodore C. *Battleship Sailor.* Annapolis, Md.: Naval Institute Press, 1982.

Matson Navigation Company. *Ships in Grey: The Story of Matson in World War II.* San Francisco: Matson Lines, 1946.

McComas, Terence. *Pearl Harbor Fact and Reference Book: Every-*

thing to Know about December 7, 1941. Honolulu: Mutual Publishing, 1991.

Melosi, Martin V. *The Shadow of Pearl Harbor: Political Controversy over the Surprise Attack, 1941–1946*. College Station, Tex.: Texas A & M University Press, 1977.

Millis, Walter. *This is Pearl! The United States and Japan—1941*. New York: Morrow, 1947.

Miyamoto, Kazuo. *Hawaii: End of the Rainbow*. Rutland, Vt.: Charles E. Tuttle, 1964.

Morgenstern, George Edward. *Pearl Harbor*. New York: Devin-Adair, 1947.

Ogawa, Dennis M. *Kodomo No Tame Ni: For the Sake of the Children: The Japanese American Experience in Hawaii*. Honolulu: University of Hawaii Press, 1978.

Ollila, John E. *"I Was at Pearl Harbor": The Life and Times of John E. Ollila*. Wichita, Kans.: Haag-Sumpton, 1984.

Porteus, Stanley D. *And Blow Not the Trumpet*. Palo Alto, Calif.: Pacific Books, 1947.

Prange, Gordon W. *At Dawn We Slept*. New York: McGraw-Hill, 1981.

——, with Donald M. Goldstein and Katherine V. Dillon. *Dec. 7, 1941: The Day the Japanese Attacked Pearl Harbor*. New York: McGraw-Hill, 1988.

——. *Pearl Harbor: The Verdict of History*. New York: McGraw-Hill, 1986.

Rusbridger, James, and Eric Nave. *Betrayal at Pearl Harbor: How Churchill Lured Roosevelt into WWII*. New York: Summit Books, 1991.

Saiki, Patsy. *Ganbare!* Honolulu: Kisaku, 1983.

Sakamaki, Kazuo. *I Attacked Pearl Harbor*. New York: Association Press, 1949.

Sheehan, Ed. *Days of '41: Pearl Harbor Remembered*. Honolulu: Pearl Harbor-Honolulu Branch 46 Fleet Reserve Association Enterprises, 1976.

Shirota, Jon. *Lucky Come Hawaii*. Honolulu: Bess Press, 1988.

Slackman, Michael, ed. *Pearl Harbor in Perspective.* Honolulu: Arizona Memorial Museum Association, 1986.

——. *Remembering Pearl Harbor: The Story of the U.S.S. "Arizona" Memorial.* Honolulu: Arizona Memorial Museum Association, 1984.

Smyser, A. A. *Hawaii's Future in the Pacific: Disaster, Backwater or Future State?* Honolulu: East–West Center, 1988.

Spector, Ronald H. *Eagle Against the Sun: The American War with Japan.* New York: Free Press, 1984.

Stephan, John J. *Hawaii Under the Rising Sun: Japan's Plans for Conquest After Pearl Harbor.* Honolulu: University of Hawaii Press, 1984.

Stillwell, Paul, ed. *Air Raid: Pearl Harbor! Recollections of a Day of Infamy.* Annapolis, Md.: Naval Institute Press, 1981.

Stinnett, Robert B. *Day of Deceit: The Truth about FDR and Pearl Harbor.* New York: Free Press, 2000.

Toland, John. *Infamy: Pearl Harbor and Its Aftermath.* New York: Doubleday, 1982.

——. *The Rising Sun.* New York: Random House, 1970.

U.S. Congress. *Pearl Harbor Attack: Hearings Before the Joint Committee on the Pearl Harbor Attack.* 79th Congress, 1st Session. 39 vols. 1946.

Van Dyke, Robert E., ed., and Ronn Ronck, text. *Hawaiian Yesterdays: Historical Photographs by Ray Jerome Baker.* Honolulu: Mutual Publishing, 1982.

Weglyn, Michi. *Years of Infamy: The Untold Story of America's Concentration Camps.* New York: Morrow, 1976.

Wisniewski, Richard A., ed. *Hawaii: The Territorial Years, 1900–1959.* Honolulu: Pacific Basin Enterprises, 1984.

Wohlstetter, Roberta. *Pearl Harbor: Warning and Decision.* Stanford, Calif.: Stanford University Press, 1962.

Yardley, Maili. *Hawaii: Times and Tides.* Lawai, Kauai, Hawaii: The Woolsey Press, 1975.

Yates, Margaret. *Murder by the Yard.* New York: Harper, 1942.

Zacharias, Ellis M. *Secret Missions.* New York: Putnam, 1946.

NEWSPAPERS AND MAGAZINES

Baldwin, Hanson W. "Our Gibraltar in the Pacific." *New York Times Magazine*, February 16, 1941.

Boyd, Ellsworth. "A Voice from the Bottom of the Sea." *Our Navy*, December 1967.

Cloward, Ralph B., M.D. "A Neurosurgeon Remembers Pearl Harbor." *Surgical Neurology*, December 1976.

Davenport, Walter. "Impregnable Pearl Harbor." *Collier's*, June 14, 1941.

Dickinson, Lt. Clarence C. "I Fly for Vengeance." *Saturday Evening Post*, October 19, 1942.

East–West Photo Journal. "Masaji Marumoto: A Personal History. Part 1: The Formative Years." Winter 1980.

Forbes. "A Mixed Blessing." February 22, 1988.

Fortune. "Hawaii: Sugar-coated Fort." August 1940.

——. "Fear and Loathing of Japan." February 26, 1990.

Fox, Barry. "I Remember Pearl Harbor." *Harper's*, January 1943.

Fuchida, Mitsuo. "I Led the Air Attack on Pearl Harbor." Ed. by Roger Pineau. *United States Naval Institute Proceedings*, September 1952.

Hawaii Business. "The Billionaires Next Door," "The Japaning of Hawaii," "The Orient Express," and "A Teed-Off Public." January 1990.

——. "The Value of the Land" and "The New King in Town." April 1990.

Honolulu Magazine. Centennial Issue, 1888–1988: 100 Years of Paradise. Honolulu, November 1987.

Horton, Tom. "Waikaloa Wonderland." *Spirit of Aloha*, April 1989.

Knaefler, Tomi. "Divided Families." A series of articles running in *Honolulu Star-Bulletin* during December 1966.

Mackay, Margaret Mackprang. "Honolulu Flashes." *Asia*, April 102.

Paradise of the Pacific. Honolulu, 1935–1945.

Pearl Harbor-Gram. Newsletter of the Pearl Harbor Survivors Association.

Shearer, Lloyd. "Takeo Yoshikawa: The Japanese Spy Who Fingered Pearl Harbor." *Parade*, December 7, 1969.

Stewart, Lieutenant Commander A. J. "Those Mysterious Subs." *United States Naval Institute Proceedings*, December 1974.

War Research Laboratory, University of Hawaii. Reports on race relations during war now found in Hawaiian War Records Depository.

Yoshikawa, Takeo. "Top Secret Assignment." *United States Naval Institute Proceedings*, December 1960.

UNPUBLISHED MANUSCRIPTS

Akita, George. Diary. Courtesy of George Akita.

Bicknell, George W. "Security Measures in Hawaii During World War II." On deposit in the Hawaii War Records Depository.

Martinez, Daniel A. "Japanese Naval Aircraft Crash Sites at Pearl Harbor, Dec. 7, 1941: A Resource Study." June 1986. Available at *Arizona* Memorial Visitor Center.

Mellen, Kathleen Dickenson. "The Hawaii That Was." Courtesy of Robert Van Dyke.

Swenson, J. Patricia (Morgan). "The Pearl Harbor Blitz: An Account of Events on or about December 7, 1941, in Honolulu as Seen and Experienced by a Honolulu Girl." 1961. Courtesy of Patricia Swenson.

INDEX